SHIPS and SEAMEN of the AMERICAN REVOLUTION

SHIPS

and SEAMEN
of the
AMERICAN REVOLUTION

*— vessels, crews, weapons, gear,
naval tactics, and actions
of the War for Independence*

written and illustrated by
Jack Coggins

PROMONTORY
PRESS

Library of Congress Catalog Card Number: 74-27879
ISBN 0-88394-032-9
Published by arrangement with Stackpole Books
Printed in the United States of America

Contents

Chronology of the Naval War of the Revolution

1764	British schooner *St. John* fired on by Rhode Islanders.
1769	Revenue sloop *Liberty* burned at Newport, R.I.
1772	Revenue schooner *Gaspée* taken and burned at Providence, R.I.

1775

June 12	Armed schooner *Margaretta* taken by patriots at Machias, Me.
June 15	Two sloops commissioned by Rhode Island, first by any public authority.
September 2	General Washington commissions first of squadron of schooners.
September 7	*Hannah* takes *Unity*—first capture by a Continental vessel.
October 30	Naval Committee formed.
November 5	Hopkins appointed commander in chief of fleet at Philadelphia.
November 10	Marine Corps established.
December 13	Congress provides for building of 13 frigates.
December 14	Marine Committee formed. (Later superseded Naval Committee.)

1776

February 17	Hopkins sails for New Providence.
March 3	Marines land at New Providence, march on Nassau.
March 17	British evacuate Boston.
March 23	Congress authorizes privateering.
April	Washington forms Hudson River defense flotilla.
April 6	Hopkins's squadron fights *Glasgow*.
May 10	John Paul Jones appointed to command *Providence*.
June 25	General Howe anchors in New York Bay with first of expeditionary force.
June 28	British fleet under Sir Peter Parker beaten off in attack on Sullivan's Island, Charleston, S.C.
July 12	Fleet under Admiral Lord Howe arrives at New York Bay.
August 21	Jones sails in *Providence* on first independent cruise.
September 7	Bushnell's *Turtle* attacks British warship in New York Bay.
September 15	British land on Manhattan; New York taken.
October 11	Battle of Valcour Island.
October 18	British naval force burns Falmouth, Me.
October 27	Jones, with *Alfred* and *Providence*, sails from Rhode Island.
December 1 (?)	Lambert Wickes in *Reprisal*, carrying Ben Franklin, reaches France.
December 8	British occupy Newport.

1777

February 17	Nicholson buys *Dolphin*, sails her to Calais.
Early April	*Lexington* arrives at Nantes.
May 1 (?)	Conyngham sails in *Surprise*.
May 28	Wickes in *Reprisal*, with *Lexington* and *Dolphin*, sails on cruise from St.-Nazaire.
May	French seize *Surprise*, detain Conyngham and crew.
June	*Revenge* purchased; Conyngham released, takes command.
July 16	Conyngham sails in *Revenge* on beginning of successful two-year cruise.
September	After successful cruise, *Reprisal* and *Lexington* ordered home by French. *Lexington* captured; *Reprisal* lost in storm.
September 26	British take Philadelphia.
October 12	Howe's fleet off Chester.
October 22	British attack on Fort Mercer beaten off; British lose *Augusta*, 64; *Merlin*, 18.
November 1	Jones sails with *Ranger* from Portsmouth, N.H.
November 10	Bombardment of Fort Mifflin begins.
November 15	Fort Mifflin falls.
November 20	Mercer abandoned.
November 21	Most of American squadron upriver burned to prevent capture.

1778

January 5	Battle of the Kegs.
March 13	Treaty between France and American colonies announced.
April 13	D'Estaing sails from Toulon for America.
April 23	Jones attacks Whitehaven.
April 24	*Ranger* takes *Drake*.

May 6	Small British expedition up Delaware; 44 American vessels sunk or burned.
June 28	British ships leave Delaware Bay.
July 8	D'Estaing arrives at mouth of Delaware River.
July 11	French fleet off New York.
July 22	D'Estaing sails for Narragansett Bay.
July 27	Battle of Ushant.
July 29	French anchor off Rhode Island.
August 5	British retire into inner harbor at Newport, destroy all vessels unable to enter.
August 9	Howe anchors off Point Judith.
August 10	D'Estaing puts to sea.
August 11	Indecisive engagement; fleets separate in gale.
August 21	French leave Newport for Boston.
September	Dominica seized by French force from Martinique.
November 14	D'Estaing sails from Boston for Martinique.
December 13	Barrington arrives at St. Lucia, lands troops.
December 14	D'Estaing arrives at St. Lucia.
December 15	French attack British ships at anchor, are beaten off.
December 18	French attack on British shore positions heavily defeated.
December 29	D'Estaing leaves island.
December 30	St. Lucia capitulates.

1779

January 6	Barrington relieved by Vice Admiral John Byron.
June 18	St. Vincent taken by d'Estaing.
July 2	D'Estaing anchors off Grenada.
July 4	Grenada surrenders.
July 6	Byron arrives; is defeated in indecisive action.
August	Combined Franco-Spanish fleet off Plymouth; has command of English Channel.
August 14	Jones sails with *Bonhomme Richard* and squadron from Lorient.
August 14	American squadron destroyed in Penobscot.
August 31	D'Estaing arrives off Savannah, Georgia.
September 23	*Bonhomme Richard* takes *Serapis.*
October 9	Franco-American assault on Savannah beaten off.
October 18	D'Estaing embarks his troops and sails for France.
October 28	Board of Admiralty established.

1780

January 16	Rodney defeats small Spanish fleet near Gibraltar.
February 10	British warships and transports arrive at Charleston.
February 15 (?)	Rodney sails for West Indies from Gibraltar.
March	De Guichen arrives at Martinique from France with 16 ships.
March 27	Rodney arrives at St. Lucia.
April 17	Rodney engages de Guichen off Dominica.
May 10	Rodney intercepts French fleet bound for St. Lucia. Indecisive engagements on May 15 and May 19.
May 11	Charleston falls to British.

July 12	French squadron from France under de Ternay arrives at Newport.
July 13	Rear Admiral Thomas Graves arrives at New York with reinforcements from England.
Late July	British blockade de Ternay in Newport.
August 9	Franco-Spanish fleet captures large British convoy.
Mid-August	De Guichen sails for France.
September 14	Rodney arrives at New York.
October 4-16	Violent hurricanes in West Indies. Severe British losses.
December	Britain declares war on United Provinces (Holland).

1781

January 28	Wilmington, N.C. occupied by British expedition from Charleston.
February 3	Rodney takes Dutch island of St. Eustatius.
March	French squadron at Newport sails for Chesapeake.
March 16	Arbuthnot intercepts; French retire to Newport after action.
March 22	Rear Admiral de Grasse sails from Brest.
April 28	De Grasse arrives at Martinique.
April 29	Action between Hood and de Grasse; Hood retires to rejoin Rodney.
June 2	Tobago falls after French attack.
June 9	Rodney encounters de Grasse; no action.
July 5	De Grasse sails for Cap François.
August 1	Rodney sails for England.
August 25	French squadron sails from Newport for Chesapeake.
August 28	Hood arrives at New York.
August 29	Robert Morris made Agent of Marine.
August 30	De Grasse arrives in Chesapeake with 28 of line and troops.
August 31	Graves and Hood sail for Chesapeake with 19 of line.
September 5	Battle of the Capes.
September 10	De Grasse and Newport squadron join, reenter Chesapeake.
September 19	Graves reaches New York.
September 30	Siege of Yorktown begins.
October 18	Graves sails for Chesapeake with 23 of line and troops.
October 19	Cornwallis surrenders.

Introduction

The war of the American Revolution was fought mainly on land and won mainly on the water. It may be that the spirit of the Colonial soldier, the genius of the American commander in chief, the corresponding blundering of the British commanders on land and of their ministers in England, and the difficulties of stamping out a rebellion which had widespread popular support in a vast underdeveloped country thousands of miles from home would have made the results inevitable. Certainly the forces of the Crown faced no easy task. But an important factor, and one not always remembered, was that the Continental Congress relied heavily on aid from abroad, aid which included not only muskets and powder, but ultimately ships and men as well. This aid could only be brought by water, and to do it required, in the words of the great American naval historian, Rear Admiral Alfred Thayer Mahan, "a sea power to counterbalance that of England."

So great was the dependence of the Colonists on overseas trade that many in England believed that the rebellion could be suppressed by naval force alone. Among these was the Secretary of War, Viscount Barrington. In letters written in 1774 and 1775 to the Secretary for the Colonies, the Earl of Dartmouth, he voiced the opinion that: (1) the army could not subdue the Colonists, and even it it did, it would be necessary to keep a large force permanently garrisoned in America, an expedient as distasteful to the British taxpayer as to the Colonists themselves, and (2) the troops once withdrawn, the pressure of a strict enforcement of the Navigation Acts; the close blockade of recalcitrant coastal towns; the complete interruption of all coastal trade and fishing; and the destruction, if necessary, of all shipbuilding facilities, docks,

etc. would soon bring the revolutionaries to their knees.

This idea had its merits. For in the absence of the actual presence of the enemy—a presence which had much to do with inflaming the populace—it would have been difficult, if not impossible, to keep even the most patriotic at fighting pitch. And with the steady deterioration of the American economy, very possibly love of liberty (which, contrary to song and story, did not burn high in every American bosom) would have taken second place to self-interest. Then such concessions as were deemed practicable could have been made, with face saved all around.

Had such a plan been carried out, history might have been written very differently. As it was, the naval effort made against the Colonists was, from the British standpoint, disappointing. Partially because of misdirection at the highest levels in London, partly through the apathy or blundering of the naval commanders on the spot, a really tight blockade, coupled with the systematic destruction of American shipping and shipyards, was never attempted. In consequence, there was fairly free intercourse between America, Europe, and the West Indies, and privateering flourished. And while the latter did not directly affect the outcome of the war, the former did.

The average American history book tends to treat the naval side of the war as a series of ship-vs.-ship incidents and dwells more on its military aspects. But the struggle for North America was fought not only at Trenton, Monmouth, Camden, and King's Mountain. It was fought in the cold, gray seas of the western approaches off Ushant; off Cadiz, and in the shadow of grim Gibraltar; and in the clear tropical water of the West

Indies. Renowned as was the long fight of the *Bonhomme Richard* and the *Serapis,* and the capture by the *Thorn* of two English sloops of war, it was not by such isolated incidents that independence was won. Ships' actions there were in plenty, and the privateers who swarmed out of the American ports did grievous hurt to England's merchant marine. But the decisive factor was the often complicated and sometimes almost bloodless behind-the-scenes maneuvering of the fleets of the great naval powers.

Because a detailed history of the worldwide sea war of 1778-1783 is beyond the scope of this book, the story is confined in the main to a few actions involving American seamen or having a direct bearing on the fortunes of the revolted Colonists. Perhaps more important, the book attempts to give a picture of what naval warfare was like in those times, with a brief look at the ships, the guns, and the men.

Action at Machias

Chapter 1

Acting-Lieutenant Moore, of the Royal Navy, commanding the armed schooner *Margaretta,* four 3-pounders and fourteen swivel guns, stirred uneasily in his pew. The sermon this Sunday morning, June 11, 1775, was no longer or duller than other such sermons, but there was some indefinable something in the air which made him nervous. Perhaps it was the sly, half-guilty glances of the congregation, or the part sheepish, part defiant look of the men who had been hanging around the town wharf when the ship's boat put him ashore. Yet, with all the talk of war and revolution around Boston the good people of Machias, Maine, had shown no sign of anything but friendliness to him and loyalty to the Crown.

Strange, though, there seemed to be few men in church, few save boys and oldsters, that is. And, come to think of it, no officers on the *Margaretta.* They were here in the same pew! If that crowd of men by the dock took it into their heads to—What was that loud buzz of voices at the church door? Armed men, by heaven! With a yell to his officers to follow, the lieutenant sprang out of his pew. Then, as preacher and congregation gaped, he jumped out of the window and legged it for the shore.

On board the *Margaretta,* lying at anchor close to the shore, all was peaceful and quiet. The men were enjoying the slackness of a Sunday routine in port. Suddenly the quiet ashore was broken by confused shouting and the sound of pounding feet. The astounded petty officer in charge of the deck saw his captain and officers flying pell-mell down the street, followed by a mob armed with pitchforks, fowling pieces, cutlasses, scythes, and sickles. But the petty officer was an old veteran, not to be flustered by trifles like this. Bellowing for a boat to be manned and sent ashore, he loaded one of the swivels and discharged it over the heads of the mob. The scream of the one-pound ball brought the onrushing patriots to a halt and gave the panting officers time to scramble into the boat as it grated on the beach.

While the irate commander of *Margaretta* prepared his tiny vessel for action the patriots ashore were busy. The schooner had come to Machias as escort to two small sloops, *Unity* and *Polly.* These two vessels had brought provisions from Boston and, in return, were to take back lumber for the use of the British garrison. This the patriots were determined to prevent, and they set about unloading both sloops. Meanwhile Moore slipped his cable

13

Patriots from Machias Boarding the Armed Schooner MARGARETTA

and, after a brisk exchange of fire with some of the patriots, who lined the shore and shouted demands for the schooner's surrender, cautiously dropped downstream to a safer anchorage.

But the patriots of Machias were determined to show that Maine stood for liberty as much as Massachusetts. Choosing one Jeremiah O'Brien as their leader, some forty of the hardiest boarded *Unity* and, accompanied by twenty more in a small schooner commanded by Benjamin Foster, proceeded down the bay with the intention of taking *Margaretta* by boarding. It was a brave scheme. The British schooner carried forty men, and with her cannon and swivels was a formidable opponent for a pair of unarmed vessels. Only a few of the Colonists had firearms; the rest were armed with assorted edged weapons, pitchforks, and axes.

Lieutenant Moore, meanwhile, had set sail down the bay, but had been delayed when, in an accidental jibe (that is, a change of course which brought the wind over the stern from a different quarter) the mainsail came over hard enough against the backstays to break the boom. The *Margaretta* was far enough ahead, however, to be able to stop a vessel she met and take a spar out of her, also some provisions and a Mr. Robert Avery of Norwich, Connecticut. The delay in shipping the new boom in the place of her damaged one, however, gave the Americans time to catch up. Cutting away his boats, Moore again attempted to escape, but the patriots were by now close aboard. The *Margaretta* let fly with a broadside which killed one man, but answering shots from the sloop killed the man at the schooner's helm and she came up into the wind.

With a crash the American vessels slammed alongside and the Colonists tried to board. Muskets flashed and steel met steel as the crews fought hand to hand. The *Margaretta*'s captain may have been cautious but he was no coward. He stood on the poop cheering on his men, and throwing hand grenades (hollow iron spheres filled with powder and touched off with a lighted fuze). Then a shot brought him down and the Colonists swarmed over the schooner's side with pitchforks and axes. The *Margaretta*'s

crew, disheartened by the fall of their captain, were driven below, and the ship was won.

An account by Joseph Wheaton, one of *Unity*'s crew, tells how the *Unity* chased the Britisher: "...in about two hours we received her first fire, but before we could reach her she had cut our rigging and Sails emmencely; but having gained to about one hundred yards, one Thomas Neight fired his wall piece, wounded the man at the helm and the Vessel broached too, when we nearly all fired. At this moment Captain Moore imployed himself

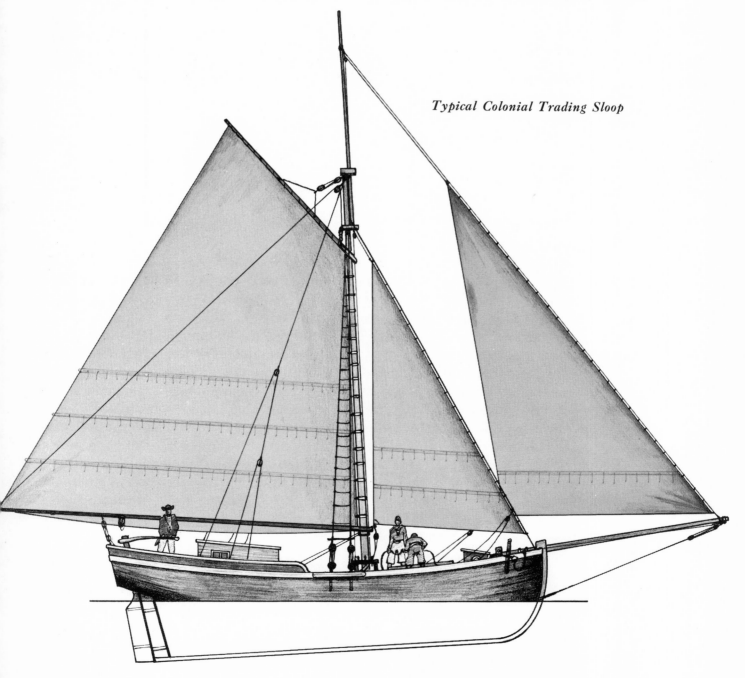

Typical Colonial Trading Sloop

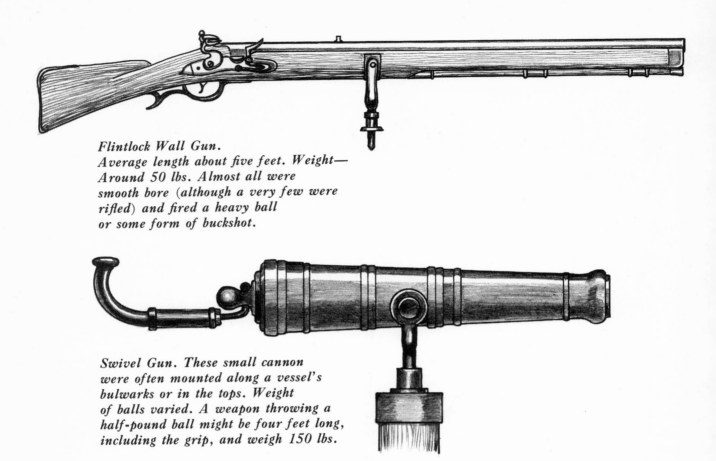

Flintlock Wall Gun.
Average length about five feet. Weight—
Around 50 lbs. Almost all were
smooth bore (although a very few were
rifled) and fired a heavy ball
or some form of buckshot.

Swivel Gun. These small cannon
were often mounted along a vessel's
bulwarks or in the tops. Weight
of balls varied. A weapon throwing a
half-pound ball might be four feet long,
including the grip, and weigh 150 lbs.

at a box of hand grenades and put two on board our Vessel, which through our crew into great disorder, they having killed and wounded nine men. Still two ranks which were near the prow got a second fire, when our bowsprit was run through the main shrouds of the Margaretta and Sail, when Six of us Jumped on her quarter deck and with clubed Muskets drove the crew from their quarters, from the waist into the hold of the Margarette; the Capt. lay mortally wounded, Robert Avery was killed and eight marines & Saylors lay dead on her deck, the Lieutenant wounded in her cabin. Thus ended this bloody affray."

It was a smart little fight; over 25 men, more than a fourth of those engaged, were killed or wounded. And for a group of half-armed farmers and fishermen to take a government ship, even a small one, was a great achievement. News of the victory spread rapidly, and it did much to boost the morale of men about to do battle with the world's greatest naval power.

It was fitting that the General Court of Massachusetts, in a resolution dated June 26, 1775, declared, "...the thanks of this Congress be, and they are hereby given to Capt. Jeremiah O'Brien and Capt. Benjamin Foster and the other brave men under their command, for their courage and good conduct in taking one of the tenders belonging to our enemies..."

Britannia's Rusty Trident

Chapter 2

The capture of the *Margaretta* on that June night of 1775 began a naval war that was to continue for more than six years. The men of Machias set out to take one of His Britannic Majesty's vessels, but we may doubt that even the most optimistic dreamed of challenging the full might of the Royal Navy. For O'Brien's lumber schooners were just about all the fleet that the Colonists had, and arrayed against it was the greatest navy in the world. Yet in 1781, at a place called Yorktown, American and French naval vessels would help an American general—whose name few, if any, of the captors of the *Margaretta* had ever heard—administer a final defeat to the forces of the Crown.

For a clearer idea of how this could come about it is necessary to review the position of the great powers and the Colonies in the period between the end of the Seven Years War in 1763 and the outbreak of war between Britain and France in 1778.

The Treaty of Paris between Great Britain, France, and Spain had ended with the island kingdom a worldwide empire. New territory was acquired in the Mediterranean, Africa, India, and the Far East, but the chief gains were in America. France ceded Canada and Cape Breton Island, with the Mississippi

the boundary between Louisiana and the British colonies. In the West Indies, she gave up Grenada, St. Vincent, Dominica, and Tobago. Spain ceded the Floridas (which in those days extended westward to the Mississippi) in return for Havana, which a British force had captured in 1762.

Not unnaturally, the loss of much of her oversea empire was resented bitterly by France, while Spain was galled by the British flag flying over Gibraltar, Minorca, and Florida. The Dutch, rivals of the British in maritime trade, also had a few old scores to pay off. It would have seemed only common sense, therefore, for Great Britain to have made every effort to keep her naval establishment at a high level of efficiency, especially as she must have been well aware that the French were building up their fleet at a great rate. This she failed to do. Pitt, the great Prime Minister, architect of British victory, was out of office, and the government had fallen almost completely into the hands of King George III and his party. The lessons of sea power could not penetrate a mind, narrow to begin with, scarcely educated, and whose one ambition was to rule. The dockyards and the vessels in ordinary (those out of commission, or as we would say, "in mothballs")

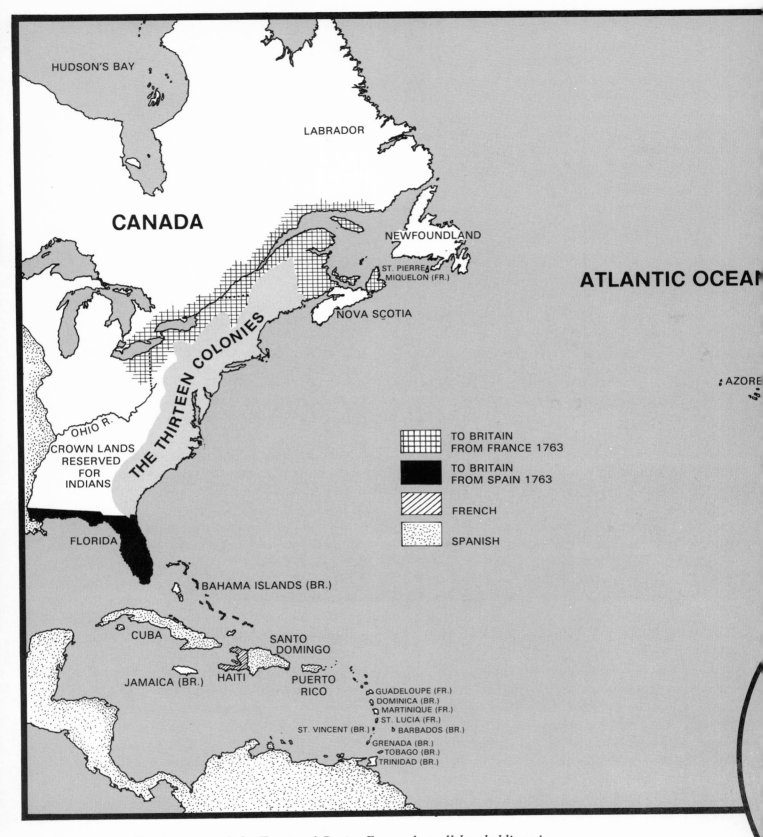

HUDSON'S BAY

LABRADOR

CANADA

NEWFOUNDLAND

ST. PIERRE
MIQUELON (FR.)

ATLANTIC OCEAN

NOVA SCOTIA

THE THIRTEEN COLONIES

OHIO R.
CROWN LANDS
RESERVED
FOR
INDIANS

AZORE

TO BRITAIN
FROM FRANCE 1763

TO BRITAIN
FROM SPAIN 1763

FRENCH

SPANISH

FLORIDA

BAHAMA ISLANDS (BR.)

CUBA

SANTO
DOMINGO

JAMAICA (BR.)   HAITI   PUERTO
RICO

GUADELOUPE (FR.)
DOMINICA (BR.)
MARTINIQUE (FR.)
ST. LUCIA (FR.)
ST. VINCENT (BR.)   BARBADOS (BR.)
GRENADA (BR.)
TOBAGO (BR.)
TRINIDAD (BR.)

*By the terms of the Treaty of Paris, France lost all her holdings in
North America except the tiny islands of St. Pierre and Miquelon off the
coast of Newfoundland. In the West Indies the islands of Guadeloupe,
Martinique, St. Lucia, and Marie Galante (just off Guadeloupe) were
returned to French hands. Spain lost Florida and Minorca in the Mediterranean.
In India, British power was in the ascendancy, the French being driven from
the continent and allowed to retain only a few trading posts.*

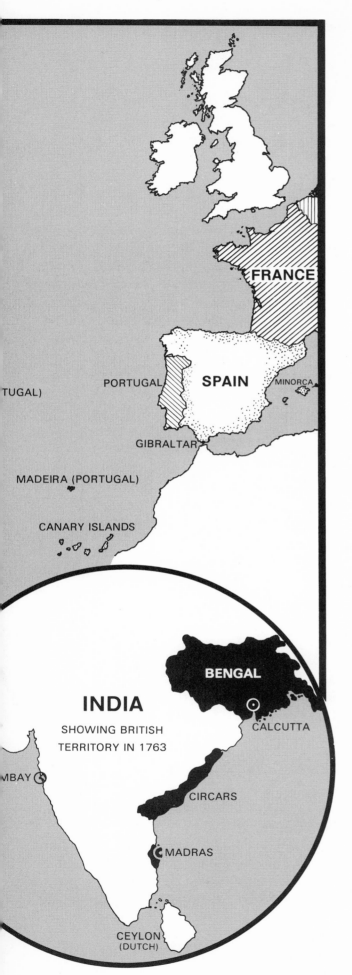

INDIA

SHOWING BRITISH
TERRITORY IN 1763

FRANCE

PORTUGAL   SPAIN   MINORCA

(TUGAL)

GIBRALTAR

MADEIRA (PORTUGAL)

CANARY ISLANDS

BENGAL

CALCUTTA

MBAY

CIRCARS

MADRAS

CEYLON
(DUTCH)

were neglected, and even the vital stockpile of oak timbering was in a dangerously low state. There was also a shortage of trained seamen. With the cessation of hostilities in 1763 many officers went ashore on half pay, and ships' crews were discharged to find other employment, beg, or starve. The bold tars who had sailed with Hawke against Conflans might well sing:

> Ere Hawke did bang
> Monsieur Conflang,
> You gave us beef and beer:
> Now Monsier's beat.
> We've nought to eat,
> Since you have nought to fear.

Thus when in early February, 1775 the bill to "restrain the trade and commerce of Massachuset's Bay and New Hampshire; the colonies of Connecticut and Rhode Island, and Providence Plantation in North America..." was introduced in the House of Commons, there were doubts whether the Royal Navy was equal to the task of policing the waters of North America and at the same time affording adequate protection to Great Britain itself and to British possessions overseas.

During a debate in the House on February 13, a member insisted that "our present naval force was by no means adequate to the execution of our professed intentions; for that the squadron we designed for America would answer no purpose of stopping their commerce; or if we did send a sufficient one, our own coasts, comparatively speaking, must be left totally defenseless; as he was well informed, that France alone had 75 men of war of the line now, more than one half of which were manned, and fit for actual service. He then gave an account of a conversation which passed lately between him and a French gentleman well acquainted with the state of their navy; from which he was full satisfied that the whole of our force, in every part of the world, would not be sufficient to defend us at home, should we blindly rush into a civil war."

The Royal Navy vessels stationed in North America in January of 1775 totaled only twenty-four, scarcely an overwhelming force to patrol a coastline of many thousands of miles, from Florida to Nova Scotia.

Disposition of North American Squadron, Vice Admiral Samuel Graves, Jan. 1, 1775

Ship	Guns	Men	Station
Boyne	70	520	Boston
Somerset	68	520	Boston
Asia	64	480	Boston
Preston	50	300	Boston
Tartar	28	160	Halifax
Mercury	20	130	Boston
Glasgow	20	130	Boston
Rose	20	130	Rhode Island
Fowey	20	130	Virginia
Lively	20	130	Salem
Scarborough	20	130	Piscataqua River (New Hampshire)
Swan	16	100	Rhode Island
Kingfisher	16	100	New York
Tamer	14	100	South Carolina
Cruizer	8	60	North Carolina
Savage	8	60	East Florida
Canceaux	8	45	New Hampshire
Diana	6	30	Just purchased
Hope	6	30	Rhode Island
Magdalen	6	30	Philadelphia
St. John	6	30	East Florida
Halifax	6	30	Maine Coast
Diligent	6	30	Maine Coast
Gaspee	6	30	Maine Coast

Despite the growing crisis the squadron was reinforced but slowly, and by the end of June, two weeks after Bunker Hill, Graves had only received the addition of five small sloops: Otter, 16; Nautilus, 16; Falcon, 16; Merlin, 16; and Senegal, 14, all ship-rigged. A letter from the Admiralty to Graves, dated August 3, listed six ships, four of 50 and two of 44 guns, and seven frigates slated to join his force in the near future—not a large reinforcement, especially as three of his largest ships were to return to England.

Buildup of the home fleet was slow, and when the War of Independence escalated into a worldwide struggle with France, Spain, and Holland, the Royal Navy, large though it was, found itself dangerously overextended. When war with France broke out in 1778, the French fleet had 80 ships of the line in good order, and a large number of frigates and lesser vessels. Moreover, due to her maritime conscription, she could at once man 50 ships of the line. England, on the other hand, was barely able to man 40. Spain, in 1779, had nearly 60 ships of the line, while to oppose these fleets the Royal Navy had but some 275 ships of all classes, of which less than 150 were ships of the line. Of these, only four were first-rates and barely 20 second-rates (see Chapter 4 for rating of ships by gunpower), while the majority were 74's and 64's. In contrast, at the end of the previous war, 365 vessels had flown the naval flag.

However, in 1775, when hostilities commenced in America with the action at Lexington and Concord, the French and Spanish menace was far in the offing, and the Royal Navy was able to bring overwhelming strength to bear on the American seacoast.

There is no indication that those in charge of British naval affairs were unaware either of the Colonists' potential strength or of the fact that sea power was bound to play a most important role in suppressing the rebellion. The actual output of Colonial yards may have come as a surprise, but as long ago as 1690 a fourth-rate, the Falkland, had been built by a private yard at Portsmouth, New Hampshire. Subsequently, other naval vessels had been built, with the result that there were in the Colonies shipwrights either experienced in naval construction (which even in those days differed from that of the merchant marine) or who had acquired the knowledge via the apprentice system.

Colonial designers were both competent and inventive. In consequence, many American vessels were noted for their speed and handiness. It is not surprising that the frigates authorized by Congress were splendid examples of their type, larger and faster than vessels of the same class built for the Royal Navy. One, *Hancock,* when examined by her British captors, was described as "the finest and fastest frigate in the world."

Of yards capable of turning out merchant vessels there were many, and it has been stated that, by 1770, almost one-third of the merchant vessels flying the British flag were American-built and American-manned.

This sizable fleet, plus the men engaged in a flourishing fishing industry, indicates a large reservoir of manpower with experience at sea. As American naval officers were to find out, it takes more than a tarpaulin jacket and cutlass to make a man-of-war's man. But at least the raw material was there. While of the captains and mates many were men of great experience and skill, it should be noted that although there were many Colonials capable of commanding a merchant vessel, few had actually been in combat. Naval command calls for other qualities besides seamanship. Few merchant captains, used to independent command, could adapt to naval discipline, while none knew anything of tactics. As it was also unfortunately true that many of those appointed to command owed their preferment to political "pull" and favoritism, the Continental Navy was, with a few brilliant exceptions, poorly officered. Had the commanders been of the same caliber as the ships, the naval record would have been brighter.

As ignorant of strategy as most of its commanders were of tactics, the Congress had given little thought to the employment of its warships, or their supply once at sea.

The defection of a considerable proportion of her merchant marine was a serious blow to British sea power. Almost as serious was the loss to the Royal Navy of a source of prime seamen. The revolt of the Colonies is estimated to have cost the British fleet 18,000 men.

No power was more aware than Great Britain of the havoc which privateers could wreak on weak or defenseless merchant vessels—nor of the immense effort, in terms of warships and men, involved in convoy and escort duty. In the Seven Years War, from 1756 to 1760 alone, French privateers had taken over 2,500 merchantmen. In 1761, despite the fact that the French naval forces had been beaten time after time and French merchantmen all but driven from the seas, over 800 British vessels were lost. But the British were also well aware that the snapping up of 800 vessels, mostly coasters and small craft, could not seriously cripple the trade of a nation whose merchant ships numbered some 8,000 sail. They were also aware that the activity of privateers, though they alarmed the merchants and sent up the insurance rates, could no more hinder the movements of the British fleet or properly armed and escorted convoys of troops and supplies than a swarm of gnats could halt the progress of an elephant.

From American naval forces, they knew they would have little to fear. Individual ships of small size might be built and equipped, but the construction of a large fleet of ships capable of lying in the line of battle, with their attendant frigates and smaller craft, was entirely beyond any but a first-class power. For the revolted Colonies, torn with war and internal dissensions and jealousies and all but penniless, to attempt such a thing was out of the question. Nor, if by some miracle the ships themselves could be constructed, were there gun foundries capable of arming them.

And so, despite the efforts of such small naval forces as could be scraped together and hundreds of privateers, the British fleet dominated the seacoast of America. It cut off, more or less effectively, the Colonists from overseas aid; and it transported the British army from position to position along the lengthy coastline—landing troops here, evacuating others there, while maintaining them with supplies and reinforcements.

If the military campaigns were ill-conceived or bungled, it was not the fault of the British sailor. And it was only the pressures developing from a worldwide conflict, plus the ill effect of the mismanagement of naval affairs by the responsible ministers in King George's government, which momentarily allowed control of the seas to slip from the navy's grasp.

But that one moment was enough. The arrival of De Grasse from the West Indies, the unskillful handling of the British fleet under Graves in the indecisive Battle of the Capes, and the successful passage of the French squadron, with eighteen transports and all the heavy siege artillery, from Newport to the Chesapeake was sufficient to ensure the fall of Yorktown. That six months later De Grasse was himself a prisoner, after his defeat by Rodney at the Saints, could not alter the fact that the war in America was virtually lost. It had been lost because the maintenance of British power in America depended upon the command of the sea. When that command, spread thin from the Indian Ocean to the Baltic, faltered, British rule over the thirteen colonies came to an end.

Strength of the Royal Navy in 1763, 1775 and 1783

	End of Seven Years War	Beginning of Revolutionary War	End of Revolutionary War
Ships of the Line (60 to 100 Guns)	141	131	174
Small Two-Deckers and Frigates (20 to 56 Guns)	142	98	198
Sloops of War (8 to 18 Guns)	57	38	85
Bombs	14	2	4
Fire Ships	11	1	17
Total	365	270	478

In the Beginning

Chapter 3

With each day of the rebellion it was becoming clearer that what had started as an armed protest was rapidly turning into a struggle for complete independence. For months small vessels—some state-owned, others owned privately—had been putting to sea in the hope of picking up British merchant vessels bringing in supplies to the forces of the Crown. Now the Congress in Philadelphia —after many delays and much argument— was seriously considering the "ways and means for furnishing these colonies with a naval armament."

There was much opposition to the Continental government taking any part in naval warfare—the feeling being that any attempt to oppose the might of the Royal Navy would be suicidal. But finally (October 5, 1775) the naval aspects of the war were referred to a committee of three: John Adams, John Langdon, and Silas Deane. On October 30, four more members were added, and the Naval Committee came into being.

On December 11, the Naval Committee's report was read, debated, and adopted. A squadron of frigates was to be built, "Five ships of 32 guns, five of 28 guns, three of 24 guns, making in the whole thirteen." These ships, the first of many to be ordered for what would become the U.S. Navy, were to be ready in 1776. But the Colonies needed vessels at once, and steps had already been taken to fit out as men-of-war such merchantmen as could be secured.

Anticipating the need for a naval force, Washington had acquired vessels for the purpose of intercepting supplies for the British Army in Boston. For sailors he drew on the regiments recruited in the Massachusetts coastal towns, many of whose men were seamen. The first ship of his little navy was the schooner *Hannah,* Captain Nicholas Broughton.

"You, being appointed a Captain in the Army of the United Colonies of North-America," read Broughton's instructions, "are hereby directed to take the command of a detachment of said Army and proceed on board the Schooner HANNAH, at Beverly, lately fitted out and equipped with arms, ammunition and provisions, at the Continental expense. You are to proceed, as commander of said Schooner, immediately on a cruise against such vessels as may be found on the high seas

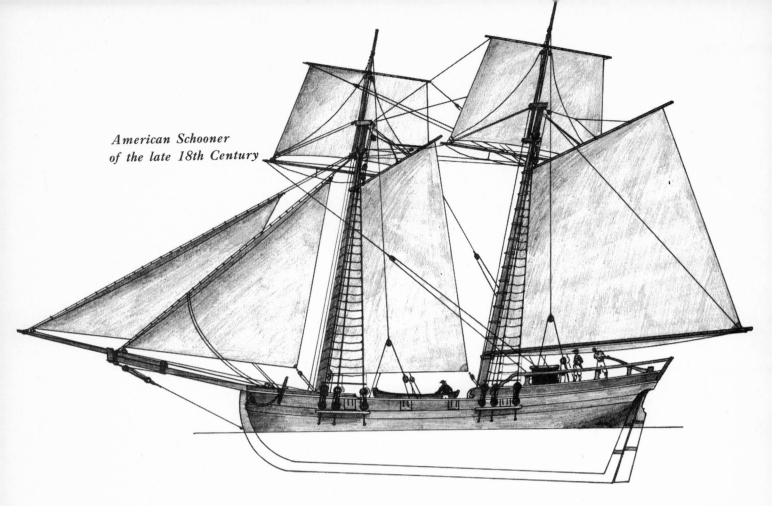

American Schooner
of the late 18th Century

or elsewhere, bound inwards and outwards, to or from Boston, in the service of the Ministerial Army, and to take and seize all such vessels laden with soldiers, arms, ammunition or provisions, for or from said Army, or which you shall have good reason to suspect are in such service."

Disposition of prizes was arranged, treatment of prisoners prescribed, a signal system organized. Powder being scarce, the captain was to refrain from wasting any of it on salutes.

The order, signed by Washington, was dated September 2, 1775. Broughton sailed on September 5 and, after being chased twice by naval vessels, was able to snap up a prize on his second day out. "Next morning," went his report, "I saw a ship under my lee quarter; I perceived her to be a large ship. I tacked and stood back for the land; soon after I put about and stood towards her again and found her a ship of no force. I came up with her, hailed, and asked where she came from; was

answered, from Piscataqua, and bound to Boston. I told him he must bear away and go into Cape Ann; but being very loth, I told him if he did not I should fire on her. On that she bore away and I have brought her safe into Cape Ann Harbour." This ship, *Unity*, loaded with naval stores and lumber, was the first captured by a vessel in the Continental service. (It is not to be confused with the sloop *Unity* taken at Machias. Duplication of names was common—and a cause of confusion to present-day researchers and readers. A vessel was usually identified by her port of registry, painted on the counter under her name, e.g., *Sally*, Boston; *Polly*, Yarmouth, etc.)

Other vessels, including the schooners *Lee, Warren, Lynch, Franklin,* and *Harrison* and the brigantine *Washington* were soon at sea. They had no great success at first, and the men, forced to keep the seas in the winter gales, became mutinous, swearing that they had enlisted as soldiers, not marines. Washington himself wrote, "The plague, trouble and

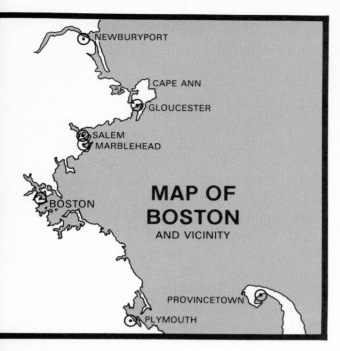

MAP OF BOSTON
AND VICINITY

NEWBURYPORT

CAPE ANN

GLOUCESTER

SALEM
MARBLEHEAD

BOSTON

PROVINCETOWN

PLYMOUTH

vexation I have had with the crews of all the armed vessels is inexpressible. I do believe there is not on earth a more disorderly set."

However, the men may have had some cause for complaint, for Washington's agent reported: "After repairing on board the brig [*Washington*] Saturday night, enquiring into the cause of the uneasiness [a mild term, seeing that they had refused duty] among the people and finding it principally owing to their want of clothing, and after supplying them with what they wanted, the whole crew, to a man, gave three cheers and declared their readiness to go to sea the next morning."

Part of the trouble was want of success, not warm clothes, and the good fortune of Captain John Manley of the *Lee* did much to put heart in the soldier-sailors of Washington's squadron. *Lee* made several prizes, among them the brigantine *Nancy* loaded with a most valuable cargo of military stores and ordnance. Included in the booty was a 13-inch brass mortar, "the noblest piece of ordnance ever landed in America."

On January 1, 1776, Manley was appointed commodore of the squadron. His flagship was the schooner *Hancock*, and in her Manley continued to harass the merchantmen supplying "the Ministerial Assassins at Boston." As well as Washington's vessels there were a few belonging to Massachusetts, Providence, and Connecticut, plus a handful privately owned. These little ships took many prizes; twenty-seven were advertised to be sold at Ipswich and Plymouth in February and March alone. After Boston was evacuated, Washington took the army to New York, leaving Artemas Ward in command. The "Army's Navy" continued to do good work all through the year until it was disbanded by order of the Marine Committee early in 1777. Not only did the little squadron take valuable merchantmen but on at least one occasion captured transports with troops aboard.

These captures so annoyed the British that an investigation was made. Admiral Shuldham, in command of the North American Station until relieved by Admiral Howe in 1776, even suggested in a letter that supplies should be sent in obsolete 40-gun frigates with all armament removed but the upper tier of guns. He went on to write: "...for however numerous our Cruizers may be or however attentive our Officers to their Duty, it has been found impossible to prevent some of our Ordnance and other valuable stores, in small Vessels, falling into the hands of the Rebels..." He praised the officers on blockade duty, saying that their service during "the rigor of this long and severe Winter in constantly keeping the Sea on their respective Stations is unprecedented and incredible." And he finishes

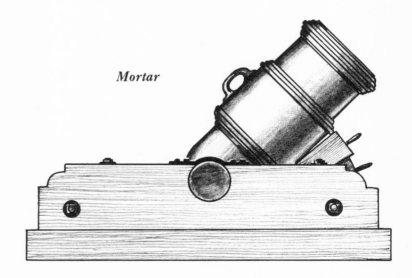

Mortar

by complaining of "The very few Ships I am provided with to enable me to co-operate with the Army, Cruize off the Ports of the Rebels to prevent their receiving supplies, or protect those destined to this place from falling into their hands."

Shuldham's letter is in itself fitting tribute to the small Colonial force which first kept the seas in spite of all the King's cruisers could do to stop them.

But while the men of Massachusetts were twisting the lion's tail, a more powerful squadron was being acquired and fitted out in the port of Philadelphia. It was an odd collection of vessels. There was *Alfred* (ex-London packet *Black Prince*), named the flagship and armed with 24 guns. Another ship, *Columbus*, was given 18 or 20 guns (accounts differ). Two brigs, the *Andrew Doria* and *Cabot*, and the sloop *Providence* carried 14, 14, and 12 small guns respectively. The sloop *Hornet*, 10 guns, and the 8-gun schooners *Wasp* and *Fly* made up the squadron.

Esek Hopkins, an old sea captain from Providence and brother of a member of the Naval Committee, was named commander in chief of the fleet. He was fifty-seven, and his only recommendation as a naval man was that he had commanded a privateer in the French and Indian War. There is some doubt as to whether Hopkins was to be commander in chief of all the naval forces of the Congress, which would have made him equal in rank to Washington, or just of the one then fitting out in Philadelphia. The officers of the other vessels were also named: Dudley Saltonstall to *Alfred;* Abraham Whipple to *Columbus;* Nicholas Biddle to *Andrew Doria;* John Hopkins, the commander in chief's son, to *Cabot.* *Providence* was to be commanded by John Hazard; *Hornet* by William Stone; *Fly,* Hoysted Hacker; and *Wasp* by Charles Alexander.

One winter morning Commodore Hopkins, his captains and lieutenants boarded a ship's boat at the foot of Walnut Street in Philadelphia. The boat made its way through the floating chunks of ice to where *Alfred* lay at anchor. Boatswain's pipes shrilled in the best Royal Navy tradition as the commodore and his officers gathered on the quarterdeck. Then, as crowds ashore cheered and cannons roared a salute, the commodore's flag lieutenant hoisted the first colors raised on an American man-of-war. What did that first flag look like? No authorities seem to agree. Some say it was striped red and white; some, plain yellow; some, white. It certainly had a rattlesnake on it somewhere. But the flag itself was not of as much importance in American naval history as the lieutenant who hoisted it; his name was John Paul Jones. (Mr. Jones, by the way, did not approve of the new ensign. "I could never see," he wrote, "how or why such a venomous serpent should be the combatant emblem of a brave and honest folk, fighting to be free. I abhorred the device.")

Hopkins's squadron was ready by the middle of January. Orders had gone out for "every Officer in the Sea and Marine Service and all the Common Men belonging to each, who have enlisted into the Service of the United Colonies on board the ships now fitting out, that they immediately repair on board their respective ships as they would avoid being deemed deserters...." Hopkins had hoped to sail at once, but there was ice on the river, too thick a crust for the squadron to crash their way through. It was not until February 17, 1776 that the little fleet left the Delaware.

The original plan was for the cruise to begin with operations in the Chesapeake. Here loyalist Governor Dunmore of Virginia had gathered a flotilla of small craft, supported by a 28-gun frigate and a couple of sloops of war. With this squadron he was raiding both shores of the bay and the rivers emptying into it. Hopkins was to "enter the bay, search out and attack, take or destroy all the naval forces of our enemies that you may find there." He was then to clean out all enemy forces on the coast of the two Carolinas, and having accomplished this task he was to go at once to Rhode Island and perform the same feat there.

No small order! But there was an "out" in the form of an "if." "If bad winds or stormy weather or any other unfortunate accident or disaster disable you so to do, you are to follow such course as your best judgement" etc.

Hopkins had made up his mind before sailing that, regardless of orders, he was going to take his fleet to the West Indies, specifically the island of New Providence in the Bahamas, where there was known to be a large supply of gunpowder. The rendezvous was fixed at Abaco and the fleet arrived there on March 1 —minus *Hornet* and *Fly,* which had become separated from the rest of the squadron.

On March 3, 270 sailors and marines under Marine Captain Samuel Nicholas landed on New Providence and marched on Nassau. Fort Montague, which lay between the landing place and the town, was abandoned by the garrison after they had fired a few shots. Hopkins issued a manifesto declaring that he had come for "powder and warlike stores belonging to the Crown, and if I am not opposed in putting my design in execution, the persons and property of the inhabitants shall be safe." Evidently this was all the King's loyal subjects on New Providence were worrying about, because there was no opposition and Nicholas was allowed to march into town next morning and take possession of Fort Nassau.

The fort yielded considerable military booty. The loot included 71 cannon, 15 brass mortars, and 24 barrels of powder. The Governor had sent off 150 barrels of the precious powder the night before, but the ordnance taken from the two forts would be very welcome to the Congress and it was with some satisfaction that Hopkins ordered his armada to set sail for home. As an added bonus, off the eastern end of Long Island his ships picked up two small prizes: the 6-gun tender *Hawk* and the 12-gun bomb-vessel *Bolton.*

The night of April 5-6 was warm, the sea smooth and the breeze light. The American vessels were coasting gently along in the familiar waters between Block Island and the

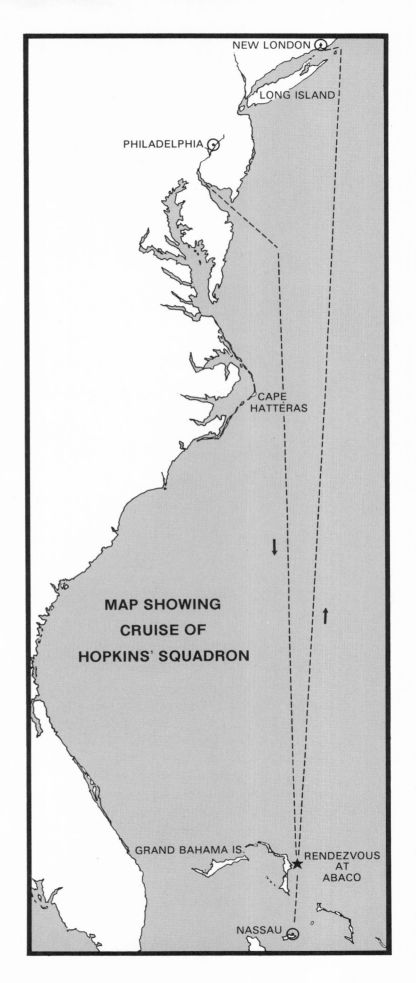

MAP SHOWING
CRUISE OF
HOPKINS' SQUADRON

Rhode Island shore. The squadron was not in close formation, and it is possible that the lookouts were preoccupied with the coming distribution of prize money and the prospects of a fling ashore. At any rate, about 2:30 A.M. a strange sail appeared almost in the midst of the little fleet. Shouts and the shrilling of pipes brought the sleepy crews tumbling out of their hammocks as the black mass of the stranger's hull loomed out of the darkness. The stranger hailed *Cabot,* who answered and then let fly with her broadside of seven 6-pounders. The reply was immediate and devastating. Splinters flew and severed rigging snaked down from aloft. Once more the stranger's guns flamed through the smoke; then the badly damaged American brig hauled off.

As the battered *Cabot* fell away, *Alfred* surged up in her place, and a running fight began which lasted until about 4:00 A.M. Soon *Providence* opened fire, followed by *Andrew Doria.* Ringed by the flashes of American guns, the stranger was in a perilous position. *Alfred* alone, with her 24 guns, should have been a match for the enemy but, as Lieutenant Jones wrote in *Alfred's* logbook, "...an unlucky shot having carried away our wheel-block and

ropes, the ship broached to and gave the enemy an opportunity of raking us with several broadsides before we were again in condition to steer the ship and return the fire."

Evidently *Andrew Doria* was not too closely engaged. "We receiv'd several shott in ye hull & riggen, one upon the Quarter through the Netting and stove ye arm chest upon the Quarter Deck and wounded our Drummer in ye Legge"; so went her lieutenant's report. Compared to *Cabot,* who had four killed and seven, including her captain, wounded, and *Alfred,* with six killed and six

NEWPORT

NEW LONDON

FISHERS ISLAND

BLOCK ISLAND

MONTAUK POINT

MAP OF BLOCK ISLAND
AND VICINITY

wounded, *Doria* got off lightly. In addition, the flagship had received "several shot under the water, which made the ship very leaky; We had besides the mainmast shot through and the upperworks and rigging very considerably damaged."

The strange vessel was *Glasgow,* 20, Captain Tyringham Howe commanding. Taking advantage of the disabling of *Alfred's* wheel, Howe set as much sail as the shattered condition of *Glasgow's* spars and rigging allowed and made for Newport. "Bore away," went her captain's report, "...and made Sail for Rhode Island, with the whole fleet within Musket shot on our Quarters and Stern. Got two Stern chase guns out of the Cabin and kept giving and receiving a very warm fire."

Columbus was prevented by the light airs from getting into the initial action at all. Whipple reported, "...before that I had got close enough for a Close Engagement, the Glasgow had made all sail for the Harbour of Newport. I continued Chase under all Sail that I had, except Steering Sails and the Wind being before the Beam, she firing her two Stern Chaces into me as fast as possible and my keeping up a Fire with my Bow Guns and now and then a Broadside, put it out of my power to get near enough to have a close Engagement."

Glasgow should have been battered into a wreck, but the American gunners had aimed too high. She had taken ten hits in her mainmast, some 250 holes had been torn in her sails and she was badly cut up aloft, but her only casualties were one man killed and three wounded by musketry. Her escape from the middle of Hopkins's squadron, after inflicting far more damage than she received, did her captain and crew much credit.

The American squadron with its prizes arrived at New London, April 8. At first Hopkins's exploits were accorded great acclaim. He was a popular man, both with his sailors and the public generally, and received the congratulations of Congress. But as time went on, people thought more and more about the escape of *Glasgow* and less about Hopkins's actual accomplishments. Also the southern members were not happy that their enemy Dunmore still roamed the Chesapeake as before. There were investigations, and both Whipple and Hazard were court-martialed. Whipple was acquitted but *Providence's* captain was relieved of his command. Ultimately Hopkins's leadership on this and other occasions was brought into question, and finally he, too, was dismissed from the service.

Actually America's first naval commander in chief and his men had not done too badly. They had brought back some much needed artillery and supplies, captured some small vessels, and put a scare into the British authorities in the West Indies. That they could not follow this first success with some other exploit was unfortunate. But the difficulties of keeping a squadron such as Hopkins's fully manned and equipped ready for sea were beyond the resources of the Congress. The trouble was that few landsmen could appreciate these difficulties and so the naval men were frequently blamed for conditions beyond their control. It was scarcely Hopkins's fault that with the scratch collection of shipping that Congress had seen fit to give him he could not rid the seas of British warships. It is to be hoped that the old privateersman took his fall as philosophically as he did his sudden elevation to the heights of command.

The Warship

Chapter 4

The function of the warship has always been to bring to bear on the enemy as large an offensive armament as possible, whether it be boarding parties of spearmen, arrows, stones, bundles of flammable material, cannon balls, armor-piercing shell, torpedoes or bombs. Since the introduction of gunpowder and the gun into Western naval warfare, sometime in the fourteenth century, warships had progressed from small vessels with a few crude bombards pointing over the "gunwales," to ships, some of which were over 2,700 tons, and carrying as many as 120 guns.

In the fifteenth and early sixteenth centuries there was little distinction between vessels built for trade and armed for their own defense, and those built expressly for war purposes. But as the number and weight of guns increased, structural modifications were necessary to bear the weight of the guns, the shock of recoil and of enemy missiles, while the large number of men necessary to work the guns meant increased accommodation space for gun crews as well as ship handlers. So the merchant type with much hold space, but with no pressing need for heavy timbering or great speed, gradually diverged from the swifter, heavily armed war vessel. By the time of which we write the two had long since

gone their separate ways. Some merchantmen, usually the fastest and handiest, could successfully compete with warships of the smaller classes. But, all other factors being equal, a larger merchant ship had no chance against a warship of comparable size. The only possible exceptions were the Indiamen. These were large strongly built vessels specially designed by the great trading companies of England, France, and Spain for the long and dangerous passage to the Far East. They were, as a type, powerfully armed and carried large and well-disciplined crews. Such a one was *Bonhomme Richard*, once owned by the Compagnie des Indes.

The naval architects of the eighteenth century were faced, as are modern designers, with problems involving length, beam, gun-power, speed, stability, living and stowage space. If the hull had too little beam, she might be fast but unstable, a poor platform for her guns. If too broad, she would probably be slow. She needed guns at bow and stern, but if these were made too fine (which also meant a faster ship), there was little room and less weight-carrying ability fore and aft. The more guns she was to carry, the more decks she needed to carry them on. And the more decks, the less stability. The bigger the hull, the

Bow and Stern View of British 100-gun Ship
ROYAL GEORGE, Launched 1756.
Note the anchor at the cat head, below, and
the ornate stern carvings and galleries.
Insert is a 90-gun ship of the same period.

more sail required to drive it, but high masts also meant loss of stability (an unstable ship was known as being "crank"). On the other hand, without sufficient weight aloft to steady it, a hull might have a short jerky roll, which greatly added to the difficulties of gun aiming. And so, like most modern designs, the results were a compromise.

The problem, basically, revolved around the naval gun itself. From its introduction right down to the adoption of the shell and the rifled bore, the gun was inefficient. In proportion to the damage it could do to a heavily timbered hull, it was far too cumbersome and required too many men to work it. It was also exceedingly difficult to aim and fire from a rolling deck and even under ideal conditions was not capable of great accuracy.

In consequence, the tendency was to design ships to carry as many guns as possible, with the hope that the cumulative damage would be sufficient to cause the enemy to strike her colors.

Like their present-day counterparts, eighteenth-century constructors found that the best way to solve their problems was to increase the overall size of their ships. In our own century we have seen the fleet destroyer outstrip in tonnage the light cruisers of World War I, cruisers attain the size of dreadnoughts, and the battleship swell from 15,000 tons to giants of 64,000 tons. During the eighteenth century both the French and Spanish built ships of greater tonnage in all classes. The British, unfortunately for them, were hampered by Navy Board scales of dimensions, "establishments," which set limits on the tonnage of any particular class. Thus their designers of the middle of the eighteenth century were restricted to tonnages "established" in 1719—with the result that, as one admiral complained, "Our 70-gun ships are little superior to their 52-gun ships." The consequences of trying to cram increasingly heavy armament into hulls too small adversely affected British naval operations throughout the next war. It was a recognized fact that

when in pursuit of an enemy force the leading ships of the British fleet were always vessels previously captured from the French (and much coveted by British captains), while any laggards snapped up by the pursuers were usually ex-Royal Navy vessels. Captured French and Spanish vessels were carefully studied, and sometimes copied, but as a general rule, a British vessel of any given rate was inferior in size and therefore in design to an adversary of the same class.

Ships of the line, the battleships of their day, varied but little in appearance. They all had a great deal of freeboard, and many were noted for the cabins and galleries which graced their sterns. A certain amount of fancy work embellished their upper works, but nothing like the ornately carved and gilded sterns, bulwarks, and stems of a hundred years before. Gone were the lofty sterns and forecastles of former days, and in the smaller vessels the flush deck was becoming common. Larger warships still showed considerable "tumble home"—the effect of making the spar or upper deck less in width than the lower gun deck. This kept the center of gravity more amidships for greater stability.

Most vessels of any size were ship-rigged—that is, square-rigged on all three masts. The illustration shows a typical ship-rigged vessel of the period. The lateen yard, on the mizzen, was going out of style, and many new vessels had gaff spankers, which had been introduced in the Royal Navy about 1750. Extra drive was obtained with studding sails, in general use in Navy vessels by the time of the Revolution.

Smaller ship types differed considerably, although perhaps not as much as the many names—brigs, snows, cats, sloops, pinks, schooners, brigantines, barks, and others—might indicate. Some of these terms referred to differences in rig and others to minor variations in hull design. Also, terminology had a habit of changing from one period to another. Thus the earliest sloops in the Royal Navy were small armed craft, with one

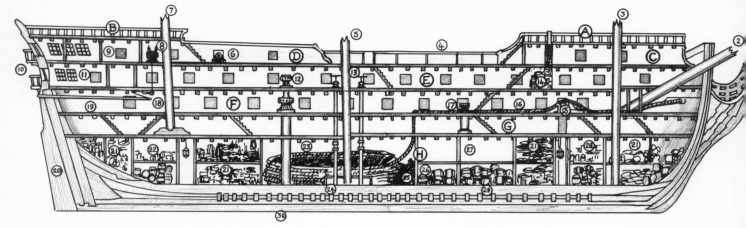

Cutaway Drawing of a Typical Two-Decker

A. Forecastle Deck
B. Poop Deck
C. Forecastle
D. Quarter Deck
E. Upper Deck
F. Lower Deck
G. Orlop Deck
H. Hold

1. Figure head
2. Bowsprit
3. Fore Mast
4. Hammock Rail
5. Main Mast
6. Gun Port
7. Mizzen Mast
8. Wheel
9. Upper cabin
10. Stern galleries

11. Lower cabins
12. Main capstan
13. Pumps
14. Galley
15. Bitts
16. Cable
17. Forward capstan
18. Tiller
19. Warrant officer's quarters
20. Rudder

21. Stores
22. After Magazine
23. Cable Tier
24. Pump Well
25. Shot Lockers
26. Water casks
27. Cockpit
28. Forward Magazine
29. Keelson
30. Keel

mast, and probably sloop-rigged—i.e., with a couple of head sails, a gaff mainsail, and a square topsail and lower square sail, or "course." Fifty years later "sloop" referred to any vessel with all guns on the main deck, irrespective of rig. By the time of the Revolutionary War a sloop was also a vessel, often ship-rigged, commanded by an officer one grade below a captain.

The cutaway drawing shows a typical warship, a two-decker in this case. What it does not show is the cramped quarters where scores, sometimes hundreds, of men slung their hammocks "fourteen inches to a man"

between decks so low that even in a large ship a man had to stoop beneath the deck-beams. Nor can it give any idea of the dank gloom of the orlop deck close above the evil-smelling bilges, where the warrant officers had their tiny compartments. Nor of the crowded, candle-lit cockpit, where the senior midshipmen, and the masters and surgeon's mates lived—and where so many wounded sailors died after a battle.

It does give a picture of the room needed for storage of a great variety of material, from spare flannel (for cartridges) and flints, to canvas, copper sheathing, dried

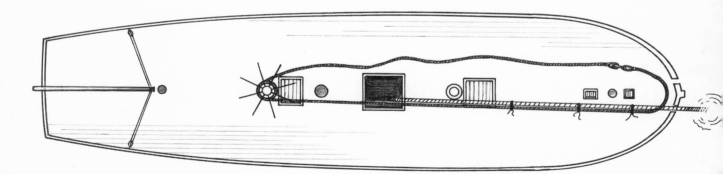

Plan of the Lower Deck of a Two-Decker. The diagram shows anchor cable nipped to messenger which was passed around capstan. On large vessels there were capstans on more than one deck, allowing more men to heave on the capstan bars.

peas, salt pork, and rope. For a warship was a self-sustaining community, designed to keep at sea for a long period of time, and she must carry in her hold food, water, and provisions enough to take her halfway round the world, if necessary.

Also shown is the relative size of the great lower masts, and the space allotted to the stout cables (some more than two feet thick) in the cable tier. In this area the anchor cables were coiled as they came in through the hawse hole—hauled in by the efforts of many men heaving at the bars of the big capstans. These cables were not attached directly to the capstans. Instead, they were fastened with a few turns of ropes called nippers to the messenger, a heavy cable joined at the ends to form a continuous circle. This went around the capstan, then back to the bow in an endless belt. As one part of it moved toward the capstan, boys (also sometimes called nippers) walked along with it, holding the cable nipped to it with the ropes. When they reached the hatchway to the cable tier, they released the nippers, the cable descended into the hold and the boys went back to the bow, repeating the process until the whole anchor cable was brought on board.

Weighing anchor was a slow process. In an emergency the cables were usually cut and the anchors either abandoned or marked with buoys fastened to the cable ends.

So many provisions were carried in casks, either because they contained liquids or to keep out water and the swarming rats, that ships of any size carried at least one cooper, to make and repair the innumerable barrels needed.

The capital ship of the period was a vessel considered to be large enough and with sufficient armament to take her place in the line of battle. These ships of the line carried their main armament on two or three decks; those of over 80 guns usually were three-deckers. In the first half of the eighteenth century 50-gun ships were included in the line, but by the time of the Revolutionary War no ship under 60 guns was regarded as fit to lie in the battle line.

Royal Navy vessels in the eighteenth century were rated according to their gunpower. First-rates had 100 guns and up; second-rates, 90-98; third-rates, 64-80; fourth-rates, 54-60; fifth-rates 30-40; and sixth-rates, 18-24 guns. Below that were sloops (smaller ship-rigged vessels carrying some 14 to 18 guns), schooners, brigs, cutters, bomb ketches, fire ships, etc. However, this system began to go out of fashion toward the end of the century, and warships were usually classed according to the number of their guns—100-gun ships, 74-gun ships, etc.

A typical 100-gun ship was some 230 feet overall, 50 feet in beam, and drew about 22 feet. Ready for sea, she cost in 1776 some £54,000, which is perhaps the equivalent today of $1,500,000. She probably carried thirty 32-pounders, twenty-eight 24-pounders, thirty 18-pounders or 12-pounders on the upper deck, and twelve 12-pounders on the quarterdeck and forecastle. After 1779 an English 100-gun ship would also carry ten carronades, although these stubby short-range weapons were never included in the rated number of guns. Other vessels carried carronades in proportion to their size; thus a 74-gun ship actually mounted 82 carriage guns (swivels were never included in rating a ship's armament), while the battery of a 36-gun frigate really totaled 44. To further confuse, the armament of any ship was subject to change; an extra pair of cannon might be mounted at one time while others might be removed, or substituted for others of different calibers.

The crews, both for sail handling and manning the guns, were necessarily large. A 100-gun ship might have a crew of 850-900 men; a 74, of 650.

The workhorse of the battle fleet was the two-decker 74. It was cheaper to build and required a smaller crew than a three-decker, while its heavy timbers and armament of twenty-eight 32-pounders, thirty 24-pounders and sixteen 9's compared favorably with the

Ship-rigged Vessel

Ketch

Brig

A snow differed from a brig in setting a sail on the lower yard of the after-mast—while the gaff of the driver is set on a trysail mast, just aft of the mainmast.

Snow

Brigantine

Schooner (with single topsail)

Topsail Sloop

British Naval Cutter

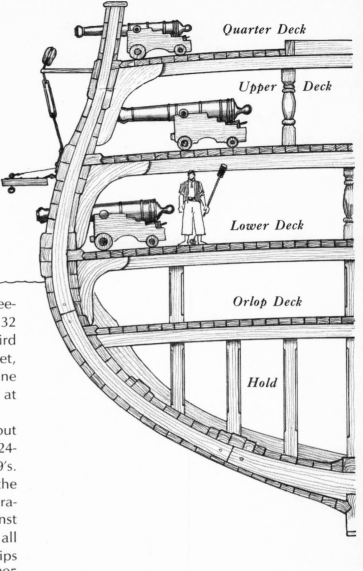

Cross section (as if sliced through just aft of the mainmast) of a typical 74-gun vessel showing the decks, deck beams, knees and side timbering.
A gunport is open and a 32-pounder run out for firing. Only in the larger men-of-war was there much head-room. In smaller vessels a man (and they were usually much shorter than the average American of today) had to duck for the deck beams.

Quarter Deck

Upper   Deck

Lower Deck

Orlop Deck

Hold

construction and heavy batteries of a three-decker. Thus, at the battle off Ushant, of 32 French ships of the line more than one-third were of this class, while of the British fleet, 74's made up one-half. Of 174 ships of the line listed (January 20, 1783) by the Royal Navy at the end of the war, 81 were 74's.

Next in numbers were the 64's, but their heavy batteries consisted only of 24- and 18-pounders, 26 of each plus a dozen 9's. They took their place in the line during the Revolutionary War period, but their comparatively light hulls and armament were against them. And in the next two decades they all but disappeared. Only three of the 27 ships of the line with Nelson at Trafalgar in 1805 were 64's, while 16 were of the 74-gun class. Of the Allied battle line of 33 sail, 22 were 74's and only one a 64-gun ship.

The drawing below of the profile of a 74 shows the various deck levels.

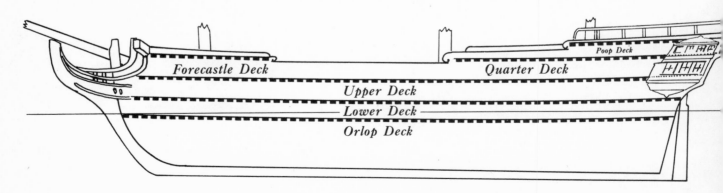

Forecastle Deck

Quarter Deck

Poop Deck

Upper Deck

Lower Deck

Orlop Deck

The fifth- and sixth-rates made up the cruiser squadrons. The frigates were by far the most numerous and efficient of this class, as well as being the best known. Their armament varied between 20 and 44 guns, but in the British service by far the greater number were 32's, followed by 28's, 44's, and 36's in that order.

Frigates were ship-rigged, and carried their main armament—sometimes of 9-, but usually of 12- or 18-pounder guns—on one deck. Lighter guns (or later, in the Royal Navy, carronades) were mounted on the quarterdeck. They served a great variety of purposes: scouting, convoy duty, anti-privateer patrols, commerce raiding, and carrying dispatches, to name a few—and no admiral ever admitted having enough of them. When the fleet formed line of battle the frigates were usually stationed on the unengaged side, ready to take a disabled ship in tow, harass a crippled enemy, or as signal repeaters, to display to ships far down the battle line the signal flags hoisted by the flagship.

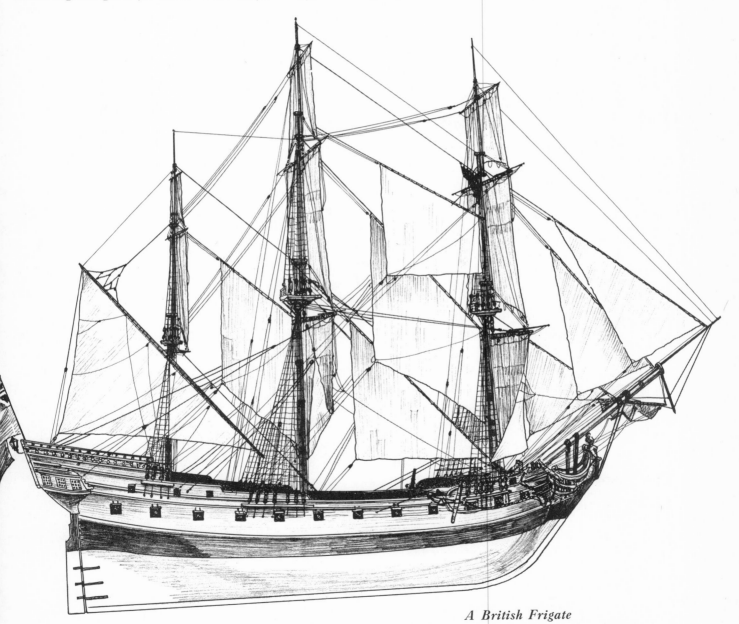

A British Frigate

Bomb Ketch

Sloops carried from 8 to 20 guns. They were usually ship-rigged and carried their armament on one deck. Brigs (square-rigged, with two masts), brigantines, and schooners were the most common of the smaller craft. They performed, on a minor scale, the same work as the frigates, but seldom operated with the battle fleet.

Bomb vessels, or "bombs" as they were called, were specially designed and rigged to carry one or two great sea mortars, throwing shells a foot or more in diameter. Usually ketch-rigged (although totally unlike anything we know as a ketch today), these vessels were easily distinguishable by their carrying their masts stepped well aft. This gave them a peculiar silhouette, but provided room for the mortars, which were customarily bedded on piles of cable (to absorb some of the shock of recoil) in a hold in the foredeck. They carried a broadside armament as well as their mortars, sometimes as many as a dozen

9-pounders. They were used for the bombardment of positions ashore, and the explosion of the heavy hollow iron spheres, filled with powder, could cause considerable damage. No ketch-rigged bombs were built for the Royal Navy after 1757; after that year bombs were ship-rigged.

Fire was a thing particularly dreaded in the days of wooden ships, and naturally had been used as a weapon in naval warfare since antiquity. Flaming arrows, balls of incendiary material, Greek fire—all had been used at one time or another. But by 1775 the use of fire at sea was confined to the occasional use of carcasses or red-hot shot—and the fire ships.

These vessels, crammed with combustibles, were sailed alongside their targets—or as close as circumstances would allow. Trains were already laid, so that a flaming torch tossed down a hatch would ignite the whole craft. Then the crew jumped into their boat, towed alongside or astern, and made their escape.

If all went well, the craft was a roaring inferno before the enemy could attempt to board and extinguish the blaze. To counteract this menace, the enemy gunners did their best to sink the fire ship before she got close while ship's boats strove to grapple the flaming hulks and tow them clear.

Their effectiveness depended largely on the courage of the commanders and crews. Vessels fired prematurely could usually be avoided, to drift harmlessly with wind and tide. But so great was the fear of these vessels that against an anchorage full of shipping even a random attack was sufficient to cause a panic. More than one squadron, sighting these fiery monsters drifting down on the tide, was stampeded into cutting its cables and making its way to sea as best it could.

Fire ships were also included with the battle squadrons, and used in the melee to destroy specified targets, but by Revolutionary War days this use of fire ships in fleet actions was dying out. Whereas in the great battles of the preceding century fire ships might

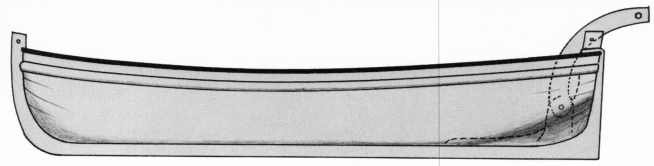

Launch—Showing Davit Used for Laying out and Recovering Anchors

Ships' Boats

36-foot Launch—Sloop Rigged

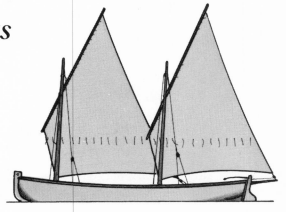

30-foot Cutter with lug sails

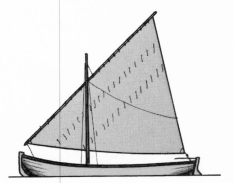

22-foot Jolly Boat—Lateen Rig

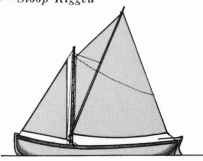

20-foot Whaleboat—Sprit Rigged

number forty or fifty, at Ushant in 1778 Keppel had but two, and neither of these was in action. This was due for the most part to the fact that fleets were far smaller (at the battle of Lowestoft in 1665, the Dutch and English fleets each numbered over 100 men-of-war) and more maneuverable, and the individual ships were more heavily gunned.

Ships carried several small boats, the number varying with the size of the ship. These were carried on deck, two or three sometimes "nested" one inside the other, and usually in the space between the main and foremasts. In larger vessels this space, which then lay between the quarterdeck and forecastle, was often decked, but only at each side, leaving gangways between the superstructures. On the open beams between the gangways were stowed the spare masts, spars, and booms, and it was on these that the ship's boats were nested. In a very small craft the larger boat (she might only have two) was often towed. In action the boats, or some of them, were sometimes hoisted out and towed. Otherwise, when needed, they were often so damaged that they could not be launched.

Boats were of various types and sizes. The largest was the launch. An old formula for determining the length of the launch was to multiply the square root of the length of the ship by 2.6. The breadth was one-fourth of this figure. Thus the launch of a 74-gun ship might have been some 36 feet long and 9 feet in beam and that of a 32-gun frigate like the *Hancock,* 31 feet long. The average small brig, such as *Cabot,* might have had a launch about 23 feet, six inches.

Next in size was the cutter. A 74 might carry four or five. The first and second cutters of ships of the line and first cutters of frigates or sloops were to be nine-tenths of the launch. The third and fourth cutters of ships of the line and second cutter of the smaller vessels was to be nine-tenths of the first cutter; thus the first cutter of our 74 would be about 32 feet 5 inches and the third some 29 feet.

A 36-foot launch might have nine oars a side; a 24-foot cutter, five. Oars were double- or single-banked—that is, rowed by two men, or one. Tholepins were usually used, although in some boats the oars worked in square notches cut in the gunwales.

Gigs were sometimes carried. They were finer lined, less in beam and draught than the cutter and thus faster. A 28-foot cutter might have a beam of seven feet and draw three feet two inches. A gig of the same length would be some five feet in beam and draw two

feet. A slightly smaller work boat was called a jolly boat.

Other boats were called quarter boats, carried on davits on the ship's quarters. Some ships carried sternboats hung on davits over the stern, and barges—in dimensions midway between cutters and gigs.

Ships' boats of the period were bluff-bowed and tubby-looking compared with similar craft today. That they were seaworthy is proved by the remarkable voyage of the *Bounty's* launch. Only 23 feet long and 6 feet 9 inches in beam, overloaded with 19 men and provisions, the little craft, under her two lug sails, made the island of Timor, 3,600 miles away from where the mutineers cast her off, without serious mishap. Bligh, who died a vice admiral, may have been a harsh and unjust commander but there is no disputing his seamanship.

Boats were rigged in various fashions. A large launch might be sloop-rigged. Smaller launches and cutters often carried lug sails on two masts. The lateen rig was sometimes used for gigs and jolly boats.

Launches were sometimes fitted with a heavy form of davit at the stern, to facilitate laying out and recovering anchors. On occasion (for landing or cutting-out operations) the larger launches and cutters carried small cannon or carronades in the bows.

Boats were usually hoisted in and out by means of tackles on the yards (main and fore) and stays. When davits were used, they were of wood. Quarter davits, which sometimes held two boats, could be lowered outboard. Some ships carried stern davits. They were fixed, projecting over the stern, and the boat was hauled up and lashed against the counter.

Shipbuilding and Repair

Chapter 5

Ships were, when circumstances permitted, "laid down" in great sheds, called mould lofts. Here the lines of the vessel were drawn out full size on the floor of the loft, scaled up from the designer's plan, or sometimes from a wooden half model. The shape and structural members once drawn to full size, the timbers were chosen and cut or hewn to shape.

Trees with natural crooks were used for "knees" and other anglelike timbers. Such trees were not easy to find, and often a vessel was held up on the stocks for want of suitably shaped timbers for the curved members. This was one of the reasons for the preference in British shipyards for English oak. For the oaks grown in the forests of northern Europe tended to grow tall and straight—fine for planking—but it was the gnarled English "hedgerow" oak, grown where its branches had opportunity to spread, that furnished the best of the "compass" timbers, as they were called.

All work was done by hand. Sawmills powered by water were very rare. Planks and other sawn timbers were cut over a sawpit with long two-man saws, one man standing on or above the timber, the other in the pit below. The shaping was mostly done with broadaxe and adz.

Timber was measured by the "load," equal to 50 cubic feet. The average oak contained about one load, which weighed in the neighborhood of a ton. The timber which went into a "74" of Revolutionary days equalled 3,700 loads, of which no fewer than 1,890 loads were compass timber and 150 more were used for knees. Planking over four inches thick was known as "thick stuff," and 410 loads of that went into the hull, as well as 360 loads of three- and four-inch planking. When it is realized that oaks were not usually cut until they were about 100 years old (more in the case of those used for exceptionally heavy pieces), it will be understood that the problem of supplying shipyards, especially in time of war, was sometimes acute.

Shipwrights in England were convinced that the slow-growing oak, *Quercus robur,* was the finest shipbuilding material in the world. They narrowed this preference down to the oaks grown in four counties—Surrey, Kent, Hampshire, and Sussex—and of these the best was held to be that from the forests of Sussex. Northern oaks, and the white oak, *Quercus alba,* of North America they held in low esteem. Actually, the live oak, *Quercus virginiana,* which grows, or grew, in a narrow

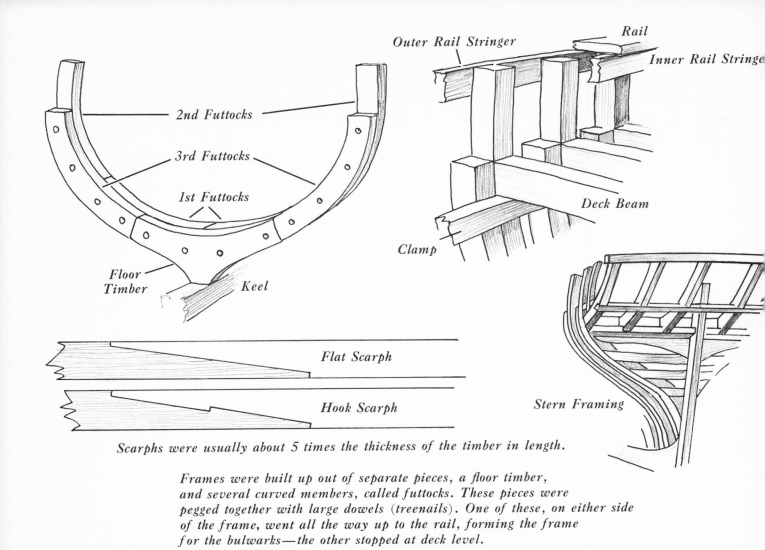

2nd Futtocks

3rd Futtocks

1st Futtocks

Floor Timber

Keel

Outer Rail Stringer

Rail

Inner Rail Stringer

Deck Beam

Clamp

Flat Scarph

Hook Scarph

Stern Framing

Scarphs were usually about 5 times the thickness of the timber in length.

Frames were built up out of separate pieces, a floor timber, and several curved members, called futtocks. These pieces were pegged together with large dowels (treenails). One of these, on either side of the frame, went all the way up to the rail, forming the frame for the bulwarks—the other stopped at deck level.

strip some twenty miles wide from Virginia to the Mississippi was equal, or superior, to the English oak. It was from such timber that the *Constitution* got her nickname of "Old Ironsides." Growing in the same range as the live oak, but in a belt some 100 miles deep, well suited for both masts and ship timber, was *Pinus palustris*, generally known as long-leaf pine, Georgia pine, or yellow pine. For some reason British shipbuilders did not discover the virtues of this splendid timber until after the Revolution. But American shipmen knew it well, and built many stout vessels from it.

The forests of America also produced other magnificent, tall, straight pines which were used for masts and spars. Lacking such trees, England imported much of this material from the Colonies and also from the Baltic countries. The Revolutionary War caused a

further dependence on the Baltic and the less developed timber industry in Canada.

Ships were usually built in the open, exposed to the weather. It was believed that this helped season the timber, and in English dockyards it was customary to leave the frame exposed for a year or more before planking. First, the keel was laid down on blocks, some four or five feet apart. The keel timbers were then joined, "scarfed" together, and fastened with huge bolts. The upright members, the stem and stern posts, were raised into position, and the various knee and angle pieces which supported them were worked into place. The frames, or ribs, were then set up, with the knees and beams which were to support the decks.

Planking was fastened to these frames with treenails (pronounced, and sometimes spelled, trunnels). These were wooden pegs which were driven into holes bored through planks and frames with augers. Treenails were usually of oak, cut from the upper part of the tree to be free from sap and knots, and well seasoned. Some were 36 inches long and 2 inches in diameter. Drilling the holes was a tricky business, and the men who used the augers were specialists in their trade. When the treenails had been driven, the ends were expanded by means of thin wedges, so locking the pegs in place. Iron bolts and nails were also used, especially in timbers above the waterline, and a blacksmith's shop was a part of every shipyard.

The planking, or strakes as shipbuilders call them, of a wooden-hulled warship was not all of the same thickness. The heaviest of these strakes were the "wales," and formulas were set up for determining the thickness and width of these wales, and of the strakes between them, for ships of various sizes. In some vessels, especially after 1800, the strakes

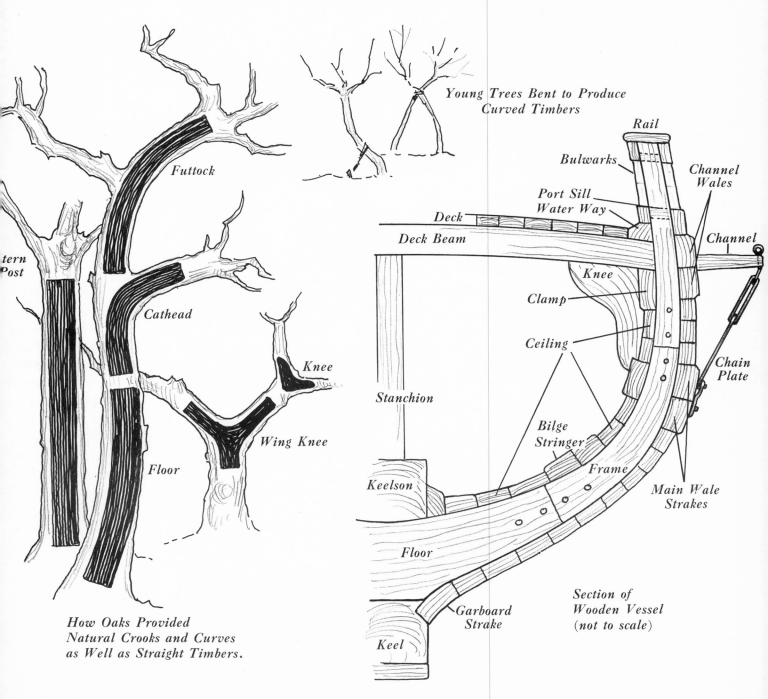

Young Trees Bent to Produce Curved Timbers

How Oaks Provided Natural Crooks and Curves as Well as Straight Timbers.

Section of Wooden Vessel (not to scale)

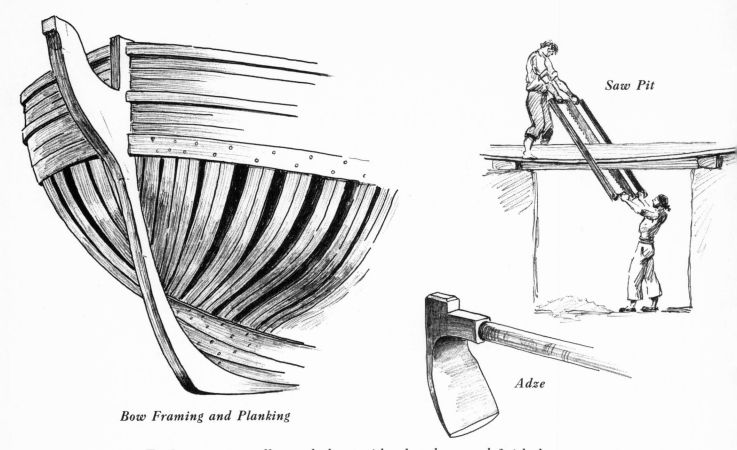

Saw Pit

Adze

Bow Framing and Planking

Timbers were usually roughed out with a broad axe and finished with an adze. A good man with a razor-sharp adze could finish a timber almost as smooth as if it had been planed.

appear flush, or almost flush, with the wales. But if you look at models of earlier ships, the wales appear prominently. There were several of these wales, placed where they not only braced the ship longitudinally but where there was extra strain, as abreast of the various decks, chain plates, etc. The gunwale, or "gunnel" as it is pronounced, is now the term for the upper timber of a small boat. Originally it was the heavy wale supporting the timber ends of the deck on which the guns of early warships were mounted.

Major European dockyards had one or more dry docks, in which vessels of the largest size were built. This was because the larger the ship the harder it was to launch. Usually anything less than a three-decker was built on the stocks, and care was taken in selecting a building site that the ground was solid enough to support the keel blocks, that the angle of

descent to the water's edge was neither too great nor too small, and that there was sufficient depth of water at the end of the ways.

Once launched, the vessel was brought alongside a sheer hulk, often an old ship of the line cut down a deck or two. The sheer hulk was fitted with a sturdy mast and sheerlegs, with their supporting tackle, with which even the heaviest spar could be lifted and lowered (stepped) into place. Masts and spars were usually of fir, pine, or spruce, spruce being customarily used for the lighter spars.

The lower masts of a large vessel were massive; an inch of diameter to a yard of length was the general rule. The mainmast of a 32-gun frigate might be some 28 inches in diameter, while that of a "74" was around 40 inches. Other masts and spars were in proportion, the foremast, for instance, being eight-ninths of the mainmast.

When possible the lower masts were made of single timbers. Such trees were hard to find, even in the great forests of North America. Perhaps one tree in 10,000 might prove suitable. A single rotten knothole could be the cause of rejection. And such select trees, felled and transported to the coast, were expensive. Prior to the Revolution a single trunk 108 feet long and 3 feet in diameter cost £110, a high price in those days. The forests of the Baltic regions, after centuries of timbering, could seldom furnish trees of such size, and in Europe it was customary to build up the lower masts out of several timbers, fastened together and bound with iron hoops.

Unlike the timbers of the hull, which were exposed to the air to season, those of the masts and spars were of resinous wood. These, to keep them sound and resilient, were stored under water, to exclude the air, and every dockyard had a mast pond in which the great spars were kept. There were also long mast houses where the timbers were worked into the required dimensions and shapes.

A Sheer Hulk Stepping a Mainmast

Each shipyard or shipbuilding town also had its rope works and walk, the latter roofed over for its length of perhaps 400 yards. Here the fibers, of hemp or some other material, were "hackled," or combed out, by drawing them through a series of steel prongs mounted on boards. The combed fibers were then spun into yarn, formed into strands, and the strands ultimately laid into rope. The amount of cordage which went into the rigging of a square-rigged vessel was staggering, and large quantities were always stored aboard for repairs and replacement.

Besides the rope walks, there were also the sail lofts, where bolts of heavy linen were converted into suits of sails. Spare sails were always carried aboard as well as stores of sailcloth and heavy storm canvas to be bent on when prolonged spells of rough weather were expected.

American ships were painted in various ways, suiting the fancy of the builders or captains. Topsides were often yellow or brown, with narrow black stripes; or black, with thin lines of yellow or white. Royal Navy ships of the period usually were painted a light yellow or varnished brown, with a wide black band, or boot, above the copper. Naval vessels were often painted red or brown inside on bulwarks and overhead. This was to make the blood, with which they were often liberally spattered in action, less noticeable. Spars were usually varnished brown, while the standing rigging, blocks, and deadeyes (the wooden fittings with which the shrouds were set up) were tarred black.

The Kedge-Anchor, or Young Sailors' Assistant gives a recipe for blacking a ship's standing rigging. "To a half barrel of tar add 6 gallons of whiskey, 4 pounds of litharge, 4 pounds of lamp black, 2 buckets of boiling beef-pickle, or hot salt water out of the coppers, if the other cannot be had conveniently; mix well together and apply immediately."

At one time the ornamentation was elaborately carved and gilded but by the late 1700's this useless and expensive decoration was dying out. What scroll work and carving was still used was more likely to be picked out in yellow or some appropriate color.

One of the greatest destroyers of the old "wooden walls" was dry rot. It was more to be feared than the guns of the enemy. Clever men sought to combat its ravages for centuries, but as long as ships were built of wood the problem was never solved. Dry rot is a fungus growth which penetrates the fibers of wood, and ultimately reduces it to powder. On the surface it often manifests itself by a toadstool-like growth, and can spread from diseased timber to sound. It seldom occurs when timber is completely dry, or always immersed, but its spores prefer a moist, warm, stagnant atmosphere. The use of unseasoned timber and improper ventilation were two of the main causes. In normal times sufficient stocks of well-seasoned timber were at hand in the yards, but in an emergency, when a "crash" building program cleared the shipyards out of proper material, green timber was used with disastrous results.

In an age of iron and steel the effect of dry rot in ships, and so, ultimately, on strategy and even national policy is hard to comprehend. But so prevalent was this scourge that some vessels, built of inferior green timbers, were pronounced unserviceable less than three years after being launched. When it is realized that perhaps 4,000 great trees were used in the hull of one ship of the line, it will be seen what a drain such a building program put on a nation's forests.

Another enemy of the wooden ship was the teredo, or ship worm. While oak, with its tannic acid, was not as palatable to this pest as some other woods, worm damage was always a serious problem. These mollusks, some species of which may reach a length of three feet, burrow rapidly into wood, to considerable depths, and so close together that a mere paper-thin wall separates one tunnel from the next. Some vessels returned to the dockyards with their hulls so honeycombed with holes

Fothering a Sail Over a Shot Hole

made by these borers that they leaked like sieves, and only luck and constant pumping got them home at all.

Harold A. Larrabee in *Decision at the Chesapeake* quotes Rear Admiral Thomas Graves as complaining: "The wooden bottoms in the Chesapeake and at Carolina are eat up presently, the small men-of-war upon the out posts here, are so perforated by the worm, we find a necessity of hauling them frequently on shore to prevent their sinking, this will oblige me to keep every thing upon copper in this country, and to send home as convoys all the wooden bottoms..."

Through the centuries men tried by various means to check the ravages of these marine tunnellers. Hulls were coated with tar, smeared with chemical substances containing poisons, sheathed in lead (which was fairly successful), even covered with hides. Then, in 1761, the British 32-gun frigate *Alarm* went to sea with her hull plated with thin sheets of copper. The experiment was a success, although for some years galvanic action, set up between the copper sheathing and iron bolts in the hulls gave some trouble. Later, copper fastenings were used in the underwater portions of all coppered hulls.

Coppered bottoms were also freer of the barnacles and marine growth which normally accumulated on vessels' hulls. This mass of vegetation naturally affected a vessel's speed, and when the accumulation reached serious proportions the vessel had to be careened in some convenient location and the hull scraped. The effects of coppering are frequently mentioned in official reports, especially in the Revolutionary War period, when some ships were coppered and others were not. One uncoppered vessel might slow down a whole squadron, with possible unfortunate results.

Temporary repairs to a damaged hull were sometimes made by "fothering" a spare sail or large piece of canvas over the hole or leak. The canvas, preferably doubled, was lowered under the hull with ropes at each corner, and drawn over the leak. The ropes and the pressure of the water kept the sail in place. While by no means watertight, this often served to allow the pumps to keep ahead of the incoming water.

When ships were damaged or needed work done on their bottoms and no dry dock was available, they were hove down, or careened. This was a major operation. Guns and stores were landed, and ballast removed. All yards were sent down and the topmasts and topgallant masts were struck. All openings, such as gunports and scuttles, were caulked tight. Battens were nailed on the decks, to serve as footholds when the decks were at a steep angle.

The ship was anchored bow and stern, and the shrouds on the lower masts (fore and main) were strengthened (on the side opposite that which was to be hove down) with preventer tackle. Usually spars were lashed to the lower mastheads and made fast inside the bulwarks as an additional precaution. Several outriggers, fastened through the gunports, also supported tackle which helped relieve the strain on the masts.

When everything was securely braced, extra heavy tackles were secured to the fore and main mastheads and to points firmly anchored on shore. The hauling parts were then taken to capstans and the ship pulled over on her side. Work was done from stages or rafts.

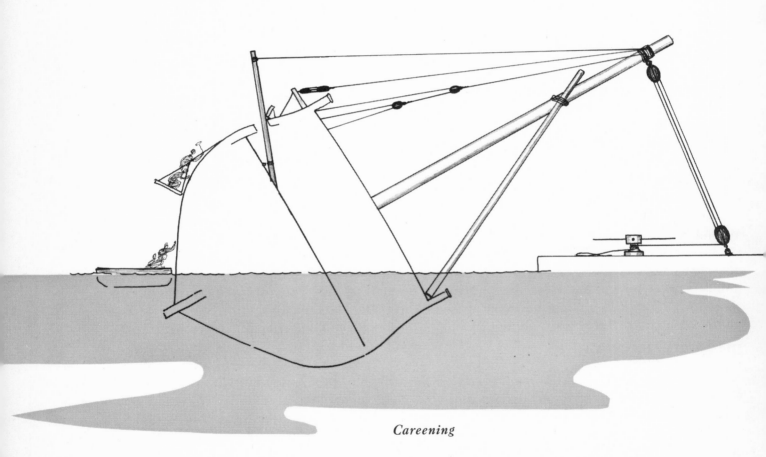

Careening

Valor at Valcour Island

Chapter 6

There were few actions between Colonial and British forces which could be classed as naval battles. Such engagements as there were involved only a few vessels, and none were of any great strategic importance. With one exception. On October 11, 1776 at Valcour Island, near the western shore of Lake Champlain, was fought an action which may well have decided the fate of the Revolution. Most of the vessels, at least on the American side, had a peculiarly homemade look—weird craft which could not have faced even a fresh breeze on the ocean. They were manned by an equally strange collection of fighting men; only a handful could be called sailors. As perhaps was to be expected, they lost their battle —but their fight was as much for time as anything else. And time they won, time for the weak Colonial forces to gather, arm, and train; time that was to be a vital factor when "Gentleman Johnny" Burgoyne and his redcoats came down the lakes in the summer of 1777 in the invasion that ended at Saratoga.

The hero of Valcour Island was a man damned in American history as a traitor. Whatever the reasons for his defection—real or fancied slights by Congress, debts, disgust at the way the war was being handled, or a

genuine conviction that the Colonies could not win in the long run—while his sword was still at the disposal of the Colonies Benedict Arnold fought with a fire and determination second to none among Washington's generals. His fantastic march to Quebec, over heartbreaking country and in appalling weather, is an example of what the drive and furious energy of an outstanding commander can accomplish. That the Canadian venture ended in a sad defeat beneath the walls of that northern fortress was no fault of his. It was due in great part to his indomitable will that the disease-stricken remnants of the American forces were led down the Richelieu River to the comparative safety of Ile-aux-Noix and, ultimately, Ticonderoga.

Arnold was general (or admiral) enough to see that the British would use the lakes as an invasion route to cut the revolted Colonies in two. And he was desperate enough to make a superhuman effort—and force others to make superhuman efforts—to scrape together a fleet capable of at least delaying the British advance. So during the summer of 1776 the woods around Crown Point, Ticonderoga, and Skenesboro rang with the blows of axes and the crash of falling timber.

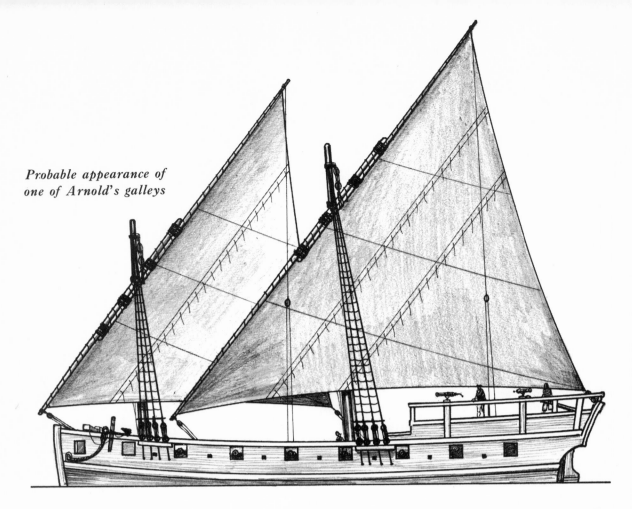

Probable appearance of one of Arnold's galleys

Wood there was in plenty, but even axes were lacking at first. Of shipbuilding tools—adzes, saws, chisels, augers, hammers, grindstones—there were none. Nor were there skilled carpenters, except a handful who had enlisted in the army. And where in that wilderness were bolts, nails, canvas, rope, blocks, paint, or tar to be had?

But Arnold demanded a fleet and a fleet there was. Although the coastal yards were busy building warships and privateers, four companies of ship's carpenters, fifty to a company and each man with his own tools, trudged in from Massachusetts, Rhode Island, Connecticut, and even Philadelphia. Sailmakers came too, and riggers and blacksmiths, and by August 20, Arnold's little squadron was ready to set sail.

It was a strange collection. There was the *Royal Savage* (schooner, eight 6-pounders and four 4-pounders), captured the previous year at St. Johns. This vessel, and two small schooners, *Liberty* and *Revenge,* and the sloop

Enterprise comprised the original flotilla. But this was not enough. The British general, Sir Guy Carleton, was building an invasion fleet at the northern end of the lake and Arnold needed more firepower. There was neither enough time nor skilled labor to build large vessels of conventional design. So two types of smaller craft were constructed—row galleys and gondolas. The row galleys were round-bottomed, some 72 feet long and 20 feet in beam. Their armament was mixed, *Washington* carrying two 18-pounders, two 12-pounders, two 9-pounders, and four 4-pounders, as well as a 2-pounder and eight swivels on her quarterdeck. *Trumbull* carried one 18-pounder, one 12-pounder, two 9-pounders, six 6-pounders, and swivels. They were rigged with triangular lateen sails, on two short masts, for ease of handling. The gondolas were flat-bottomed, some 45 feet long, carrying three guns: a 12-pounder and two 9's. One mast carried two square sails, and each had a crew of 45. The row galleys each carried 80 men.

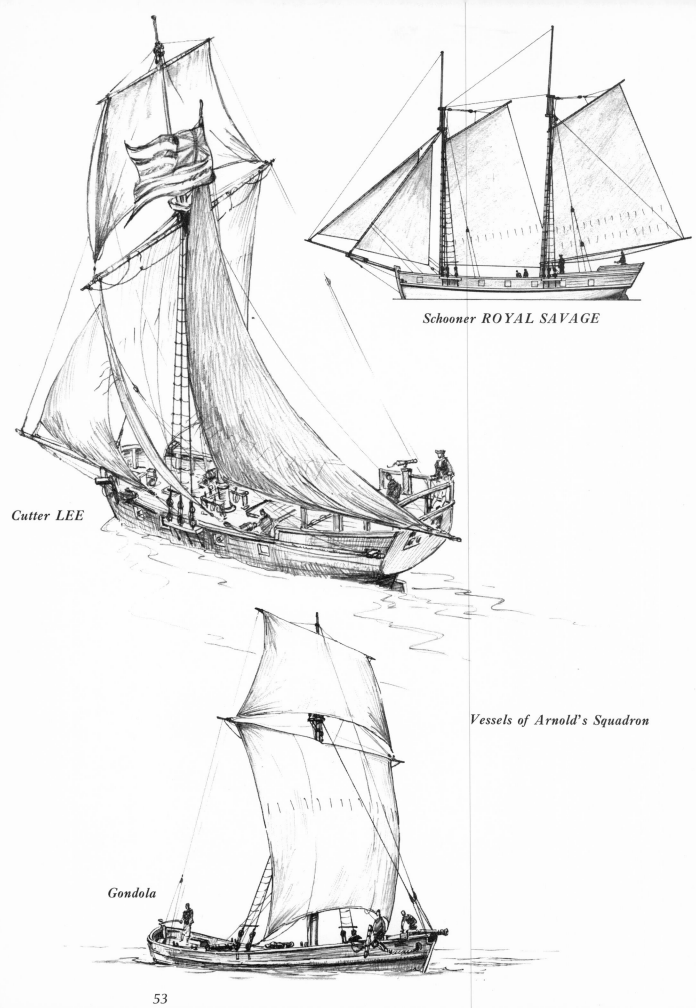

Schooner *ROYAL SAVAGE*

Cutter LEE

Vessels of Arnold's Squadron

Gondola

53

British Radeau THUNDERER

Carleton, with the British fleet in the St. Lawrence to furnish him with trained men and materials, had lost no time in constructing a small navy at his end of the lake. Working with great rapidity, his workmen had rebuilt a gondola, *Loyal Convert*, carrying seven 9-pounder guns. This *Loyal Convert* was the ex-American *Convert*, built on the St. Lawrence. After capture by the British, she was taken apart and transported to St. Johns, where she was reassembled. Twenty gunboats were also built, each carrying one gun in the bow, and a great sailing raft, or radeau, *Thunderer*,

carrying six 24-pounders, six 12's, two howitzers, and a crew of 300 men. But the pride of his fleet was the *Inflexible*, a three-masted ship with eighteen 12-pounders. She and two schooners (*Maria*, fourteen 6-pounders, and *Carleton*, twelve 6-pounders) had been taken to pieces below the rapids on the Richelieu and reconstructed at St. Johns. How well the British and Canadians worked is shown by the fact that the *Inflexible* was rebuilt, rigged, and equipped in 28 days. Even so, Carleton's armada was not ready to sail before October 4.

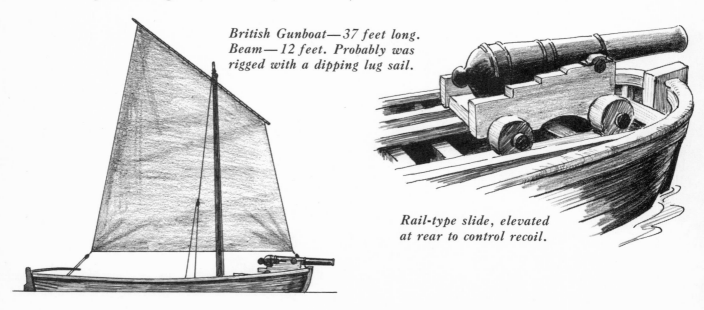

British Gunboat—37 feet long. Beam—12 feet. Probably was rigged with a dipping lug sail.

Rail-type slide, elevated at rear to control recoil.

Besides the fighting ships there were thirty longboats and some 400 bateaux, hauled up the rapids to transport troops and supplies.

Part of Arnold's squadron was completed by August 20, and he sailed in *Royal Savage* from Crown Point on August 24. Gales forced him to put into Buttonmould Bay, and it was not until the beginning of September that he reached the northern end of the lake.

Had Arnold's fleet been more powerful he undoubtedly would have sought to attack the British and smash the invasion before it began. But the broadsides of Carleton's fleet could throw almost twice the weight of metal as those of the Americans, his men were trained seamen under Royal Navy officers, and his larger vessels carried men of the Twenty-ninth Regiment acting as marines. Arnold's squadron, on the other hand, was manned largely by landsmen. Of his force, which did not exceed 700 men at the time of the action, Arnold wrote: "We have a wretched, motley crew in the fleet. The Marines are the refuse of every regiment, and the seamen, few of them were ever wet with salt water." Arnold was a man of action, but his actions were usually tempered with caution. To meet the British head on in an open engagement was to invite disaster.

After some maneuvering the American general found a favorable position in the channel between Valcour Island and the shore. Here he was joined by three more galleys (*Washington, Congress,* and *Trumbull*), and two gondolas (*Jersey* and *Spitfire*).

The anchorage at Valcour Island was hidden from vessels advancing from the north by a heavily wooded promontory projecting from the island on its west side. Arnold's plan was to form a line of battle in a crescent inside the southern end of the channel. Then, if the chance presented itself, he could sail out and fall on the rear of the unsuspecting British as they passed. Or he could force them to attack him at a disadvantage, against the wind and in the teeth of a converging fire from his crescent of guns.

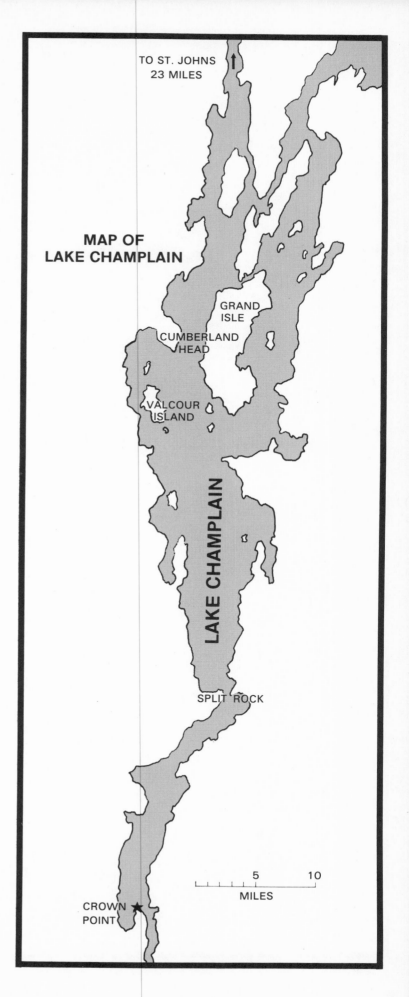

MAP OF
LAKE CHAMPLAIN

TO ST. JOHNS
23 MILES

GRAND
ISLE

CUMBERLAND
HEAD

VALCOUR
ISLAND

LAKE CHAMPLAIN

SPLIT ROCK

5   10
MILES

CROWN
POINT

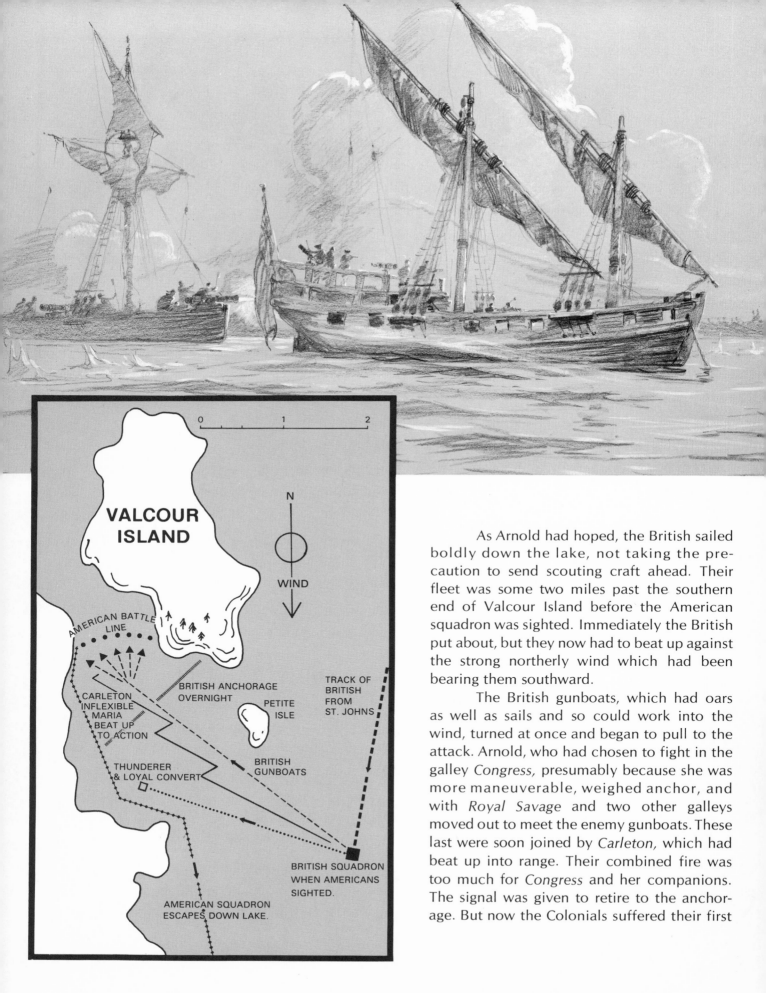

VALCOUR ISLAND

0 1 2

N

WIND

AMERICAN BATTLE LINE

BRITISH ANCHORAGE OVERNIGHT

CARLETON INFLEXIBLE MARIA BEAT UP TO ACTION

PETITE ISLE

TRACK OF BRITISH FROM ST. JOHNS

THUNDERER & LOYAL CONVERT

BRITISH GUNBOATS

BRITISH SQUADRON WHEN AMERICANS SIGHTED.

AMERICAN SQUADRON ESCAPES DOWN LAKE.

As Arnold had hoped, the British sailed boldly down the lake, not taking the precaution to send scouting craft ahead. Their fleet was some two miles past the southern end of Valcour Island before the American squadron was sighted. Immediately the British put about, but they now had to beat up against the strong northerly wind which had been bearing them southward.

The British gunboats, which had oars as well as sails and so could work into the wind, turned at once and began to pull to the attack. Arnold, who had chosen to fight in the galley *Congress,* presumably because she was more maneuverable, weighed anchor, and with *Royal Savage* and two other galleys moved out to meet the enemy gunboats. These last were soon joined by *Carleton,* which had beat up into range. Their combined fire was too much for *Congress* and her companions. The signal was given to retire to the anchorage. But now the Colonials suffered their first

loss. *Royal Savage* had been damaged aloft by the British fire. In trying to tack into the narrow channel she went aground on the southern end of Valcour Island. Her crew made great efforts to refloat her, but she was finally abandoned. Some of her crew, escaping to shore, fell victims to Carleton's Indians, who swarmed in the thick woods of both the island and the mainland across the channel.

About noon the action became general. The American vessels—the schooner *Revenge;* sloop *Enterprise;* cutter *Lee;* galleys *Trumbull, Washington,* and *Congress;* and the gondolas *Providence, New Haven, Boston, Spitfire, Philadelphia, Connecticut, Jersey,* and *New York*—were all engaged. Of the British forces the unhandy radeau *Thunderer* and the gondola *Loyal Convert* were too far downwind to take any part in the action, while the square-rigged *Inflexible* could not be brought to within close range until the end of the action, thus depriving Carleton of his most powerful ships.

The twenty gunboats with four armed longboats and *Carleton* kept up a hot fire, but the American cannonade was heavy. *Carleton* was the target for many American guns, Arnold sighting some of the guns of *Congress* himself. The British schooner, which had anchored some 350 yards from the American line, was badly knocked about. Her cable spring, which held her broadside to the wind, was shot away; and she swung to her anchor, head to wind. In this position she was raked by the American fire and, lacking bow guns, could make no reply. A young midshipman, Edward Pellew (who later achieved fame as Admiral, Viscount Exmouth) climbed out on her bowsprit, amid a hail of cannon shot and musketry, and attempted to set her jib. The sail would not fill. Then two boats pulled up, Pellew threw them a line, and the battered schooner, half her crew killed or wounded, was towed around and out of action.

The British gunboats had suffered, too. One was sunk, and about 5 P.M., after *Inflexible* had finally come within effective range, they retired some hundreds of yards. From their new position they kept up a long-range fire until dusk, when the whole force anchored and awaited daylight to renew the action.

The *Royal Savage* had been set afire by the British, and the flames lit the still water of the bay as the American commanders came aboard *Congress* to report.

The American squadron was in bad shape. *Congress* had been hulled twelve times, *Washington* had lost almost all her officers, *Philadelphia* hit so badly between wind and water that she sank shortly after the action, and the others hit repeatedly. Worse still, ammunition was running low. A renewal of the battle in the morning would have meant the destruction of the American vessels. The only solution was an immediate retreat, and under cover of darkness, the shattered squadron got under way.

In dead silence and with all lights out (except a lantern, carefully shaded so as to show a glow only directly behind, in the stern of each ship) the American vessels slipped through the British line. By first light they were some ten miles down the lake, off Schuyler Island. Here Arnold, whose *Congress* had brought up the rear—the post of danger—decided to anchor and make repairs. With him were *Washington* and the gondolas *Providence, New York,* and *Jersey. Jersey* ran aground and was too full of water to be got off. *Providence* and *New York* were shattered beyond repair and they were sunk. Pumps working hard, the two remaining galleys started down the lake.

Astern the British were in sight, and ahead, four American gondolas which had lagged behind the main body. The British came down fast with a favorable breeze, the schooner *Maria* in the lead. Arnold opened with his stern guns, but at Split Rock the pursuers caught up. Attacked by *Inflexible, Carle-* *ton,* and *Maria, Washington* was forced to strike her flag. But *Congress* and the gondolas kept up a ragged fire, until Arnold's ship was almost a wreck. At last, with no chance of escape left, Arnold ordered the gondolas run ashore and fired. Guns still banged aboard *Congress* as she covered the retreat of the crews. Then she too was beached and fired, Arnold remaining aboard until she was well and truly alight. Then he leaped ashore, organized his weary crews, and led them through the woods to Crown Point.

Arnold and his men had been heavily defeated. Eleven of his sixteen ships had been taken or destroyed, and eighty men were casualties. Yet the effects of his action were far-reaching.

Because Arnold had demanded the construction of an American squadron, Carleton had been forced to do likewise. This, the preliminary maneuverings and the battle itself had consumed so much precious time that he considered it was too late in the season to besiege Ticonderoga and advance to the Hudson before winter put an end to campaigning. Had he been able to take Ticonderoga in the summer and press on to Albany, the disaster at Saratoga might never have occurred and the British forces from the North could have linked up with Howe's advance up the Hudson. At that stage in the Revolution such an event could well have meant the end for Washington and his hard-pressed troops.

Mahan put it like this: "That the Americans were strong enough to impose the capitulation of Saratoga was due to the invaluable year of delay secured to them in 1776 by their little navy on Lake Champlain, created by the indomitable energy, and handled with the indomitable courage of the traitor, Benedict Arnold."

When we consider that it was the defeat of Burgoyne at Saratoga which led to the entry of France into the war, this "strife of pigmies for the prize of a continent," as it has been called, assumes its true proportions.

The Tale of the Turtle

Chapter 7

Upper New York Bay was crowded with British shipping. From transport and supply ship, sloop, frigate, and ship of the line came the shrilling of whistles and stamp of feet as the crews of more than 100 vessels settled down to the day's routine. In the cabin of *H.M.S. Eagle*, 64, Admiral Lord Howe studied the charts of the waters surrounding Manhattan Island. For to "Black Dick," as his seamen called him, had been given the task of supporting his brother's army, at that moment encamped on Long Island.

Boston, threatened by the Americans' seizure of Dorchester Heights, had been abandoned by the forces of the Crown in March. Now New York was to be the new Tory stronghold. The battle of Long Island had been fought, and the beaten remnant of Washington's army was fortifying itself on Manhattan.

Suddenly a tremendous bang jarred the anchorage out of its morning quiet. Those nearest the explosion saw a tall column of water slowly collapsing into a cloud of dirty gray powder smoke. In an instant the anchorage was in an uproar. Drums beat to quarters as the King's ships prepared for action, while many of the merchant captains cut their cables and drifted down the bay on the ebb tide. For some months there had been rumors of the imminent arrival of some devilish product of Yankee ingenuity. Loyalist informers had reported on a device "to Destroy the Navy, a certain Mr. Bushnel has compleated his Machine...when you may expect to see the Ships in Smoke."

As no captain of any ship, his own or the King's, wanted to see his command go up in smoke, the alarm was understandable. Most people are afraid of the unknown, and the gallant captains of the vast array off Governors Island were no exception. If Mr. Bushnell's machine had done nothing else, it had put a scare into the British seamen. Henceforward no Royal Navy captain, anchored in an American harbor, would sleep quite so soundly.

But what was it that had raised such a din on that quiet morning of September 7, 1776? For an explanation we must turn the clock back some years, to a time when the first rumblings of unrest were heard in the Colonies and a young man named David Bushnell became interested in the possibilities of exploding gunpowder underwater.

Bushnell was the gadget-minded son of a hard-working Connecticut farmer, a youngster who read avidly anything he could get his hands on, and whose greatest ambition was to go to Yale College in nearby New Haven. He finally got there, but not until he was thirty-one. Twice as old as some of the freshmen, and desperately poor, Bushnell's position was not an enviable one. But he had come to work, and work he did (there was little opportunity to do anything else at Yale in 1771).

But there was one distraction—politics. In the best college tradition, Yale was at that time seething with discussions about the oppressive financial measures of the British government, and the lengths to which some of the Colonials were prepared to go to resist them. The Sons of Liberty, loud-spoken, hardcore patriots (if sometimes of questionable motives and morals), were a power in the land. But although tax collectors and excise men were occasionally tarred and feathered, and the barns of outspoken Tories might go up in flames on dark nights, there was little actual violence.

If the situation seemed outwardly calm, however, violence lay just beneath the surface. And it was in this atmosphere that David Bushnell began to experiment with his underwater mine. In more peaceful times his theorizing might have ended with a demonstration for his admiring friends, but Bushnell's mine now acquired a more practical value. The visible signs of the oppressor's might were the wooden hulls and menacing guns of the British men-of-war, anchored in American harbors and patrolling American coasts. What better way to strike a blow for liberty than to devise a means of sinking the enemy vessels, or at least driving them out to sea.

So along with his Greek and Latin, rhetoric and logic, arithmetic and geometry, Bushnell worked away at his drawing board. By the time the musket flashes at Concord and Lexington had touched off the flames of civil

war, plans for an underwater mine were well under way. More than that, there was a plan of a submersible to transport the mine to its target, and to fix it where it would do the most damage. While enthusiastic volunteers—many of his classmates among them—hurried off to the patriots' camp at Cambridge, Bushnell, equally enthusiastic, hurried to his home near Saybrook, there to begin construction of his "sub-marine."

Poverty Island, a little islet long since washed away by the Connecticut River, was chosen as a suitably secluded spot for the enterprise. To further confuse any talkative neighbors or Tory spies, Bushnell gave out that he had turned fisherman, and the shed built to house the strange vessel was, ostensibly, where he kept his seine. There was a fair chance that, had some snooping Loyalist entered the shed, he would never have recognized the contraption within as a vessel at all. Certainly it looked like no craft that had ever sailed on any sea since time began.

Two tortoise shells, about six by seven feet long, clamped together describes its shape best. Viewed from the side, it somewhat resembled a top. Above this peculiarly shaped hull sat a small, round, flat-topped structure with glass ports—the conning tower. A 700-pound lead keel gave her stability. The hull was of oak, of barrel-stave construction, bound with iron and reinforced inside against the pressure of the water. Seams were carefully fitted and caulked, and the hull was liberally coated with tar.

Two brass pipes admitted fresh air and exhausted foul. These air vents had check valves, similar in principle to the snorkel air-intake devices of the modern submarine. Two crank-driven propellers projected through the hull, one to drive the vessel in a horizontal plane, the other vertically. A rudder, worked by a tiller, steered the craft, and two pumps enabled water ballast, admitted by a foot-operated valve to submerge the boat, to be ejected. All shafts which passed through the hull were carefully turned on a lathe to ensure

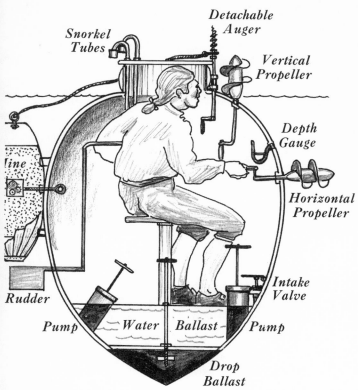

Snorkel Tubes

Detachable Auger

Vertical Propeller

Depth Gauge

Horizontal Propeller

line

Rudder

Pump   Water   Ballast   Pump

Intake Valve

Drop Ballast

Bushnell's Turtle

The mine was attached to the hull by a bolt, and the withdrawal of this bolt not only detached the mine but started the timer. After ticking for about an hour this actuated a flint gunlock, which set off the charge.

To fix the mine to the bottom of an enemy ship an auger bit was mounted in a socket on a crank-driven rod passing through the top of the hull. When under the enemy vessel, the auger was turned, screwing into the wood. When firmly imbedded, the rod was drawn, leaving the bit in the enemy's hull. A line from the bit to the mine anchored the latter to the victim.

The air in the hull was only sufficient for some thirty minutes, and in operation the submersible made her approach on the surface, with only the conning tower and air vents showing. When in danger of discovery, the valve was cracked and sufficient water admitted to submerge.

watertight seals in their bearings.

Depth was shown by a vertical glass tube, closed at the top and leading to the water outside through a brass pipe. Any increase in water pressure forced a column of water further up the glass (in principle the same as a modern depth-sounding tube). A cork, faintly illuminated with fox-fire (the phosphorescent glow sometimes given off by decayed timber) floated on the top of the water column, allowing the depth to be read by a calibrated scale. A compass, also marked with fox-fire, gave direction to the navigator.

As a safety precaution 200 pounds of the lead keel could be released from within the hull, counteracting any tendency to sink suddenly below a safe depth. This drop keel could also act as an anchor, being connected to the hull by a line.

The mine itself was an egg-shaped wooden cask containing the powder charge of 150 pounds and a clockwork timing device.

The *Turtle,* as Bushnell named his strange craft, was an exceedingly well-thought-out piece of engineering. There had been plans for, and experiments with, underwater craft long before, but Bushnell's was the first practical device. And it was not confined to theory and the drafting table. It was actually built—and it actually worked!

Bushnell's brother Ezra helped with the construction, and it was he who was to operate the craft in action. As may be gathered from the foregoing description, the submariner had as many things to do as a one-man bandsman. What with cranking the vertical and horizontal propellers, operating the ballast pumps, navigating (the tiller fitted under the steersman's armpit), and, finally, screwing the auger into the enemy hull, the captain, pilot, and crew of *Turtle* was a busy man. He also needed to be strong as well as skillful, and Bushnell's health was not good.

So it was Ezra, on leave from the Seventh Connecticut Regiment, who completed the tests and practiced himself in handling the vessel both afloat and submerged. It was now the autumn of 1776 and all was ready for an attempt on a live target. Then—disaster. The redoubtable Ezra, the only man trained to operate *Turtle,* came down with one of the fevers which chronically plagued the Continental armies. It looked as if years of planning, a full year of hard work, and all Bushnell's money had been wasted. Where could a man be found who was, in Washington's words, "hardy enough to encounter the variety of dangers, to which he would be exposed; first, from the novelty; secondly, from the difficulty of conducting the machine, and governing it under water, on account of the current; and thirdly, from the consequent uncertainty of hitting the object devoted to destruction, without rising frequently above water for fresh observations, which, when near the vessel, would expose the adventurer to discovery and almost certain death."

Finally, three men who had volunteered to man a fire ship were asked to train for the job. Of these three, Sergeant Ezra Lee was chosen to make the first attempt.

On Friday, September 6, *Turtle* was brought down from Saybrook aboard a sloop, and secured at South Ferry Landing, on the southern tip of Manhattan. Just after midnight a group of men gathered at the wharf to speed America's first submariner on his way. General Putnam was there, and perhaps Washington himself.

After a thorough check of equipment the mine was put in place, the line to the auger bit made fast, and Lee squeezed through the hatch. Lines were taken aboard two whaleboats, which were to tow *Turtle* as close to the anchorage as they dared. The target was *Eagle,* the flagship; her destruction, and possibly that of the admiral as well, would be a severe blow to the British.

The description of what followed is from Sergeant Lee's own account.

> The whaleboats towed me as nigh the fleet as they dared and then cast me off. I however hove about and rowed for 5 glasses [two and one half hours] by the ships' bells before the tide slackened so that I could get alongside a man-of-war which lay above the transports. The moon was about 2 hours high and the daylight about one. When I rowed [by rowing Lee meant turning the horizontal screw propeller] under the stern of the ship I could see the men on deck and hear them talk. I then shut down all doors, sunk down and came up under the bottom of the ship. Up with the screw [auger bit] against the bottom but found it would not enter. I pulled along to find another place, but deviated a little to one side and immediately rose with great velocity and came above the surface 2 or 3 feet between the ship and the daylight, then sunk again like a porpoise. I hove about to try again, but on further thought I gave out, knowing that as soon as it was light the ships' boats would be rowing in all directions and I thought the best

generalship was to retreat as fast as I could, as I had 4 miles to go before passing Governors Island. So I jogg'd on, as fast as I could, and my compass then being of no use to me, I was obliged to rise up every few minutes to see that I sailed in the right direction, but for this purpose keeping the machine on the surface of the water and the doors open. I was much afraid of getting aground on the Island, as the tide of the flood set on the north point.

While on my passage up to the city, my course, owing to the above circumstances was very crooked and zig-zag, and the enemy's attention was drawn towards me from Governor's Island. When I was abreast of the fort on the Island, 300 or 400 men got up on the parapet to observe me; at length a number came down to the shore, shoved off in a 12 oar'd barge with 5 or 6 sitters and pulled for me. I eyed them, and when they had got within 50 or 60 yards of me I let loose the magazine in hopes that if they should take me they would likewise pick up the magazine, and then we should all be blown up together. But as kind Providence would have it, they took fright and returned to the Island to my infinite joy. I then weathered the Island, and our people seeing me, came off in a whaleboat and towed me in. The magazine, after getting a little past the Island, went off with a tremendous explosion, throwing up bodies of water to an immense height.

Thus the first submarine attack in history ended in failure. Yet it came within an ace of succeeding. Both Lee and Bushnell were of the opinion that the auger must have struck the heavy iron bar connecting the rudder fitting to the sternpost. As Bushnell wrote: "Had he moved a few inches, which he might have done without rowing, I have no doubt that he would have found wood where he might have fixed the screw..."

It was believed that the bit would have pierced the copper with which the bottom was (presumably) sheathed. However, anyone who has tried to work underwater knows the difficulty of exerting any pressure, unless firmly anchored to the object being worked on, and it is possible that the copper resisted the point of the bit, *Turtle* bobbing down as the pressure was applied.

Still, it was a noble attempt and deserved success. Later, two more attacks were made on naval vessels in the Hudson River, both equally unsuccessful. This was after the loss of Manhattan and when the small American squadron was operating above Fort Washington. On October 9 a British force moved upstream and engaged the hopelessly out-gunned Americans. The few gunboats and sloops were no match for the King's ships. Some escaped upriver, some were beached, and the sloop carrying *Turtle* was sunk.

Bushnell and Lee escaped and later Bushnell succeeded in recovering the submarine, but it was never used again. Its fate is a mystery. It was probably destroyed after Washington's defeat at White Plains, to keep it from falling into the hands of the enemy.

Bushnell himself, after his mining exploits on the Delaware (described later in "Defeat on the Delaware"), returned to Saybrook and his inventions. Having spent all his own funds on his projects he applied to the government for aid. But money was scarce and none could be spared for experiments in submarine warfare. It is in keeping with his character that he found time to earn a master's degree at Yale in 1778. On May 6, 1779, he was captured, along with some other civilians, by a British raiding party from Long Island. Fortunately, although the British knew Bushnell only too well by reputation, they did not know him by sight. Steps were immediately undertaken to effect his exchange, and in consequence his stay in a British prison hulk was mercifully a short one.

Within a week after his release he petitioned Governor Jonathan Trumbull for an appointment to the newly formed Corps of Sappers and Miners. Trumbull obliged with a captaincy. In this capacity Bushnell served (at Yorktown, among other places) until June, 1783, when he was appointed Commandant of the Corps. On being mustered out, he is said to have sailed for France. Returning to this country (if, indeed, he ever left it), he settled in Georgia, under the name of Dr. Bush. He became a man of some property, practiced medicine, and taught school in Columbia County. He died in 1826 at the age of eighty-four.

As a pioneer in the art of the submariner, Bushnell deserves much credit—far more than was accorded him in his own time. He designed, built, and tested a submersible that actually functioned—and functioned well enough to make a submerged attack on an enemy vessel. It was only bad luck, against which no man is proof, that denied him the success which should have been his. Had brother Ezra been in command of *Turtle* when she made her attack on *Eagle*, both Bushnell's future and the immediate future of the submarine might have been very different.

The Privateers

Chapter 8

At the outbreak of the Revolution the British flag went unchallenged on the seas. Yet the ports of the colonies were filled with shipping and swarmed with seamen. There was a desperate need for a naval force, but of organized navy there was none. It was obvious that any offensive action against the British at sea had to be undertaken in private ships manned by merchant seamen.

Fortunately for the Colonials, there were captains in their merchant fleets who had sailed against the French and Spanish in previous wars, and many others who had smelled powder on more than one occasion. Seafaring was a risky business in those times. It was less than sixty years since the notorious Blackbeard had terrorized the seas. The deeds of Roberts and Kennedy were still remembered, and a few ancients could still recall seeing the tattered remains of Captain Kidd and some of his crew, hanging in chains above the mud flats of the Thames. Piracy was still rife in the Caribbean (and would be for another fifty years), while those who sailed to the Mediterranean or to the Far East must be prepared to fight off Moor, Malay, Chinaman, and the riff-raff of a dozen seas. Cannon were as familiar articles of equipment as anchors, and the prudent captain saw to it that his gun

crews were frequently exercised, the supply of powder and projectiles adequate, and the small arms in good order.

So when hostilities actually commenced, there was great activity among seafaring men. Slow, unwieldy merchantmen, unfitted for warlike enterprises, were stripped of their armament, while those vessels considered suitable as ocean raiders received extra ordnance—and while they were fitting out, their officers went recruiting. It was seldom difficult to find crews for privateers. In addition to the spirit of adventure, which doubtless motivated many men, there was the lure of prize money. This certainly was the main reason why numerous shipowners were eager to equip their ships as privateers and send them to sea. The capture of a fine ship with a valuable cargo meant big money to the privateer's owners, and varying percentages of the "take" went to the officers and crew. Naturally, the biggest share went to the owners, to reimburse them for the expenditures of fitting out a ship and manning her, with the ever present risk of losing their investment to some cruising British man-of-war. The captain received the next largest share, and so on down through the officers, petty officers, and seamen to the lowliest ship's boy. A successful voyage or two could make the fortunes of the owners, and a rich man of the captain. Enough was left so that even a cabin boy might receive more for one cruise than he could hope to make in several years' work ashore.

In a sense, a privateer was little more than a licensed pirate. The "license" was a commission or letter of marque issued by a warring government, empowering vessels of private ownership to capture or destroy any enemy shipping they encountered. Those operating under such a document, recognized as legal by the maritime powers, were held to be belligerents, and were entitled to be treated as such if captured. Knowing the conditions in which prisoners of war were held in those days, one may wonder whether this was much of an advantage. But armed robbery on the high seas without sanction of government was piracy, and even incarceration in some miserable prison was better than hanging.

It should be pointed out, however, that during the Revolution the British government, while not *actually* treating American privateersmen as pirates and hanging them outright, still maintained that they *were* legally pirates, serving as they did a government which the British did not recognize. Their treatment, and that of captured "rebel" seamen in general, was in most cases extraordinarily severe, and Mill Prison, Portsmouth, acquired almost as evil a reputation as the prison hulks of New York.

(Most historians and writers class privately owned vessels which operated against the enemy under government commission as "privateers." To be precise, a privateer was a vessel fitted out as a warship and primarily intended to cruise against enemy merchantmen. It was not uncommon, however, for a government commission to be issued to an armed cargo-carrier, in which case the vessel was known as a letter of marque. The distinction is a nice one, but one customarily made in contemporary accounts and which, if not understood, may cause confusion among modern readers.)

As far as the American government was concerned, privateering was a mixed blessing. Every British vessel taken or sunk was a blow to that nation's economy, and in some small degree exerted a little pressure on the side of the peace party. Every British warship on convoy duty meant one less for offensive action. On the other hand, although perhaps over 1,000 British vessels fell victim to the American privateersmen, these losses had little material effect on the outcome of the war. Insurance rates leaped, and trade was partially disrupted, but British merchantmen still plied the oceans in great numbers, and inevitably many fine American vessels, with their crews, fell into British hands.

More important was the effect of privateering on the manning of the ships of the Continental Navy. Warships went to sea to fight. Their prime duty was to seek out and destroy the enemy. But as a rule the privateer fought only if absolutely necessary. The plunder of a fat merchantman, undermanned and undergunned, was his reason for being at sea. Any fighting was incidental, and an encounter with an adversary of anything like the same strength was usually avoided like the plague. As opposed to the navy man, who could expect little except harsh discipline and hard fighting, the privateersman looked for a relatively easy voyage and a pot of gold at the end of it.

As an added inducement privateer owners offered higher pay to seamen—twelve to sixteen dollars a month as opposed to eight for a navy man, plus the fact that the percentage of prize money was higher. So the cream of the adventurous and enterprising went to the privateers, while Continental ships were often immobilized for months for want of crews.

The above is not meant to infer that the privateer captains lacked courage. On occasion they fought, and sometimes beat, King's ships their equal or superior in weight of armament. But a commerce raider had to

rely on her heels. Damage received in a stand-up fight might cripple her sufficiently to send her limping back to port before her voyage had barely begun. Worse still, it might leave her the prey to the first cruiser that might happen along. So, by and large, the rule was "fight only if you must."

Privateers were of all shapes and sizes, but speed was a prerequisite. Fortunately for the Colonials, their shipbuilders had already begun to turn out vessels noted for their fine lines and superior sailing abilities. Ships of this type could overtake the lumbering mer-

chantmen of the day and outrun all but the fleetest of the British cruisers.

At the beginning of the war almost anything that could float was pressed into service. Armament was at a premium, and some vessels put to sea unarmed, hoping to fill their empty gunports from the first merchantman they could bluff or carry by boarding. Later in the conflict ships were specially designed as privateers. Some of these were quite large, and whereas in 1775 and 1776 many vessels were mere cockleshells mounting 4 or 6 guns and with crews of 25 or 30 men, by

1781 some privateers carried 24 guns, and crews of 150 men or more. These were formidable craft, able, if necessary, to trade blows with even a Royal Navy sloop or small frigate. At times they teamed up in "wolf packs," and proved as dangerous to a convoy, and as difficult to combat, as their undersea counterparts of World War II.

A feature of the average privateer was the extra large crew. This was to provide prize crews for the vessels which, hopefully, the privateer might take on a successful voyage. Upon capturing a ship a prize crew, just enough men to work the ship, was put aboard under an officer (or petty officer if he were able to navigate). The victim's officers were usually taken aboard the captor, while the crew was confined below decks in the prize. As these men often outnumbered the prize crew, great precautions had to be taken to prevent their escape. When space permitted, a part or all of the crew would be transferred to the victor—something often not possible in the privateer's typically "racy" hull, crammed with men and supplies. Leg irons for prisoners was a common solution to this vexing problem. On more than one occasion, the prisoners were able to break out and retake the ship. The crew of a small merchant ship—a few elderly seamen (the press gangs were taking the cream of the younger men) and ship's boys—were not much of a menace. But crews of naval vessels or privateers were a different matter.

A case in point was that of the Continental brig, *Lexington*, 16 four-pounders. In December, 1776, she was homeward bound from the West Indies with powder and military stores when she was taken by the British frigate *Pearl*, 32. A high sea was running, and the British captain, who would normally have taken most of *Lexington*'s crew of some 80 men aboard, transferred only four or five. Wind and sea increased during the night, and thinking that under the conditions there would be no danger from the prisoners, the prize crew became careless. Choosing a moment when the prize master and deck officer were below,

the prisoners swarmed on deck, knocked down the guards, and retook the ship. A leader in this exploit was Master's Mate Richard Dale, who later won recognition under John Paul Jones as second-in-command of *Bonhomme Richard*.

Lexington went safely into Baltimore with her prisoners. The British officer in charge of the prize was, on his release, court-martialed and dismissed the service.

Even merchant crews could strike back on occasion. The privateer *Yankee*, 9, cruising in British waters, took two merchantmen. Captain Johnson, *Yankee*'s commander, although his crew numbered only 43, put prize crews aboard each, and the three ships cruised in company. The prisoners on both merchantmen succeeded in recapturing their vessels and then proceeded to attack *Yankee*. Shorthanded now, the unfortunate Captain Johnson was forced to surrender, and was taken triumphantly into Dover, prisoner to his own prizes.

The first Americans to sail against the enemy did so without any authorization at all. Later on in 1775 some revolted colonies issued papers empowering ships' captains to take such British ships as they came across. But it was not until March, 1776, that Congress began the general issuing of letters of marque. This delay was due to the hesitation on the part of the Colonials, many of whom still hoped for some form of reconciliation with the mother country, to take so drastic a step. But from that time until the end of the war British commerce was never free from the threat of American privateers. Their deeds in many cases went unrecorded. A thousand tales of high adventure have been lost—terse entries in the log of some long-forgotten ship, or told around the roaring fire of a vanished grog shop. A few have survived, enough to show that the American privateersman was as tough a customer as any who sailed the seven seas.

A good privateersman was a mixture of gall and guts, of bluff, bravery, and good seamanship, with a fair slice of luck thrown in. Such a one was Jonathan Haraden of Salem. An outstanding seaman, Haraden first served as lieutenant in the Salem privateer *Tyrannicide*, 14, Captain J. Fiske. *Tyrannicide* was a good vessel in which to begin a naval career. On her first voyage in 1776 she captured a Royal Navy cutter and later in the same cruise took the schooner *Despatch*, 8, after a sharp little fight. The following month she took the ship *Glasgow* and in August the brig *St. John* and the schooner *Three Brothers*.

The spring of 1780 found Haraden faring forth on his own as captain of the 180-ton *General Pickering*, 16. As was often the case with privateers, *Pickering* carried a cargo—in this instance, sugar for Bilbao. En route the ship fell in with a British cutter of 20 guns and succeeded in beating off her heavier antagonist after a hard two-hour fight. Not many hours later *Pickering* was forging through the darkness when the lookouts made out a vessel ahead. Silently the crew went to their stations, while Haraden made a quick estimate of the stranger's strength. She was schooner-rigged and appeared to carry more guns than *Pickering*, but Haraden had the great advantage of surprise.

Without hesitation he ran his ship alongside the stranger, shouted that *Pickering* was an American frigate of the largest class and that if the schooner did not surrender he would blow her out of the water. The stranger, caught totally unprepared, hauled down her flag, and *Pickering*'s second officer went aboard with a prize crew. The stranger proved to be the English privateer *Golden Eagle*, 22. Her captain was a bitter man when he found

he had been tricked into striking to a weaker ship. But "all's fair in love or war," and Haraden's bluff had worked.

Followed by her prize, *Pickering* was about to enter Bilbao, when a large vessel was sighted working her way out. *Golden Eagle*'s captain informed Haraden that the strange sail was the privateer *Achilles*, 42, of London. Haraden might well have given so powerful an enemy a wide berth, but he had just bluffed *Golden Eagle* into surrendering, and it was possible that her captain was trying a little bluffing on his own. He stood on with a light breeze until the stranger was hull-up, when his telescope revealed that *Golden Eagle*'s commander had told the truth.

Achilles beat slowly toward *Pickering*, retaking *Golden Eagle* but unable, because of the light wind, to come to grips with the American before nightfall.

When the two vessels finally closed, vantage points on the shore were crowded with Spaniards come to see the show. Haraden had chosen a position near land, where shoals would force the attacking Britisher to approach under a raking fire from *Pickering*'s broadside. As luck would have it, the wind died, and *Achilles* had to endure *Pickering*'s fire for some two hours before her captain rounded-to and brought his broadside to bear. Foiled in his efforts to close, the British captain hammered away at *Pickering*. But Haraden's guns, though few in number, were well served, and after three hours the battered *Achilles* had had enough. She hauled off and made haste to get away, even abandoning *Golden Eagle* and her prize crew to the victorious Haraden.

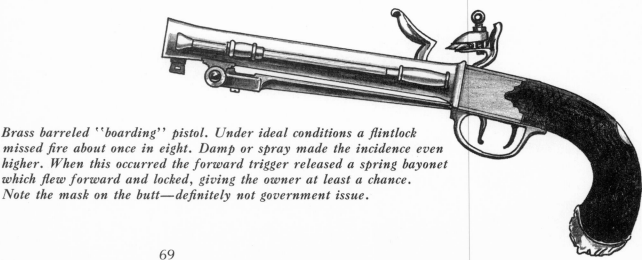

Brass barreled "boarding" pistol. Under ideal conditions a flintlock missed fire about once in eight. Damp or spray made the incidence even higher. When this occurred the forward trigger released a spring bayonet which flew forward and locked, giving the owner at least a chance. Note the mask on the butt—definitely not government issue.

Considering the disparity in force it was a notable victory. One witness said that "the *General Pickering,* in comparison with her antagonist, looked like a longboat by the side of a ship." Haraden well deserved the enthusiastic welcome he received from the Spaniards when he went ashore. And as a fitting climax on his return voyage he took three armed merchantmen off Sandy Hook. Haraden was to win other hard-fought actions, and it is said that the number of guns on the vessels he captured during the war totaled over 1,000. But his duel with *Achilles* under the eyes of thousands of Spaniards was perhaps his finest exploit, and one that ensured him his place in the lists of great American sea-fighters.

Privateersmen were a versatile lot, as witness the career of one of the greatest—

Silas Talbot. A Massachusetts man of poor parents, Talbot began his life at sea at the age of twelve as a cabin boy in a coaster. By the time he was twenty-one, he was master of a vessel, and had built himself a house in Providence, Rhode Island. He was commissioned as a captain in the army in 1775, fought around Boston, and went with his regiment to New York. Here he volunteered for duty with the fire ships, with which the Americans hoped to destroy the British warships in the Hudson River. Talbot chose as his target the 64-gun *Asia,* and to make more certain of reaching his objective unobserved, he ordered his crew not to fire the trains leading to the combustibles until the vessels actually touched.

As the fire ship's target loomed up ahead, the alarm was raised and round shot ripped through the vessel's hull. A few mo-

ments later the fire ship, with her load of tar barrels and turpentine-soaked wood, crashed into *Asia*'s side and the trains were fired. The flames spread so rapidly that Talbot was badly burned before he could get clear in the ship's boat. Frantic efforts by her crew saved *Asia*, but the attack so alarmed the British they abandoned their positions and dropped down below New York. For this operation Congress promoted Talbot to a major. He was twice wounded in the gallant defense of Fort Mifflin, and in 1778 greatly distinguished himself in the fighting around Newport. Here he took a large galley mounting eight guns, his own vessel a small schooner with two 3-pounders. This exploit brought him promotion to lieutenant colonel.

Tory privateers were such a nuisance at this date that Washington suggested that a small sloop, *Argo*, twelve 6-pounders, be fitted out and proceed against these vicious pests, under the command of Colonel Talbot. One such, *Lively*, 12, of New York was taken on Talbot's first cruise, and shortly after two

heavily laden vessels from the West Indies, bound for New York, were snapped up.

Most of Talbot's early prizes gave up without much of a struggle, but his sixth proved a tougher nut to crack. A sail sighted early one morning turned out to be a large vessel, well armed, and crammed with men. She was the English privateer *Dragon*, fourteen 6-pounders, and for four and one-half hours the two vessels pounded away at each other within pistol shot. *Argo*'s quarterdeck was almost swept clear of men, Talbot's speaking trumpet was holed in two places, and a round shot sliced off the tail of his coat. The action ended when the Englishman's mainmast tottered and came crashing down, by which time water from shot holes in *Argo*'s waterline was almost up to her gundeck. Holes were plugged, pumps manned, and other damage repaired, while *Dragon* was sent into New Bedford under a prize crew.

The job of getting *Argo* shipshape was scarcely completed before another English privateer was sighted. She was the brig *Hannah*,

A snow-rigged privateer. A similar snow, the 16-gun vessel—FAIR AMERICAN—
was 68-feet on the gundeck and 24' beam. She was very fast, and after
her capture the British Admiralty is said to have made the model of her
now at the Naval Academy. Vessels like this carried a large amount of canvas.
Note the Royals, topgallant, studding sails, and the ''ringtail'' on the driver.

twelve 12-pounders and two 6's, and Talbot went for her without hesitation. Another sharp fight began, but a second American privateer hove in sight, and *Hannah*'s flag came down. When *Argo* reached port, "she was so much shivered in her hull and rigging by the shot which had pierced her in the last two engagements that all who beheld her were astonished that a vessel of her diminutive size could suffer so much and yet get safely to port."

Talbot's adventures had only begun. After more successes in *Argo* he was given command of the powerful privateer *General Washington,* twenty 6-pounders. On his first

cruise he took two prizes; then his luck changed. Off Sandy Hook he stumbled into a British squadron and had to run for it. Under normal circumstances he might have outdistanced his pursuers, but it was soon blowing a gale. In such weather a larger, more heavily sparred vessel could often carry on when a smaller one had to take in sail. One enemy ship of the line carried away her foreyard but *Culloden,* 74, overtook Talbot and brought *Washington* under her guns. There was no arguing with a "74," and Talbot was forced to strike. His treatment was a fair sample of what could be expected by a captured American seaman. Courteous treatment from one officer, then a stretch in the notorious *Jersey*, followed by a horrible voyage to England in the ship of the line *Yarmouth*. Seventy-one men, many of them officers, were crammed in a twelve-by-twenty space in the lower hold, only three feet high, for fifty-three days of a stormy passage. Eleven died in this noisome dungeon, where the survivors crawled and lay in their own filth; then Mill Prison, little if any better than *Jersey*. Released a few months later, Talbot reached France. He sailed for home as a passenger in an American brig—only to be taken two weeks later by a British privateer. The privateer's captain treated his prisoners well, and declaring that Talbot had suffered enough, transferred him to an English brig bound for New York. From British-held Manhattan Talbot made his way to Huntington, Long Island, and thence across Long Island Sound to Fairfield and, ultimately, to Providence.

In after years, ex-cabin boy Silas Talbot, then a captain in the United States Navy, commanded the frigate *Constitution*—a fitting end to a distinguished career.

Some privateer actions ended in dramatic fashion. In September, 1778, the privateer *General Hancock*, 20, under Captain Hardy, encountered the British letter of marque *Levant*, 32. Hardy answered the Britisher's hail with a broadside, and both ships were soon shrouded in powder smoke as the gun crews settled down to work. An hour went by, and Hardy, peering through the smoke, no longer saw the enemy's colors flying. To his hail asking if *Levant* had struck there came the answering shout, "No! Fire Away!" For another two hours both ships blazed away yardarm to yardarm. Hardy was wounded and carried below, and his first lieutenant took command. Suddenly a brilliant flash lit the smoke. A violent shock threw the stunned Americans off their feet as with an ear-splitting crash *Levant* blew up. A chance shot or, more likely, an accident aboard had touched off her magazine. Smashed timbers, cordage, and shattered

bodies rained down through a dense pall of smoke to crash on the American's deck. When the smoke lifted, only wreckage-strewn water marked the place where *Levant's* broken hull had gone down. *Hancock's* boats picked up eighteen survivors, but more than eighty went down with their ship.

The fate which overtook the brig *Holker* of Philadelphia was no doubt shared by more than one of her kind. *Holker*, a fast vessel of sixteen guns built especially as a privateer, proved a fantastically successful venture for her owner, Blair McClenahan, as well as a small gold mine to her officers and men. She took prize after prize, either cruising alone or in company. She was particularly fortunate when teamed with another McClenahan-owned vessel, *Fair American*. Her first captain, Geddes, retired a rich man, and so did another of her skippers, Roger Keane.

Not all *Holker's* captures were easy ones. She fought some ding-dong battles but always managed to win back to port, usually with a prize or two. Luck had sailed with her for four years, but at last that fickle lady shipped elsewhere. On a dark, squally morning, in the waters between St. Lucia and Martinique, the lookouts made out a sail. She proved to be that nemesis of many a privateer—a British frigate. *Holker's* captain ordered all sail set that the brig could carry. Away she went with the frigate *Alcmene* in pursuit. Officers intently watching the American brig from *Alcmene's* quarterdeck saw that their quarry was gradually increasing her lead. A rain squall blotted her from view; then she came into sight again, heeling well over to the press of wind. Again she vanished as an even more violent squall swept down, thick curtains of rain trailing from the boiling inky blackness overhead. The pursuing frigate smashed her way through the confused sea and as the squall roared away, eager eyes sought for the flying privateer. No sail broke the horizon—nothing, except floating wreckage and some bobbing heads. *Holker's* captain in his efforts to avoid capture had carried sail too long. Forty-seven men from the capsized brig were rescued, but the little privateer would take no more prizes.

Exactly how many American privateers took part in the Revolutionary War will never be known, as many small craft were armed and went to sea without any commissions, either state or Continental.

The Calendar of Naval Records of the American Revolution, published in 1906 and printed by the Library of Congress, lists 1,697 private armed vessels to which letters of marque were issued by the Continental Congress. The Calendar also lists 14,872 guns and 58,400 men, but the number of guns and men is not complete as thirty ships did not list their armament, and eighteen furnished no lists of men.

Privateers Listed by Class of Vessel

Ships	301
Brigs and brigantines	541
Schooners, sloops, etc.	751
Boats and galleys	104

Privateers Listed by State

New Hampshire	43
Massachusetts	626
Rhode Island	15
Connecticut	218
New Jersey	4
New York	1
Pennsylvania	500
Maryland	225
Virginia	64
South Carolina	1

Letters of Marque as Issued by Year

1776	34
1777	69
1778	129
1779	209
1780	301
1781	550
1782	383
1783	22

To these must be added those commissioned by the states, estimates of which run as high as 2,000. Just as varied are the estimates of the number of prizes taken. These range from some 600 to close to 3,000. A breakdown of Lloyd's list, given below, shows 560 British merchantmen taken to the end of 1777 alone. Of these, 103 were retaken or ransomed, but even allowing that government ships took as many as 100 during that period, it seems unlikely that over the next five years, when a far greater number of commissions were issued, captures by American privateers amounted to less than 250 vessels. On the other hand the 3,000 figure, even if it includes those ships retaken or ransomed, almost equals the total number lost by the British during the whole war.

When William Laird Clowes was preparing his *The Royal Navy, a History*, the Secretary of Lloyd's compiled a list from the firm's records which gave the following figures for the war period:

British merchantmen taken or destroyed	3087	
Retaken or ransomed	879	Total 2208
British privateers taken	89	
Retaken	14	Total 75
American and Allied merchantmen taken	1135	
Retaken or ransomed	27	Total 1108
American and Allied privateers taken	216	
Retaken	1	Total 215

While the total of British vessels taken includes those captured by government war vessels, both state and Continental (which Maclay puts at 196), plus those taken by the French, Spanish, and Dutch, the number which fell victim to American privateers must still have been very large. American naval forces, both government and private, are also credited with capturing some 16,000 British seamen—a figure which compares favorably with the numbers of the enemy captured by the land forces, including those surrendered at Saratoga and Yorktown.

French lugger of 1775. Fast vessels like these, carrying large crews, caused great losses to Britain's merchant fleet.

Besides harassing the enemy, the hard school of the privateers produced many fine officers for the Continental service and for the future United States Navy. Truxton, Barney, Decatur, Talbot, Porter, Barry—to name a few—all at one time or another went privateering.

Prize money loomed so large in the eyes of the seamen of the old days that the subject is worth a short section of its own.

There is no doubt that in both British and Continental service the whole system of the awarding of prize money was inequitable, and an injustice to many fine commanders and hard-working crews whose duties, necessary and often dangerous, kept them at sea in

appalling conditions in circumstances where the chances for prize money were small or nonexistent. It was also one of the reasons why it was far easier to recruit seamen for a privateer than for a naval vessel. And in the Royal Navy it was always easier to obtain a crew for a swift sloop of war or frigate whose captain might expect detached duty, with increased opportunity for taking prizes, than for a line-of-battle ship, which would almost certainly remain attached to a squadron.

On the other hand, at a time when pay, especially on the lower deck, was pitifully small it was an incentive, in that it always held out the glittering promise of rich reward. Like fabled Eldorado, it was the dream of captain

Grand Union Flag. Adopted Sept. 3, 1775. In use as navy ensign until after the Declaration of Independence.

DON'T TREAD ON ME

First Navy Jack. First flown by Hopkins' squadron, December 1775.

AN APPEAL TO HEAVEN

Flag flown by Washington's squadron, 1775.

First Stars and Stripes

and cabin boy alike. And no idle dream, either. On occasion great sums were awarded. Admirals and captains were sometimes made rich men for life. After the capture of Havana in 1762, for instance, £736,000 in prize money was divided. The admiral's share was a whacking £122,697, a huge sum in those days. Many a thrifty petty officer was able to settle down after his service was over as owner of a fishing vessel, farm, or tavern. Traditionally, Jack spent his share in riotous living, aided by assorted grog-shop owners, dolls, and doxies.

Even the lowly cabin boy came in for a windfall occasionally. In 1779 one fourteen-year-old, after only a single month in *Ranger,*

is said to have received $700.00, one ton of sugar, some 35 gallons of rum, and 20 pounds apiece of cotton, ginger, logwood, and all-spice.

How prize money was awarded was often a source of argument and dissatisfaction. The prize, or prizes, was sent into some specified port, where agents of the government, or private owners, sold ship and cargo. Sometimes the vessel was purchased by the government and taken into the Service. Naturally, the value of ship and cargo would vary from place to place and time to time. John Paul Jones, for instance, was enraged (he became enraged very easily, and very often) at the low prices fetched by his prizes from the

Bonhomme Richard expedition. *Serapis* was sold to a French merchant for some $48,000, and the whole share allotted to *Bonhomme Richard's* officers and crew was only about $26,583, gold.

In the event that an enemy vessel was destroyed in action, a sum of money was sometimes awarded to the victor.

The distribution of prize money was also the cause of much bitter recrimination. For one thing, the Congress began by appropriating the lion's share—two-thirds—of all prize money taken by Continental ships for the government. This forced contribution to

the cause of liberty may have appealed to the idealistic among the legislators, but it raised a howl of protest from the sailors. Privateers shared full value—and it was this fact, coupled with higher pay and looser discipline, that made it so hard to recruit for Navy ships. So great the outcry, that in October, 1776, Congress upped the Navy's share from one-third to one-half on all merchantmen and allowed full value on all captured warships and privateers. This helped, but was still unfair as opposed to Royal Navy practice in which the captors were given full value for any type of ship.

Ensign usually flown by privateers and merchantmen, 1776-1795.

White Ensign. One of the three ensigns in use by the Royal Navy. The flag officers of the Fleet—admirals, vice admirals and rear admirals—were classed in squadrons of the red, white and blue. An admiral of the white, with all the ships of his squadron, flew the above flag.

Red Ensign. The ensign flown by all British merchantmen. Also by the Royal Navy ships of the Red Squadron. The squadron of the blue flew a similar flag with a deep blue fly instead of a red.

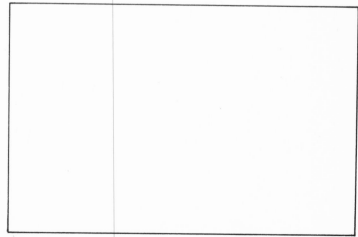

The French naval flag as flown by deGrasse and his captains was plain white.

In 1776 Congress ruled that the prize money awarded should be divided into twentieths, after the government had taken its half. The commander in chief received one-twentieth, or 5 per cent of the proceeds from the sale of all prizes taken by the ships under his command, whether he was present or not. Two-twentieths went to the captain who made the capture (or was divided among all the captains of a squadron). Three-twentieths was divided among masters, Navy lieutenants and captains of marines; two and a half twentieths was divided among master's mates, chief gunners and carpenters, surgeons, chaplains, if any, and marine lieutenants; midshipmen and other petty officers got three-twentieths, and the remainder of eight and one-half twentieths was shared by the rest of the lower deck: seamen, marines, ship's boys, etc.

This was straightforward enough when it came to a single ship but the equitable division among a fleet of various-sized ships was another matter. Should a small sloop receive as large a slice of the money as a frigate, for instance. Congress said it should, but some captains disagreed (John Paul Jones, for one; when he commanded his squadron aboard *Bonhomme Richard*, he ordered that the British prize system should be used in his little fleet).

Under the Royal Navy system, the number of a ship's crew was multiplied by the sum of the calibers of her armament, the resulting figure indicating the proportion to the whole of that particular ship. If, for instance, a vessel had a crew of 80, and mounted fourteen 6-pounders and one 12, she would have a factor of 7,680, or 80 times 96 (84 plus 12). A frigate mounting thirty-two 12-pounders, with a crew of 250, would have a factor of 96,000. Supposing the total for all the ships of the squadron came to 192,000, the frigate would get 50 per cent of the money while the first vessel's share would be only 4 per cent.

Compared to the money that might be won by the capture of a rich prize, the wages of the Continental Navy man, as established by Congress in 1775, were small indeed. A captain only received $32.00 per month; a lieutenant or master $20.00; a chief petty officer $15.00, and an able seaman $6.66. In November, 1776, the pay of officers was raised. The captain of a larger ship (over 20 guns) then received $60.00; of a smaller, $48.00. Lieutenants and masters of the same type of vessels got $30.00 and $24.00.

Such pay, however, was not considered too bad in those days, even allowing for the fact that an officer was expected to pay his mess bills while on board. Meanwhile, just over every horizon, like the pot of gold at the foot of the rainbow, lay the laden enemy merchantman, promising a handsome bonus for all hands.

The Prison Hulks

Chapter 9

Ask a New Yorker or a man from Brooklyn where the New York Naval Shipyard is—or was—and he can tell you. Ask him for Wallabout Bay and he may give you a blank stare. But a New Yorker of Revolutionary days would have known well enough, for during the years that the city was held by the British the Wallabout had an evil reputation.

Few of the tens of thousands who travel in that vicinity every day know that in that little indentation on the Long Island shore, which up to a year or two ago housed one of the world's greatest naval yards, was once anchored a grim flotilla of dreary hulks. Or that every day on the muddy shores of Wallabout Bay, the silence then unbroken except for the screams of scavenging gulls, sad little parties of pallid scarecrows, prisoners of war, buried the previous night's toll of comrades, dead of disease and malnutrition. For almost seven years one or more of those dread hulks were anchored there, and many of the estimated 11,000 American seamen who died in the prison hulks in New York Harbor were buried on the beaches and mud flats nearby.

All prisons were a disgrace in the eighteenth century—filthy, verminous, and disease-ridden. But the foulest peacetime jails were jolly taverns compared with the British hulks at their worst. It is true that treatment differed from time to time, and that occasionally efforts were made to make the prisoners' lives a little less miserable. But the overall record is a black one, and does no credit to those in authority—naval, military, or civilian.

Typical of these hulks was the *Jersey*, nicknamed the "Hell Afloat." Once a stately ship of the line, she ended her days as a floating prison, cursed by thousands, many with their dying breaths. The ports from which her sixty-four guns had once flashed at the enemy were nailed shut, and along her hull two tiers of holes, twenty inches square and some ten feet apart, let in a little light and air. At the break of the quarterdeck was a ten-foot barricade, loopholed for musketry and with a door at each side where ladders led down to the waist. There were cabins aft for the officers, and space where the guards and crew slung their hammocks. *Jersey's* crew consisted of a captain, two mates, a dozen seamen, and some marines. There was usually a draft of some 30 British or Hessian soldiers aboard also.

The hull had been stripped of all fittings, only the flagstaff and bowsprit remaining; even the rudder had been removed. A spar amidships supported a derrick for hauling in

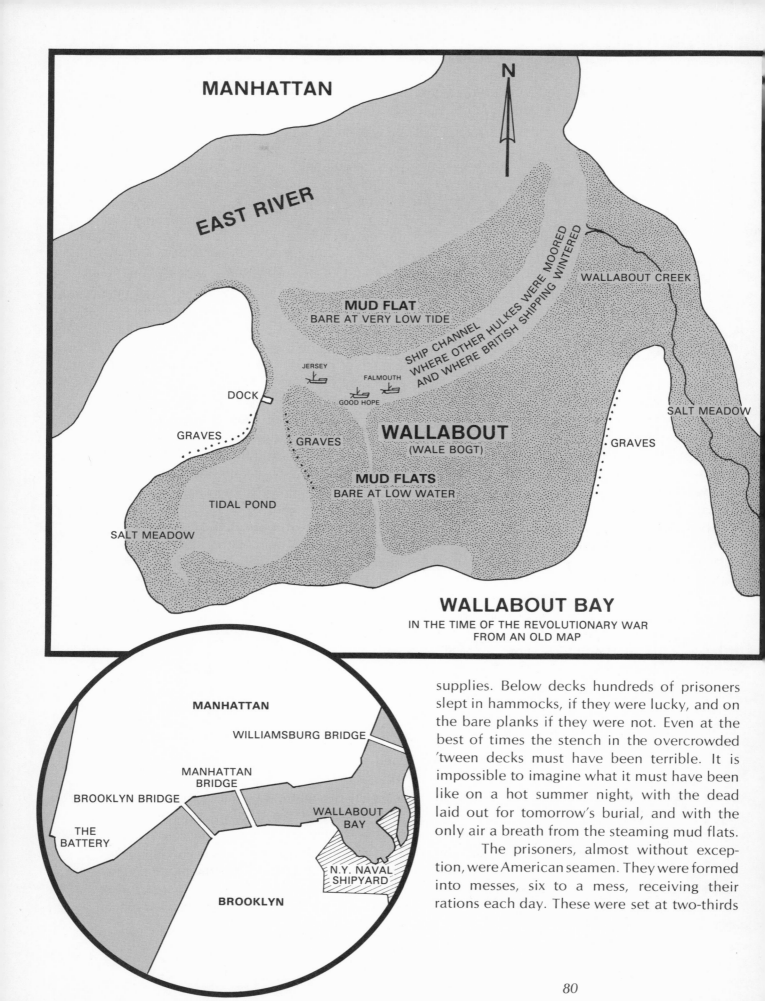

MANHATTAN

EAST RIVER

N

WALLABOUT CREEK

MUD FLAT
BARE AT VERY LOW TIDE

SHIP CHANNEL
WHERE OTHER HULKES WERE MOORED
AND WHERE BRITISH SHIPPING WINTERED

JERSEY

FALMOUTH

GOOD HOPE

DOCK

SALT MEADOW

GRAVES

GRAVES

GRAVES

WALLABOUT
(WALE BOGT)

MUD FLATS
BARE AT LOW WATER

TIDAL POND

SALT MEADOW

WALLABOUT BAY
IN THE TIME OF THE REVOLUTIONARY WAR
FROM AN OLD MAP

MANHATTAN

WILLIAMSBURG BRIDGE

MANHATTAN
BRIDGE

BROOKLYN BRIDGE

WALLABOUT
BAY

THE
BATTERY

N.Y. NAVAL
SHIPYARD

BROOKLYN

supplies. Below decks hundreds of prisoners slept in hammocks, if they were lucky, and on the bare planks if they were not. Even at the best of times the stench in the overcrowded 'tween decks must have been terrible. It is impossible to imagine what it must have been like on a hot summer night, with the dead laid out for tomorrow's burial, and with the only air a breath from the steaming mud flats.

The prisoners, almost without exception, were American seamen. They were formed into messes, six to a mess, receiving their rations each day. These were set at two-thirds of the British navy ration. The navy allowance was:

Sunday	1 lb. biscuit, 1 lb. pork, 1 lb. peas
Monday	1 lb. biscuit, 1 lb. oatmeal, 2 oz. butter
Tuesday	1 lb. biscuit, 2 lb. beef
Wednesday	1 1/2 lb. flour, 2 oz. suet
Thursday	same as Sunday
Friday	same as Monday
Saturday	same as Tuesday

There was no provision for fresh vegetables, and scurvy was naturally one of the diseases which afflicted the prisoners. Food on all ships was horrible in those days. Salt pork or beef pickled in brine was the usual fare, so tough that some sailors carved trinkets out of extra hard chunks. Biscuits were generally moldy and full of weevils, while the water was often so long in the cask that it had to be strained before drinking. Sailors of that period took such fare for granted, so the bitter complaints about the vileness of the prison food by men who survived to write of their experiences indicates that the supplies which found their way to the prison hulks were far worse than average. Much was probably condemned for navy use, and one shudders to think of hungry men confronted with a cask of putrid pork on a hot July day.

Prisoners were allowed on deck during the day, carefully watched by the armed guard. At sunset they were sent below, the hatches covered with gratings, and sentries posted at every hatch. No lights were allowed below, and movement in the crowded spaces in almost total darkness must have been a hazardous procedure. The after part of the gun deck was reserved for officers, more by custom than any set regulation.

There were frequent attempts at escape, some of them successful. At times prisoners managed to wrench out the window bars and dropped or lowered themselves into the water. They were then faced with a long swim, for the shore was patrolled for some distance. Thus escape by this route entailed a swim of at least two miles—a great distance for a man weakened by near starvation and confinement. One man writes of a successful break by about thirty-five men, who rushed the sentries, disarmed them, and seized a little schooner

lying alongside. The escapees managed to get her safely away, presumably with the tide toward Hell Gate.

There was one other avenue of escape (other than the one-way journey to the mud flats), taken by quite a few who despaired of surviving long confinement in the disease-ridden hulks. This was to join either the Royal Navy or one of the British regiments stationed in the West Indies, assurance being given that they would not have to serve against their countrymen. Among those who thus escaped the horrors of *Jersey* was Ebenezer Fox, one

British Soldier. Coat red, facings, collar and cuffs of the regimental color.

of those young men who wrote up their adventures in after years and so gave us some personal glimpses of life during the Revolutionary War.

Fox was captured when the state ship *Protector* was taken by two British frigates, and spent several months in *Jersey*. He wrote of the 1,000 or more prisoners already aboard:

> They were covered with rags and filth; visages pallid with disease, emaciated with hunger and anxiety, and retaining hardly a trace of their original appearance. They were shriveled by a scant and unwholesome diet, ghastly with inhaling an impure atmosphere, exposed to contagion, in contact with disease, and surrounded with the horrors of sickness and death.

Determined to get off the "Hell Ship" while he was still alive, he consented to enlist in a regiment stationed in Jamaica. His one idea, he wrote, was to desert and somehow get back home. This he did, after some hair-raising adventures.

Besides *Jersey* there were *Whitby, Scorpion, Prince of Wales, John, Stromboli, Good Hope, Falmouth,* and *Hunter.* These three last were at one time or another designated as hospital ships, and the most seriously ill were transferred to them. That they did not quite meet the standards of a modern hospital ship is shown by the following, written by a survivor.

> The Hunter had been very newly put to the use of a hospital ship. She was miserably dirty and cluttered. Her decks leaked to such a degree that the sick were deluged with every shower of rain. Between decks they lay along, struggling in the agonies of death, dying with putrid and bilious fevers, lamenting their hard fate to die at such a fatal distance from their friends; others totally insensible and yielding their last breath in all the horrors of light-headed frenzy.

In partial defense of the British authorities it appears that, spasmodically, attempts were made to treat the prisoners as human beings. One prisoner, captured in June, 1779 and assigned to *Jersey*, wrote:

There was nothing plundered from us, we were kindly used by the Captain and others that belonged to the ship. Our sick were attended to by physicians who appeared very officious to recover them to health. Our allowance for subsistence was wholesome and in reasonable plenty, including the allowance by the Continental Congress sent aboard....on the whole we were as humanely treated as our condition and the enemy's safety would admit.

Again, in 1782, a report by six American captains, on parole, stated that they found the prisoners "in as comfortable a situation as it is possible for prisoners to be aboard ship, and much better than they had any idea of."

It must be remembered that even in peacetime contagious diseases took a fearful toll both ashore and afloat. In the armed services, where many men were brought in close proximity under conditions far from ideal, the toll was even higher. It is estimated that at least ten men died of disease in the Continental armies to every one killed by the enemy. Jails were notorious pest holes, and louse-born "jail fever," or typhus as we call it, often carried off prisoner, turnkey, and judge alike.

However, nothing alters the fact that, even judged by lenient eighteenth-century standards, the New York prison hulks were things of horror. Many a privateersman, with the shadow of the "Hell Afloat" and her sister ships hanging over his head, must have fought a little harder to avoid capture. Or, as undoubtedly hoped by the British, refrained from going privateering at all.

Besides the hulks at New York, American prisoners were confined in various other places, among them Mill Prison at Plymouth; Forton Prison, Portsmouth; Halifax, Nova

Scotia; and Antigua in the West Indies.

Conditions in all these prisons were on the whole very bad. Mill Prison housed many American seamen, and if it had not been for the charity of many sympathetic English people who provided extra food and clothing, many more would have perished than actually did. As it was, the death rate was low as compared to that of the New York prison hulks. Americans were always regarded as more rebels and traitors than belligerents. Spanish and Dutch prisoners of war regularly received better treatment.

Hessian Grenadier, Regiment of Von Rall. Blue coat; facings, cuffs and turnback, cap and pompon red. Cap plate brass.

Treatment of prisoners en route to England or back to New York varied with the individual commander. Some received adequate food and opportunities to enjoy fresh air and exercise; others were transported in irons in quarters so cramped and foul that many died during the voyage.

Those held on Antigua complained of the heat, foul water, poor food, and the usual diseases which afflicted all whites in tropical climates in those days. On the other side of the coin, British prisoners confined in jails ashore or in prison ships in Boston and New London were equally vociferous about the bad treatment accorded them.

Twisting the Lion's Tail

Chapter 10

By the time the Declaration of Independence had been signed, American national, state, and private vessels had inflicted severe losses upon British trade in American and West Indian waters. But it was evident that far more damage could be done, with much greater effect on British morale, if the war were carried to the enemy. Consequently, in the autumn of '76 we find the privateer schooner *Hawke* of Newburyport, commanded by Captain John Lee, arriving in Spanish waters after a voyage in which she captured five British vessels. These were sent back to America with prize crews aboard while Lee entered Bilbao to reprovision and refit. British representations that Lee was nothing but a pirate resulted in his arrest and seizure of his ship. But Silas Deane, our first Commissioner in France, protested to the French, who in turn interceded with the Spanish, who thereupon released *Hawke* and her captain.

Meanwhile, the privateer *Union* of Cape Ann, 10 guns, 8 swivels, and a crew of 40 under Isaac Soams, was also operating off the Spanish coast.

The first of the Continental cruisers to operate in European waters was the 16-gun brig *Reprisal,* Captain Lambert Wickes. Wickes had, in October, 1776, been put under orders of the Congressional Committee of Secret Correspondence to take Benjamin Franklin to France. That mission accomplished, *Reprisal* was to cruise in the English Channel and do what damage she could. She sailed about November 1 and arrived in Quiberon Bay about the first of December. Wickes took two small vessels en route, and these are believed to be the first prizes sent into French ports. After refitting she cruised in the Bay of Biscay and took a ship, a snow, and three brigs. The snow, which mounted 16 guns, showed fight and *Reprisal* suffered some casualties before the Britisher hauled down her flag.

With the arrival in French waters of American war vessels there began the long, drawn-out quarrel between representatives of the French and British governments and the American Commissioners as to the status of such American ships in French ports and the disposal of prizes and prisoners taken by these vessels.

The British, as was natural, demanded that French ports be closed to American "pirates" and that no vessel be allowed to be purchased, fitted out, and manned on French soil. It was a reasonable request, particularly the last proviso. The ports of northern France were all too close to Britain's trade routes to countenance their unlimited use by an enemy power. France was not yet ready to commit herself to war on behalf of the revolted colonies, and her ministers were therefore compelled to temporize; they smoothed ruffled English feathers while at the same time giving the Americans enough support to keep them reasonably content—and fighting.

The exchanges at ministerial level followed a pattern, one long familiar to diplomats. Those following the arrival in Nantes of the prizes taken by Wickes were typical. When word reached the British Ambassador, Lord Stormont, that *Reprisal* was in port, with prizes, he wrote a sharp note of complaint to the French foreign minister, the Comte de Vergennes. That worthy replied soothingly that *Reprisal* had been ordered to sail at once. Some ten days later Stormont somewhat testily pointed out that *Reprisal* was still in Lorient and that, far from being returned to their rightful owners, two of the prizes had been sold!

The Comte courteously replied that the sale of the prizes was to be doubted, while Captain Wickes had been definitely ordered to sea immediately. Two weeks later Stormont was complaining bitterly that not only was *Reprisal* still in port, undergoing repairs, but that all five prizes had been sold, and to Frenchmen, at that!

This, replied Vergennes, was deplorable. The Minister of Marine, M. de Sartin, would cause a full investigation to be made. But strangely enough, the minister's investigation uncovered no explanation of how five prizes—five British vessels—could have been condemned and sold without his Most Christian Majesty's government being the wiser.

And so it went. When the heat was really on, when the government felt that the patience of the British authorities had reached the breaking point, then some concessions would be made: a prize returned, a captain and crew briefly imprisoned (but in a French gaol, never handed over to the British), an American war vessel warned off before entering French territorial waters.

As for the American Commissioners, they played a careful game. Officially, as far as the French were concerned, they piously disclaimed any knowledge or responsibility of prizes bought and sold, or of French-based warships. They had, they wrote, "ordered no Prizes into the Ports of France," while *Reprisal* "had orders to cruise in the open sea and by no means near the Coast of France." But in a letter to the Committee of Secret Correspondence they warned that the bringing of prizes into French ports "has given some trouble and uneasiness to the court and must not be too frequently practiced."

There were more secret agents lurking in every seaport than there are on today's TV programs and bookstands. Everyone spied on everyone else, and there were numerous double agents who sold information to both sides. The comings and goings of the American Commissioners and their business agents were closely watched and the arrival and departure of American vessels reported to the British Ambassador as rapidly as the communications then in existence allowed.

The fitting out of vessels in French ports, at home or in the West Indies, was bad enough, but the British were particularly incensed by the manning of such vessels with French crews. Sailing under an American commission, with an American captain, these vessels could operate with a great degree of safety. If stopped and boarded by a British warship, the American captain and the American commissions were safely stowed away and the officer in charge of the boarding party was met by a voluble French commander, with genuine French papers and an equally genuine French crew.

It was all very baffling, but besides much tail-lashing and occasional angry roars there was little the British lion could do. Small wonder, perhaps, that when an American vessel did fall foul of a British cruiser, that the luckless skipper and crew were given "the treatment."

Sharply as the French ports were watched, however, it was still possible for Americans to move fairly freely in England.

HOY
The hoy varied in rig almost as much as in size, but usually was sloop rigged. Used as a general purpose craft for short hauls and for tenders for naval vessels.

BILANDER
The bilander's most distinctive features were its rounded bow and stern and the large mainsail, much like a sawed-off lateen.

Herring BUSS
The buss shown was the descendant of the older three masted, square-rigged craft of earlier years. The small after sail was used mainly to keep the vessel's head to wind as she drifted to her nets.

And there were sufficient sympathizers with the American cause (some of them in high places) so that Colonials could operate with some degree of safety. Thus it was that Samuel Nicholson and Joseph Hynson could meet in London, travel to Dover, and there purchase a cutter, which Nicholson sailed to Calais.

An aid to the undercover movement in agents and materiel was the well-organized smuggling racket, which had been operating between England and the continent ever since taxes and tariffs had been invented. Deal and Dover, Dunkirk and Calais, had for generations been noted for the cross-channel movement of tax-free goods. But there was scarcely a fishing village along the northern coast of France or the southern shores of England that did not harbor honest fellows who felt that the paying of duty on such items as brandy, lace, and tobacco—to name a few—was a crime against human nature. Nor were minor disturbances such as wars allowed to interrupt the lucrative trade of these patriotic citizens. There was usually room for a mysterious (and well-paying) gentleman to stow away among the casks and bales—and no questions asked at either end of the voyage.

An early arrival in French waters was the brig *Lexington*, Captain Henry Johnson. She sailed from Baltimore February 27, 1777 and arrived off Nantes in the first part of April. Already fitting out was the cutter *Dolphin*, Captain Samuel Nicholson. Nicholson had been directed by Franklin to purchase a cutter at Boulogne or Calais, if possible, but if not, to arrange for the purchase of one in Dover or Deal. There was nothing suitable available in the French ports; so, risking his neck, Nicholson went to England. In London he contacted Captain Joseph Hynson, Wickes's brother-in-law, writing with much truth, "My business are of such a nature Wont Bare Puttg to Paper." The two Americans journeyed to Dover and there bought *Dolphin*. On February 17, Nicholson sailed her to Calais and thence to Nantes.

These two vessels, with *Reprisal*, were to cruise along the British coasts, sending all prizes into French or Spanish ports. Wickes, as senior officer, issued orders that the three ships should keep together unless "chased by a Vessel of Superior Force & it should be Necessary so to do for our own preservation."

MAP OF
CRUISE OF
WICKES' SQUADRON

IRELAND

IRISH SEA

ENGLAND

LONDON

DOVER
CALAIS
DUNKIRK

USHANT
MORLAIX
ST. MALO

BAY OF
BISCAY

MAY 28,
1777

ST. NAZAIRE
NANTES

FRANCE

If the squadron did become separated the rendezvous was off the Orkneys, after cruising "through the Irish Channel or to the North West of Ireland, as you may Judge Safest and best."

Prisoners were to be removed from a prize before it went into port, and "the Prize Master must not Report or Enter her as a Prize, but as An American Vessel from a port that will be most likely to gain Credit according to the Cargo she may have aboard." So as not to accumulate too many prisoners, "to prevent their Rising & Taking your Vessel," Wickes recommended putting them aboard any "Dutch, French, Dean, Sweed, or Spainish Vessel....giving as much provision and Water as will serve them into Port."

The squadron sailed from St.-Nazaire May 28, 1777. Two days later they were chased by *Foudroyant*, 80, but got away, and on June 19 they took two brigs and two sloops off the north of Ireland. A week's cruise in the busy waters of the Irish Sea netted them fourteen more. Of the eighteen, eight were sent in as prizes, seven were sent to the bottom, and three more let go loaded with prisoners. On June 27, off Ushant, they were chased by a large warship, and *Reprisal* only escaped by throwing her guns overboard. Wickes, who was hardly in a position to censure breaches of international law, complained that "they pay very little regard to the laws of neutrality, as they chased me and fired as long as they dared stand in, for fear of running ashore."

Reprisal, sans guns, made St.-Malo safely, as did *Dolphin*, who had sprung her mast in the aforementioned chase. *Lexington* anchored at Morlaix.

While Wickes had been readying his squadron for sea, American seapower had received a welcome addition in the shape of one Gustavus Conyngham. This American seaman, Irish by birth, had been sent from Philadelphia to purchase military supplies and in Dunkirk had met William Hodge, then engaged in the business of buying vessels for the American navy. He had just purchased a

*Royal Navy Cutter. These fast vessels were used both by the Navy and the Revenue Service.
The one above—some 65-feet on the waterline and 25-feet in beam—is typical. Their deep
draught enabled them to carry a great press of canvas, although the square sails were used
only with the wind well abaft the beam. As extra canvas many cutters also carried lower
studding-sails, a ringtail, flying jib and a gaff topsail.*

lugger, *Surprise,* and suggested Conyngham to the Commissioners as a likely captain. These gentlemen, impressed by Hodge's recommendation, duly filled him out a blank commission, of which they had a supply signed by the President of the Congress.

So about May 1 Gustavus Conyngham sallied forth in *Surprise,* now mounting ten guns, and within the week was back in Dunkirk with two prizes. The British reacted violently—so violently that the French were forced to give ground. Conyngham and his crew were jailed, *Surprise* was seized, and her prizes returned. The American Commissioners protested, and Conyngham was released. A second vessel was clandestinely purchased, the fast cutter *Revenge*, 14. Despite the efforts of the British Ambassador she was fitted out; Conyngham's old crew, plus 65 French cutthroats from Dunkirk, were smuggled aboard, and she sailed on July 16 with orders "not to attack, but if attacked, at Liberty to retaliate in every manner in our power—Burn, Sink & destroy the Enemy."

Revenge cruised successfully in British waters, taking prizes in the North Sea, Irish Sea, and the western approaches. After landing in Ireland for water, Conyngham harried shipping in the Bay of Biscay, afterward putting into Ferrol. Using Ferrol and Corunna as bases, *Revenge* made many successful cruises, her prizes being sent into Spanish ports. When English pressure made Spain too hot for her, she sailed for the West Indies. There she took several more ships, including two privateers. By the time Conyngham brought her safely into the Delaware early in 1779 both captain and crew had made a record which was to haunt British ship owners for some time to come. Up to the time that *Revenge* sailed for the West Indies she is said to have taken sixty ships, of which twenty-seven were sent into port and thirty-three sunk or burned.

Reprisal refitted in St.-Malo, where *Dolphin* was converted into a packet, while *Lexington* made her repairs at Morlaix. But so insistent did Stormont become that the French were finally forced to order the return of these two cruisers to America. In September they set sail. Neither reached home. *Reprisal* foundered in a gale on the Newfoundland Banks, carrying with her the gallant Wickes and all his crew except the cook.

Lexington fell in with *Alert*, a ten-gun cutter commanded by Lieutenant Bazely. The lighter armed *Alert* went for her larger opponent and a sharp action followed. *Lexington*, short of ammunition, managed to cripple *Alert* aloft and made off. But the intrepid Bazely repaired damages, and "as soon as I got my Rigging to rights, again gave Chase

and came up with him at half past one, renewed the Action till half past two, when he Struck." *Lexington* lost seven dead and eleven wounded out of a crew of eighty-four. Of sixty men, *Alert* had three killed and three wounded.

From 1777 until the end of the war American privateers continued to wage war on British commerce. There were continued protests and occasionally the American Commissioners had to warn their countrymen. "Complaints have been brought to us of Violences offered by American vessels armed in neutral nations, in seizing vessels belonging to their subjects and carrying their flag and in taking those of the enemy while they were under the protection of the coasts of neutral countries, contrary to the usage and customs of civilized nations...."

But the war was taking a new turn. The number of neutral countries was diminishing. First France, then Spain and finally Holland, joined in the war against their old enemy. Ports which had been closed, at least officially, to American vessels now welcomed them, while the hard-pressed British had to spread the forces guarding their vital trade routes ever thinner. More American ships reached Europe—among them *Ranger*, with the great John Paul Jones. Perhaps the glamour of the little Scotsman's exploits has tended to outshine all others, but the names of Wickes and Conyngham deserve to stand high. They arrived on the scene when America still fought alone, and they carried the flag of the new navy into enemy waters with a daring and dash seldom equaled. And it was during their campaign against British shipping that an Englishman lamented: "The Thames also presented the unusual and melancholy spectacle of numbers of Foreign ships, particularly French, taking in cargoes of English commodities for various parts of Europe, the property of our own merchants, who were thus seduced to seek that protection, under the colors of other nations, which the British flag used to afford to all the world...."

Defeat on the Delaware

Chapter 11

It has usually been the custom to write off the British generals who fought in the Revolutionary War as fools or worse. Certainly they made their share of mistakes but on occasion they could perform brilliantly. General Sir William Howe proved that by smartly outmaneuvering Washington in several engagements before Philadelphia, and finally entering that most important city on September 26, 1777. Its loss was a great blow to the patriots and the British had every intention of holding it. But the baffled American forces still lay around the city, cutting off its supplies from the countryside. If it was to be held for the Crown, the sea lane to Delaware Bay and the ocean must be opened.

Could the river defenses be held, General Howe's situation would not, as Washington wrote, "be the most agreeable: for if his supplies can be stopped by water, it may easily be done by land....and the acquisition of Philadelphia may, instead of his good fortune, prove his ruin."

By the twelfth of October Admiral Lord Richard Howe's fleet was off Chester. Here it was forced to anchor, for the Delaware above that point was defended by obstructions planted in the river, by forts, and by the guns of American warships. The first of the obstructions was at Billingsport—boxlike fabrications of heavy timbers filled with stones and sunk in two rows in the channel between Billings Island and the Jersey shore. Wooden beams, tipped with iron, were set in these foundations, slanting downstream with their points some four feet below the surface. Any ship trying to pass over them was likely to tear a hole in her bottom.

But no line of obstructions—ancient pilings or modern minefield—is of much use without some means of keeping the enemy from removing it. So on the Jersey shore there was a small fort, or redoubt, armed with cannon sited to discourage any attempt at breaking a way through the line of stakes. This little fort, however, was never completed, and was but lightly held. On October 2, the Forty-second Regiment and part of the Seventy-first had landed below the fort and attacked it in the rear. The garrison retired hastily, after spiking the guns and setting fire to the barracks.

This threat removed, the line of pilings was cut and ships moved through. So much for obstacle number one.

A little below the mouth of the Schuylkill River lies Mud Island. Just south of this a triple line of obstacles ran across the channel to Red Bank, New Jersey. The Jersey end of this line of obstructions was guarded by Fort Mercer, an earthwork with ditch and abatis, mounting fourteen guns. The western end lay

under the guns of Fort Mifflin, on Mud Island. Above the obstructions lay the American squadron, consisting of the state frigate *Montgomery;* two xebecs, each carrying a 24-pounder in the bow, an 18-pounder in the stern and four 9's amidships; and thirteen row galleys, one with a 32-pounder, two with 24's and the rest with 18's. Besides these there were twenty-six half-galleys, oversized rowboats, each with a 4-pounder; two floating batteries, one mounting twelve and the other ten 18-pounders; several schooners, brigs, and sloops; and a number of fire ships and fire rafts.

Part of the squadron, under its elected commodore John Hazelwood, had already been engaged with the batteries which the British had emplaced to defend Philadelphia. The action had not exactly covered Commodore Hazelwood with glory. In his squadron was the Continental frigate *Delaware,* 24. After an ineffectual bombardment at some 500 yards range, *Delaware*'s captain, whose seamanship seems to have been as poor as his gunnery, found himself stranded by the outgoing tide. The British brought up a new battery, and forced the American crew to abandon ship. They then boarded her them-

selves. Two schooners also ran aground and were lost, and the *Montgomery* lost her masts.

But the British were to have their bad days, too. A force of about 2,000 Hessians and some artillery, under Colonel von Donop, crossed the river at Philadelphia, marched leisurely down the east bank and on October 22, attacked Fort Mercer. The fort was garrisoned by some 400 Rhode Island Continentals, and they met von Donop's grenadiers with a deadly fire. At point-blank range they fired into the masses of men struggling to mount the parapet, while grapeshot from the row galleys in the river added to the carnage.

When the Hessians finally withdrew they had lost 371 men, including von Donop.

The British had no better luck on the water. To support the Hessians, Admiral Howe ordered *Augusta*, 64; *Roebuck*, 44; *Pearl*, 32; *Isis,* 32; *Liverpool*, 28; and *Merlin*, 18 to attack the American squadron. There was a brief engagement the afternoon of the twenty-second which was renewed the next morning. The *Augusta* ran aground. She was holding her own against forts, galleys, and fire ships when suddenly she caught fire and blew up. *Merlin* also took the ground, and was destroyed by her own people. *Augusta* was the largest ship

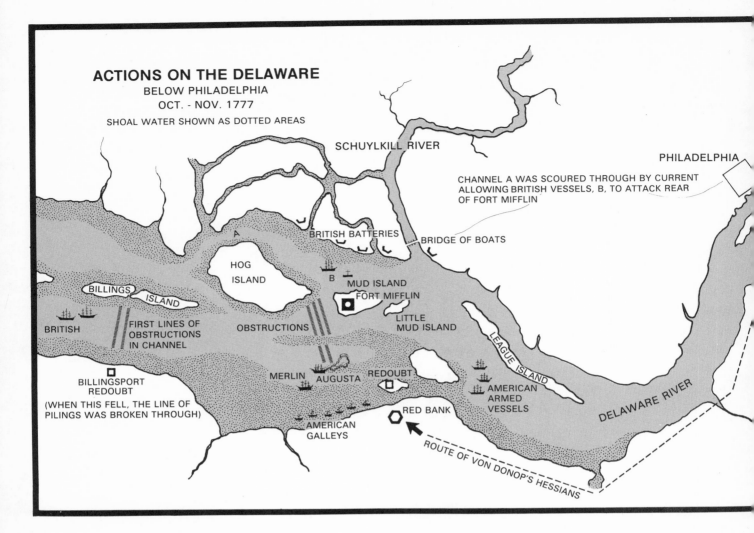

ACTIONS ON THE DELAWARE
BELOW PHILADELPHIA
OCT. - NOV. 1777
SHOAL WATER SHOWN AS DOTTED AREAS

SCHUYLKILL RIVER

PHILADELPHIA

CHANNEL A WAS SCOURED THROUGH BY CURRENT
ALLOWING BRITISH VESSELS, B, TO ATTACK REAR
OF FORT MIFFLIN

BRITISH BATTERIES

BRIDGE OF BOATS

A

HOG
ISLAND

B   MUD ISLAND
FORT MIFFLIN

BILLINGS   ISLAND

BRITISH

FIRST LINES OF
OBSTRUCTIONS
IN CHANNEL

OBSTRUCTIONS

LITTLE
MUD ISLAND

LEAGUE ISLAND

DELAWARE RIVER

BILLINGSPORT
REDOUBT

(WHEN THIS FELL, THE LINE OF
PILINGS WAS BROKEN THROUGH)

MERLIN   AUGUSTA   REDOUBT

AMERICAN
ARMED
VESSELS

RED BANK

AMERICAN
GALLEYS

ROUTE OF VON DONOP'S HESSIANS

Heavy timber crib, filled with stones, bracing an iron-tipped stake. Set below water level facing downstream.

to be destroyed in action with the Americans in either the Revolution or the War of 1812.

Fortunately for the brothers Howe there was dissension and mismanagement in the American forces. In consequence, the blockade on the Delaware was not efficiently maintained, allowing much-needed supplies to slip upstream to the city. On the British side preparations were pushed for the attack on Fort Mifflin, both by the erection of land batteries and the positioning of a floating battery mounting 24-pounders. This last was towed up a new channel (which had been scoured by the current deflected by the line of obstructions) by *Vigilant*, 20, and was finally anchored within point-blank range of an angle in the rear of the fort.

On November 10 the bombardment began, and continued for five days. Much damage was done to the badly built fort, which was termed, among other things, "A Burlesque upon the Art of Fortifications." The eastern side, facing the river, had stone walls, as did the southern face. But the other walls had only ditches and palisades, with four wooden blockhouses, each mounting four guns. The entire garrison totaled only some 450, less than half the number needed to adequately man the works.

Ammunition was scarce, and the fort's sole 32-pounder could be fired only by using British shot of that caliber which fell within the walls. A gill of rum was offered for the retrieving of such shot, a prize which attracted many contenders, despite the risk. A young soldier of the Eighth Connecticut, Joseph Martin, wrote that he often saw "from twenty to fifty of our men standing on the parade waiting with impatience the coming of the shot. It would often be seized before its motion had fully ceased and conveyed off to our gun to be sent back again to its former owners."

The bombardment went on day and night, fire being opened at regular intervals during the hours of darkness to hamper the work of repair. Finally all but two of the guns were dismounted, and the commandant, Lieutenant Colonel Samuel Smith, was so badly wounded that he had to give up his post to Major Simeon Thayer. But the worst was yet to come.

On November 15, the ship of the line *Somerset*, 64, and frigates *Roebuck*, 44; *Pearl*,

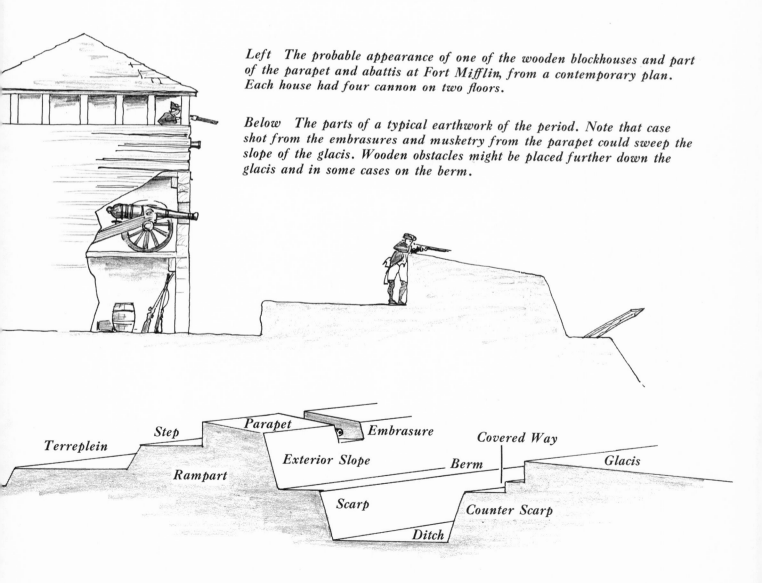

Left   The probable appearance of one of the wooden blockhouses and part of the parapet and abattis at Fort Mifflin, from a contemporary plan. Each house had four cannon on two floors.

Below   The parts of a typical earthwork of the period. Note that case shot from the embrasures and musketry from the parapet could sweep the slope of the glacis. Wooden obstacles might be placed further down the glacis and in some cases on the berm.

Terreplein   Step   Parapet   Embrasure   Covered Way   Glacis
Rampart   Exterior Slope   Berm
Scarp   Counter Scarp
Ditch

32; and *Liverpool,* 28, anchored as close to the fort as the line of obstructions would permit. As the signal for the squadron to open fire was made, some 86 guns crashed out as one. It was the most intensive bombardment of the war. An estimated 1,000 shot were fired every 30 minutes. The effect on the flimsy fortifications was devastating. Gun crews were wiped out, the remaining guns hurled from their carriages, and walls and buildings shattered. "The whole area of the fort," wrote Martin, "was as completely ploughed as a field."

By nightfall the fort, as such, had ceased to exist. The wrecked buildings were set on fire, and under cover of darkness the remnant of the garrison was ferried across the river to Red Bank. The glare of the flames revealed the evacuation of the rearguard to the British, and their journey was accomplished amid a hail of shot.

The defense had been one of the most determined of the war. Altogether 250 of the garrison were killed or wounded, their places being taken by replacements rowed across to them at night. It had but slight assistance from Commodore Hazelwood and the Pennsylvania and Continental vessels, whose guns might have been an important factor in the defense. Why these vessels played such a feeble part in the battle for the river is still a mystery. Lack of discipline and poor leadership is the probable answer. Properly handled, they could have made the attacker's task more difficult, if not impossible. Perhaps if they had been a Continental Navy squadron under Navy discipline they might have performed better. But the river fleet was a Pennsylvania affair, with all the evils which usually went with such organizations; politics, favoritism, elected officers and all.

Once Fort Mifflin was destroyed, there was little chance of holding Fort Mercer. General Cornwallis with 2,000 men crossed the river to attack the fort. In the face of an attack in strength, backed by the guns of the British fleet as well as those of shore batteries, Colonel Christopher Greene, the American commander, very properly decided to abandon the place (November 20).

Mercer's fall was the signal for the destruction of the larger vessels of the river squadron. These included the *Andrew Doria, Repulse, Champion, Surprise, Fly, Racehorse,* and the floating batteries. Blazing, the ships which were to have blockaded the enemy drifted harmlessly upstream with the tide, while disconsolate Philadelphians watched from river banks and docks. Two frigates, *Washington,* 32, and *Effingham,* 28, under

Reconstruction of a typical floating battery carrying ten 18-pounders.
Length—59-feet. Beam—22-feet. Oar holes for ten sweeps a side.

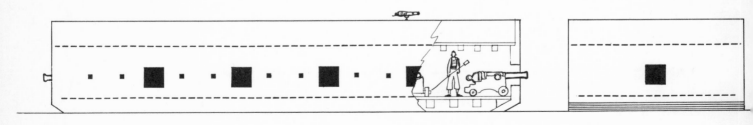

Floating batteries were built in all sizes and shapes. The above barge-like craft gives
an idea of what the floating batteries in the Delaware were like. Not all had upper decks,
but those that did used them for close-range work with swivels and musketry.

construction above Philadelphia, had previously been scuttled and the disaster was complete.

On the American side there were recriminations between the leaders of the army and navy forces involved. Charges of inefficiency and even cowardice were exchanged. The sailors contended that more could have been done by the army in the way of attacking or neutralizing the British shore batteries and in erecting batteries of their own. The soldiers, in their turn, claimed that the river squadron had been handled with excessive caution, and pointed out, quite rightly, that many of the ships so carefully preserved during the action were destroyed anyway as soon as the forts fell. The British, meanwhile, had uninterrupted passage from Philadelphia to the sea.

But not quite uninterrupted. After the loss of his submarine, David Bushnell had experimented with other types of mines, with different firing mechanisms. One of these floating mines had come close to destroying a British man-of-war off Saybrook, Connecticut. His fame and that of his floating mines had reached the Delaware Valley, and a call for his unique services went out. At Bordentown, twenty-six miles above Philadelphia, was the depot of military supplies for the American forces. Colonel Joseph Borden and some of his friends, fearing that the British might come upriver to attack such a tempting target, were anxious to devise some means of denying the river to the redcoats, and if possible drive them off it altogether.

Bushnell's floating mines seemed to offer a solution to the problem, and technical assistance, as well as materials, was supplied to the inventor. The mines were to be fastened in pairs, as had been those used against *Cerberus* off Saybrook. Only in this case the mines were to be submerged, buoyed up with kegs. A spring-lock device, acting as a detonator, would explode the powder-filled mine as soon as it rubbed against the hull of its victim.

Spurred on by the versatile Francis Hopkinson, a signer of the Declaration of Independence and Chairman of the Continental Navy Board, the work went forward rapidly. Finally, a few days after Christmas, 1777, all was ready for the attack. Some twenty kegs and mines were loaded into a whaleboat and, with Bushnell and a friend of Borden's named Carman aboard, the boat with its dangerous freight pushed off down the Delaware. It was a pitch-black night, and neither Bushnell nor Carman was acquainted with the river. In the darkness they put their deadly cargo overboard too far above the line of anchored ships, and they badly miscalculated the time it would take for the mines to drift down with the current. Floating ice in the river also delayed the arrival of the mines at their destination, and at the same time caused the British to secure their vessels to the wharfsides instead of leaving them anchored in midstream.

One pair of mines drifted down ahead of the rest. Two boys saw the floating kegs, rowed out, and began to haul one of them in their boat. There was a loud explosion and boat and boys vanished in a cloud of smoke and spray. But the accident had occurred some distance from the British sentries, and no alarm was given.

On Monday, January 5, 1778, the crew of a barge spotted another floating keg and pulled it and its attendant mine on board. It, too, exploded, killing four of the crew and wounding the rest. The alarm was given. Drums rolled, the troops ran to arms, and the citizens ran also—some to their homes, others to the wharves and the decks of whatever vessels they could clamber aboard.

Then began the so-called Battle of the Kegs. The British captains, taking no chances, let fly broadsides at everything floating. Logs, kegs, bits of driftwood, were all subjected to an intense bombardment, until darkness put an end to the "action." The incident was reported in the rebel papers with great glee, and the gallant fight put up by the British against the barrels was ridiculed in song and story. Hopkinson himself is supposed to be the author of the following poem, "British Valor Displayed: or, the Battle of the Kegs."

We are told this poem was a favorite around the campfires of Valley Forge; so Bushnell's effort had some value, if not exactly that which he had intended. We can also believe that extra-sharp watches were kept on all British vessels from that time on, and that any "unidentified floating objects" were met with blasts of grapeshot or cannon balls.

Twas early day as poets say,
Just as the sun was rising,
A soldier stood on a log of wood
And saw a sight surprising.

As in amaze he stood to gaze,
The truth can't be denied, sir,
He spied a score of kegs or more,
Come floating down the tide, sir.

Now up and down throughout the town
Most frantic scenes were acted,
And some ran here and some ran there
Like men almost distracted.

"Therefore prepare for bloody war
These kegs must all be routed,
Or surely we despised shall be,
And British courage doubted!"

The cannon roar from shore to shore,
The small arms loud do rattle,
Since time began, I'm sure no man,
E'er saw so strange a battle.

The Navies of the States

Chapter 12

The Pennsylvania State Navy, which played a part in the Delaware River campaign, was perhaps typical of the naval forces of other states. It was a local force, built with local defense needs in mind. In conception, it antedated the legislation for a Continental squadron by some three months. On July 6, 1775, a committee was appointed which approved a plan for the building of a number of small galleys about fifty feet in length and thirteen feet in beam, to be armed with a cannon of fair size. They were to be manned by not less than thirty, nor more than fifty men, officers included. Each galley had, in theory at least, a captain, first and second lieutenants, a gunner, gunner's mate, boatswain, boatswain's mate, steward, steward's mate, carpenter's mate, drummers, a fifer, seamen, and a few marines. The coats of these last were brown, faced with green, and they wore the usual cocked hat.

Action was swift. The first vessel was ordered on July 8 and launched on July 19. Meanwhile others had been ordered and by the end of August, six were in the water. There were, finally, thirteen galleys: *Experiment, Bulldog, Franklin, Congress, Effingham, Ranger, Burke, Chatham, Dickinson, Hancock, Gen. Washington, Warren,* and *Camden.* An extract from a letter dated Philadelphia, July 19, 1775 (presumably by a Loyalist) describes one of these vessels. "This day saw one of the floating Batteries [the writer was no naval expert] intended for destroying such of His Majesty's Ships as may come into the River Delawar, in length they are 40 feet Keel, flatt bottomed & are to row twenty Oars double banked, to carry a Cannon of 24 pdrs Shott in the Stern Sheets...." The thirteen galleys were actually armed with one 32-pounder, four 24-pounders, and eight 18-pounders.

Smaller craft called armed boats were also built. These ultimately included *Argus, Basilisk, Brimstone, Dragon, Eagle, Fame, Firebrand, Hawk, Hornet, Lion, Porcupine, Race Horse, Resolution, Repulse, Salamander, Terror, Thunderer, Tormentor, Viper, Vulture,* and *Wasp.* These carried a smaller weapon, usually a 4-pounder.

By the end of December, ten fire rafts were also in readiness. These rafts were thirty-five feet long and thirteen feet in beam, with rails to confine the material. They were loaded with hogsheads full of combustibles, with pinewood in between the casks, and with powdered rosin liberally sprinkled over the whole cargo.

Captain John Hazelwood, in charge of the fire rafts, was afterwards Commodore of the Pennsylvania State Navy.

In 1776 two floating batteries, *Arnold* and *Putnam,* were added to the flotilla. Floating batteries were usually square-ended scow-like vessels with heavy timber sides pierced for cannon built around a flat deck. Sometimes these superstructures were partially decked, so that swivels could be mounted on the top of the bulwarks. Armament varied, but 24- and even 32-pounders were not uncommon. A ship of war, *Montgomery,* and the fire sloop *Aetna* also joined the Pennsylvania squadron. By August 1, 1776, 27 vessels manned by crews totaling 768 were in commission.

The state ships first saw action on May 6, 1776, when several of them engaged the frigates *Roebuck,* 44, and *Liverpool,* 28, which, with their tenders, were engaged in a reconnaissance of the entrance to the Delaware. The almost bloodless action ended with the British vessels withdrawing downstream, followed as far as Newcastle by the Pennsylvania squadron.

By 1777 the Pennsylvania Navy had grown even larger, and included a shallop, *Black Duck;* a fire brigantine, *Blast;* four fire brigs, *Comet, Hell Cat, Vesuvius, Vulcano;* two fire ships, *Hecla* and *Strumbelo;* six sloops, *Defiance, Hetty, Industry, Liberty, Speedwell,* and *Sally;* a schooner, *Lydia;* the armed schooner *Delaware,* and the brig *Convention.*

After the actions noted in the preceding chapter the state ships which had moved above the city (August 21, 1777) wintered along the river. In April, 1778, on Washington's orders, the remainder of the Pennsylvania squadron was dismantled and sunk and most of the crews dismissed. On June 13 (the British by this time were preparing to evacuate Philadelphia) Commodore Hazelwood began raising his sunken vessels. Three galleys and three armed boats were fitted out, rearmed, and manned; the others were laid up.

Commodore Hazelwood and all the men except those needed to man three galleys and armed boats were discharged, with thanks, by the Pennsylvania Navy Board, in August, 1778. But there was still a little life left in the State Navy. The brig *Convention,* it was decided, was to be fitted out as a privateer. Her career was a short one, for on December 7, 1778, she was ordered sold, along with ten galleys, nine armed boats, four sloops, and one schooner.

On March of the following year the ship *General Greene* was purchased and under Captain James Montgomery took five prizes. She too was ordered sold on November 1, 1779, but it was not until February 13, 1781, that the last personnel of the Pennsylvania squadron were mustered out. Like those of other states, the effect on the war of the navy of Pennsylvania was small. On the other hand, every little bit helps, as the saying goes, and the mere presence of a fleet in being, even such a one as Commodore Hazelwood's, posed some threat and demanded some countermeasures at a time when the enemy's resources were stretched very thin indeed.

Pay Scale and Rations
of the Pennsylvania State Navy
(from the minutes of the Pennsylvania Committee of Safety, Philadelphia, Sept. 1, 1775)

Resolved, that the following be the monthly pay of the officers and Men employed in the Provincial Armed Boats:

The Commodore	30 Dollars per month
Every Captain of a Boat	20 ditto per do.
Every Lieutenant	12 ditto per do [Increased Sept. 14, 1775 to 14 dollars per month]
Surgeon of the Fleet	20 ditto per do.
Surgeon's Mate	12 ditto per do.
Every Steward of a Boat	10 ditto per do.
Every Captain's Clerk	8 ditto per do.
Every Mate and Gunner	10 ditto per do.
Every Carpenter	10 ditto per do.
Every Boatswain	8 ditto per do.

Every Cook	6 ditto per do.
Every Drummer	6 ditto per do.
Every Private	6 ditto per do.
Every Boy	4 ditto per do.

Resolved, that every Man, Officers and Privates, employed in the Armed Boats, should have the following weekly allowances of Provisions and Rum, or Malt Beer:

Seven pounds of Bread per Week, or six pounds of Flour.

Ten pounds of Beef, Mutton, or Pork.

The value of Six pence per Week in Roots and Vegetables

Salt and Vinegar

Three pints and a half of Rum, or Beer in proportion.

The navies of the other ten states (Delaware and New Jersey had none) varied considerably in size and effectiveness. For the greater part they were for local defense and consisted mostly of small shallow-draft craft, many of them row galleys and armed boats capable of operating in rivers and bays. Massachusetts was an exception, in that her fleet was in the main composed of deep-water vessels. The lists below, taken largely from Paullin's *Navy of the American Revolution*, are not necessarily complete. Undoubtedly there were some vessels taken into service on a temporary basis (as many were) whose names have gone unrecorded. Also, the dates when certain vessels went out of service—returned to owners, sold as unserviceable, destroyed, or captured by the British—were not always recorded. As in most cases where armament is concerned, there are frequent discrepancies in contemporary accounts. The weaponry of a ship of the period could be (and often was) changed from voyage to voyage and it is difficult, if not impossible, to pin down the exact armament carried by a specific vessel on a certain date. Rigs were often changed, too, and a vessel recorded as

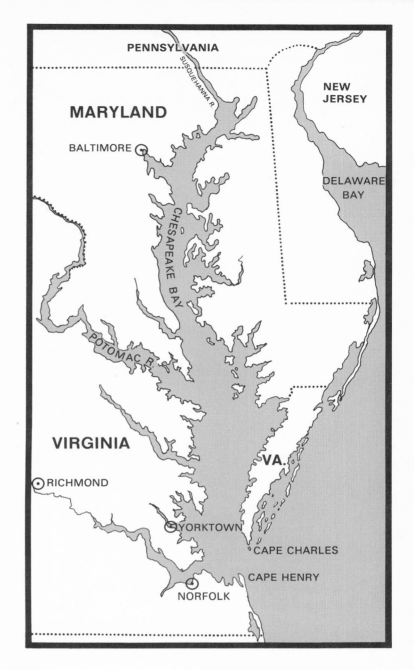

a brig on one voyage might set sail another time as a brigantine or a schooner.

The Navy of Virginia was impressive in size, if not in accomplishment. Despite considerable effort and expense it was usually poorly armed and manned, and in general failed in its main purpose, which was to defend the state's rivers and bays and drive off British vessels preying on its commerce. In two destructive raids, 1779 and 1781, the enemy burnt shipyards and towns and took or destroyed scores of vessels. In the raid of

1781, led by Benedict Arnold, a Virginia squadron—six ships, eight brigs, five sloops, two schooners, and several smaller craft—was wiped out.

A few of the larger ocean-going vessels did well, taking several prizes; for instance, the brigs *Mosquito* and *Liberty* captured the ships *Noble* and *Jane,* respectively, both with valuable cargoes. The brig *Liberty,* which remained in commission until 1787, saw longer service than any other vessel, state or Continental.

THE NAVY OF VIRGINIA
Vessels in Service in 1776

Henry	galley	*Liberty*	brig
Hero	galley	*Mosquito*	brig
Lewis	galley	*Northampton*	brig
Manly	galley	*Raleigh*	brig
Norfolk Revenge	galley	*Adventure*	brig
Page	galley	*Liberty*	armed boat
Safeguard	galley	*Patriot*	armed boat
Scorpion	sloop		

Vessels Added in 1777

Accomac	galley	*Dragon*	ship
Diligence	galley	*Gloucester*	ship
Greyhound	brig	*Protector*	ship
Hampton	brig	*Tartar*	ship
Caswell	ship	*Nicholson*	armed boat
Washington	ship		

Vessels Added in 1778

Tempest	ship	*Experiment*	armed boat
Thetis	ship		

Vessels Added in 1779

Virginia	ship	*Fly*	armed boat
Jefferson	brig	*Dolphin*	armed boat

The Navy of South Carolina was smaller than that of Virginia but was considerably more active despite a shortage of seamen (in January of 1776 the state was permitted to enlist 300 men in Massachusetts). South Carolina vessels cruised off the Carolina and Florida coasts and in the West Indies. Between 1776 and 1779 they captured some 35 prizes. As early as July, 1775, two armed barges had assisted in taking an English supply ship carrying 16,000 pounds of gunpowder, while in August of the same year the sloop *Commerce* captured the *Betsey* with 12,000 pounds more. The 40-gun frigate *South Carolina,* built in Holland as the *Indien* for the Continental Navy, then sold to France, and finally bought for the state of South Carolina, was one of the finest vessels in state or Continental service, and she mounted twenty-eight 32-pounders and twelve 12's. The ship *Bricol,* 44, was one of four major state vessels lost at Charleston when the place was taken on May 12, 1780.

THE NAVY OF SOUTH CAROLINA
Acquired 1775

Commerce	sloop	*Defence*	schooner
Comet	schooner	*Prosper*	ship

Acquired 1776

Peggy	schooner	*Rattlesnake*	schooner
Notre Dame	brigantine		

A number of galleys were built. Among these were:

Congress	*South Edisto*	*Revenge*	*Beaufort*
Lee	*Marques de Bretigny*	*Carolina*	*Rutledge*

Other vessels commissioned included:

Beaufort	brigantine	*Hornet*	brig
General Lincoln	brigantine	*Wasp*	brig
Ballony	brigantine	*Polly*	schooner
Sally	schooner	*Eshe*	schooner
Anthony	schooner	*Nancy*	schooner
Three Friends	schooner	*General Moultrie*	schooner
Lovely Julia	schooner	*Count de Kersaint*	sloop

The following vessels, all classified as ships, were purchased from France in 1780-81: *Bricole*, 44; *Truite*, 26, and *South Carolina*, 40. *Bricole* and *Truite* were lost at Charleston. *South Carolina* was captured in 1782.

Three privateers—the ships *General Moultrie*, 18; *Polly*, 16; and *Fair American*, 14—were at one time temporarily taken into state service.

The Massachusetts Navy was composed almost entirely of sea-going ships. These, though for the most part small and carrying only a few light guns, cruised far afield and took some seventy prizes. The only large vessel was the *Protector*. On June 9, 1780, she fought a 1 1/2-hour battle with the privateer *Admiral Duff*, 32, which ended when the latter caught fire and blew up. *Tyrannicide* took the privateer brig *Revenge*, 14, on March 31, 1779. The ill-fated Penobscot expedition was the largest naval operation undertaken by the Americans during the war. There the state lost three state-armed vessels, nine privateers, twenty transports, and a store ship.

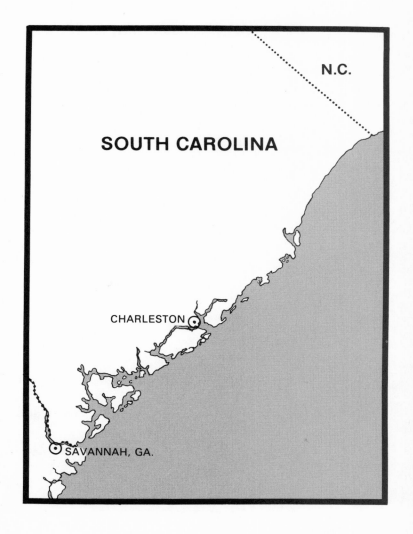

THE NAVY OF MASSACHUSETTS

Vessel	Class	Date of Acquisition	Date of Leaving Service
Machias Liberty	sloop	1775	discharged, Oct. 1776
Diligent	schooner	1775	discharged, Oct. 1776
Tyrannicide	sloop, later brigantine	1776	lost, Penobscot, Aug. 14, 1779
Rising Empire	brigantine	1776	1777
Independence	brigantine	1776	captured, 1777
Republic	sloop	1776	1777
Freedom	sloop	1776	captured, 1777
Massachusetts	sloop	1776	1778
Hazard, 14	brigantine	1777	lost, Penobscot, Aug. 14, 1779
Active, 14	brigantine (prize of *Hazard*)	1779	lost, Penobscot, Aug. 14, 1779
Lincoln	galley	1779	1781
Protector, 26	ship	1779	captured by *Roebuck,* 44, *Medea,* 28, May 5, 1781
Mars	ship	1780	1781
Defense	sloop	1781	unknown
Tartar	ship	1782	sold, 1783
Winthrop	sloop	1782	sold, 1783

The ships of the Connecticut Navy saw considerable service. Long Island Sound swarmed with Tory small craft and the state's armed boats did good service in curtailing their depredations. *Spy, Defense,* and *Oliver Cromwell* cruised as far as the Azores and West Indies, and in the spring of 1778 *Cromwell* and *Defense* took the letter of marque *Admiral Keppel,* with eighteen 6's. Ship and cargo were valued at over £22,000. Six of the nine vessels which saw service were taken in action. In all, some thirty prizes were taken by the vessels of the Connecticut State Navy.

THE NAVY OF CONNECTICUT

Minerva	brig	Ready, Oct. 1775. Crew refused duty. Returned to owner, Dec. 1775.
Spy, 6	schooner	Made first capture by Conn. Navy, Oct. 1775. Captured, 1778.
Defense, 14 6-pdrs	brigantine	Ready for sea, April 1776. Wrecked, 1779.
Oliver Cromwell, 18	ship	Ready for sea, August 1776. Captured, 1779.
Shark	schooner-rigged galley	Ready for sea, July 1776. Sent to N.Y. Captured, 1777.
Whiting	schooner-rigged galley	Ready for sea, July 1776. Sent to N.Y. Captured, 1776.

Crane	schooner-rigged galley	Ready for sea, July 1776. Sent to N.Y. Captured, 1776.
Mifflin	schooner	*
Schuyler	sloop	*
Guilford, 8	sloop	*

*Dates of entering and leaving service unknown.

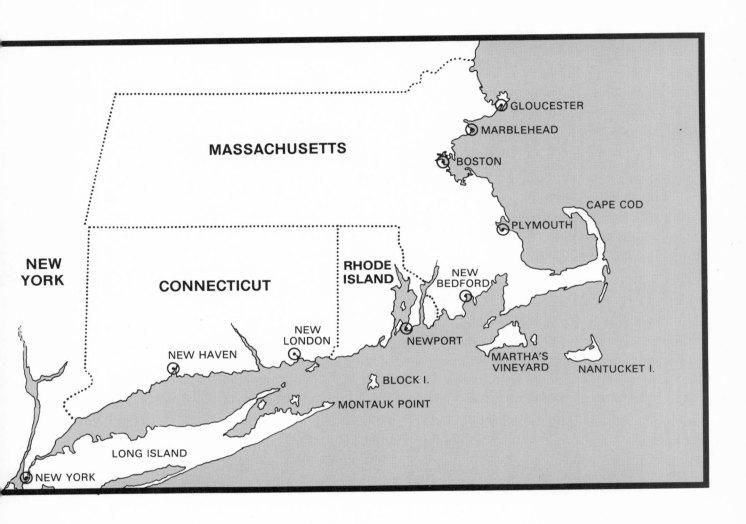

In addition to the above vessels, the Connecticut Navy included some dozen armed boats.

The state vessels of Maryland were almost all galleys or barges. These usually carried one or two fair-sized guns, with crews of some sixty-five men and with ten to fifteen oars a side. They were handy craft, well suited to the Chesapeake in which they were almost exclusively employed. Besides protecting the Maryland shores, Maryland vessels convoyed American troops and supplies, notably Washington's forces from Head of Elk down the Bay for the final campaign at Yorktown. The largest Maryland state vessel, *Defense*, carrying twenty-two 6-pounders, cruised further afield, taking prizes in the West Indies.

| Defense, 22 | ship | Acquired, March 1776. |
| Resolution | schooner | Acquired, March 1776. Tender to Defense. |

Galleys built in 1777 included:

Baltimore	Independence	Johnson	Plater (armed boat)
Conqueror	Chester	Annapolis	

A number of barges were added in 1778, including:

Somerset	Defense	Experiment	Reformation
Terrible	Dolphin	Intrepid	Protector
Fearnought	Revenge	Venus	

Besides these there was a schooner, *Dolphin,* and her tender, *Amelia.*

Georgia contributed little to the naval war. A 10-gun schooner was briefly employed in 1775 and four galleys were built in 1777. Of these *Washington* and *Bulloch* were stranded and set on fire in 1779, and *Lee* and *Congress* were captured in the same year.

The state of North Carolina was chiefly concerned with protecting shipping attempting to enter the important Ocracoke Inlet. Three brigantines—*Washington, Pennsylvania Farmer,* and *King Tammany*—were acquired for this purpose. Later in 1778, the ship *Caswell* was purchased from Virginia. She sank on station, presumably worn out, in 1779.

New York was occupied by the British from 1776 until the end of the war. The sloops *General Schuyler* and *Montgomery* and a schooner, *General Putnam,* were briefly employed, and several armed boats and fire ships attempted to halt the British advance up the Hudson when New York City was captured in 1776. New York also contributed men and supplies for Arnold's fleet on Lake Champlain.

Rhode Island chartered the sloops *Washington* and *Katy* in June, 1775. The former was soon returned to its owner and the *Katy* was bought by Congress and renamed *Providence.* In 1776 two galleys, *Spitfire* and *Washington,* each with fifteen oars a side, armed with an 18-pounder in the bows and carrying some sixty men, were built. Both were later captured or destroyed. Another galley, *Pigot,* and a sloop, *Argo,* were in service from 1779 to 1780 and the sloop Rover was briefly in commission in 1781.

New Hampshire's only state vessel was the privateer *Hampden,* 22, taken into state service for the Penobscot expedition and lost there shortly afterwards.

The navies of the states were hampered by the same difficulties which beset the navy of the Congress—lack of funds, supplies, leadership, and trained seamen.

Most states commissioned privateers, and as usual these vessels drew the majority of the available seamen. State vessels were as often decommissioned for lack of manpower as for insufficient finances or materiel.

Besides armed vessels some states operated merchant ships, exporting state produce and in return bringing in supplies for the state forces or goods whose sale added to the state revenues.

In Harm's Way

Chapter 13

To many present-day Americans John Paul Jones was the American navy. Few may have heard of the expedition to New Providence or of Valcour Island, of Wickes and Biddle, Conyngham or Barry, while every schoolboy knows about the fight between *Bonhomme Richard* and *Serapis*. But it is given to few men to become legends in their own time, and John Paul Jones was certainly not one of them. In fact, the man whom many regard as our greatest naval hero, and the founder of American naval tradition, was in his day a junior captain in the Continental Navy, often passed over for command (and often not employed at sea at all), actively disliked by many and ignored by others. Much of his term of duty with the American forces was spent in a state of angry frustration—in debate, usually acrimonious, with higher authority over lack of a suitable ship, recognition, supplies, crews, recognition, promotion, money, and again recognition. For John Paul Jones might be forced to sail with inferior crews, and in inferior ships, but honor he must and would have.

He was a strange man, this sailor to whom honor meant so much. He was born in 1747, a gardener's son, in Kirkbean on the northern shore of Solway Firth—that deep inlet on the western borders of England and Scotland which resembles an open mouth, forever about to snap up and swallow the hapless Isle of Man. But a life of digging and delving, even for such a kind master as Mr. Craik of Arbigland, his father's employer, held no joys for young John Paul (he was to add the Jones years later). From earliest boyhood the sea was his love. Spare moments were spent on the beach, out with the fishing boats, or clambering over the small coasters which called at the little port of Caresthorn nearby, on their way up the River Nith to Dumfries.

Those were stirring days for a boy who loved the sea. The Seven Years War, with its long roster of British victories, was drawing to a close. Stories of great naval battles were told and retold. No doubt little John saw himself an admiral, as he played at sea fights with the neighbor boys on the beach. So it was little wonder that when the short years of formal schooling were over, and the time come for him to leave his father's crowded cottage and seek to make his way in the world, the road he chose was the sea.

Had there been money available, and some patron to pull strings in the right places, young John Paul might well have begun his career as a midshipman in the Royal Navy. He would, under normal circumstances, have been senior to Nelson! As it was, the merchant marine was his stepping-stone to greatness, and at thirteen he was apprenticed to a Whitehaven ship owner to learn the mariner's trade. He was entered as ship's boy aboard the brig *Friendship,* then loading cargo for Barbados and Virginia. John Paul had gone to sea.

There followed three years of transatlantic voyaging, after which time (the ship owner, now bankrupt, having meanwhile released young Paul from his obligations) he found his way into the slave trade. He was learning his business, for at seventeen he was third mate in the Whitehaven blackbirder *King George* and two years later chief mate of the *Two Friends,* of Kingston, Jamaica. But life on a slaver did not suit John Paul, and in 1768 he shipped home in the brig *John.* One man's ill luck is another man's good fortune. Both master and mate died en route, and John Paul brought the vessel home so handily that the pleased owners made him master for the next voyage.

From ship's boy to master in nine years was not bad; very good, considering that there was no family influence at work on his behalf. Not only was he now a competent navigator, but able to fulfill the duties of supercargo as well (that is, handle the buying and selling of the cargo). More than that, he had been at great pains to better himself socially; had educated himself by reading, dropped his thick lowland brogue, become something of a dandy, and in general adopted the manners of a gentleman.

In 1772 John Paul was given command of a large square-rigger, *Betsy,* of London,

plying between England, Ireland, Madeira, and Tobago, and it was on his second voyage that there occurred an event which changed his whole life.

By his own account, while in port at Tobago a murderous attack was made on him by a mutinous seaman; and Paul ran the man through with his sword and killed him. This in itself would have caused little stir in those days, and Paul had immediately offered to give himself up to the local justice of the peace. The death of a mutinous seaman would scarcely have prejudiced him in the eyes of an Admiralty court; yet according to Paul, he was advised to flee, which, unaccountably, he did. Abandoning his command, he rode across the island and caught a ship just about to sail. The whys and wherefores of this incident are shrouded in mystery. Even supposing that the dead man, a native of the island, had many friends ashore, it hardly explains the sudden flight—or the change of names, from John Paul to John Jones, and then to John Paul Jones. Also mysterious are the captain's movements for the next several months. Until, in fact, October 1775, when a letter, still in existence, was addressed to him in Philadelphia.

All this, while intriguing enough, has little to do with our story. What is important is that a chain of events, beginning with the violent death of a sailor, brought a needy and out-of-work merchant captain to Philadelphia at a time when officers were being sought for the embryo Continental Navy. In this Navy, on December 7, 1775, John Paul Jones, Esq. received his commission as first lieutenant.

Our tale has to do with John Paul Jones's cruises off Britain, and his great fight in *Bonhomme Richard.* But the change from merchant skipper to famous naval captain did not occur overnight. And by the time Jones fought *Serapis* he had by daring, seamanship, and sound judgment acquired an enviable reputation, at least in some quarters. As we have seen, Jones sailed in *Alfred* under Saltonstall on Hopkins's expedition to the West Indies and was in charge of the flagship's gundeck in the fight with *Glasgow*. The inquiries and courts-martial stemming from that affair did not, of course, affect Jones; in fact, he sat on both the trial of Whipple, of *Columbus,* and that of Hazard, of *Providence.* When the latter captain was broken, his ship fell to Jones, with the rank of acting captain. Whatever doubts Jones may have had about independence from Britain and the eventual success of the American cause vanished with this, his own command.

After some routine convoy duty, Jones received a regular captain's commission dated August 8, 1776, and was given orders to ready the little sloop for an extended cruise against the enemy. It was a fortunate undertaking. He had a good crew, a stout vessel, and was his own master. The cruise netted him several prizes, some British fishing vessels were destroyed, and on two occasions Jones had the satisfaction of bringing his ship safely from under the noses of British frigates.

His next command was *Alfred* (Saltonstall had been given one of the new frigates then building). With *Hampden,* Captain Hacker, he was to make a raid on Cape Breton. Hacker managed to run *Hampden* aground in Narragansett Bay; so he and his crew shifted to *Providence.* Sailing north, the two ships took several valuable prizes, but *Providence* was leaking badly and, over Jones's protests, returned to Rhode Island. Jones carried on alone, raided Canso, and took several colliers and merchantmen and a 10-gun privateer (which was recaptured soon afterward). *Alfred* returned to Boston after a successful cruise, although two of the colliers were also recaptured before they could reach American ports.

To Jones's disgust he was relieved of command of *Alfred* and reassigned to *Providence.* Worse, his commission was reissued, now dated October 10, 1776. The Marine Committee had recommended that Congress list the captains in the Continental Navy in order of their seniority.

List of Captains in the Continental Navy in Order of Their Seniority as Established by Congress, October 10, 1776

1.	James Nicholson	frigate *Virginia*
2.	John Manley	frigate *Hancock*
3.	Hector McNeill	frigate *Boston*
4.	Dudley Saltonstall	frigate *Trumbull*
5.	Nicholas Biddle	frigate *Randolph*
6.	Thomas Thompson	frigate *Raleigh*
7.	John Barry	frigate *Effingham*
8.	Thomas Read	frigate *Washington*
9.	Thomas Grinnell	frigate *Congress*
10.	Charles Alexander	frigate *Delaware*
11.	Lambert Wickes	sloop *Reprisal*
12.	Abraham Whipple	frigate *Providence*
13.	John B. Hopkins	frigate *Warren*
14.	John Hodge	frigate *Montgomery*
15.	William Hallock	brig *Lexington*
16.	Hoysted Hacker	brig *Hampden*
17.	Isiah Robinson	brig *Andrew Doria*
18.	John Paul Jones	sloop *Providence*
19.	James Josiah	no ship assigned
20.	Elisha Hinman	ship *Alfred*
21.	Joseph Olney	brig *Cabot*
22.	James Robinson	sloop *Sachem*
23.	John Young	sloop *Independence*
24.	Elisha Warner	schooner *Fly*

As the list shows, Jones was eighteenth, a fact which enraged him and was the cause of more angry letters to his more influential friends. Actually, as a foreigner, with only a few friends to speak for him, Jones was perhaps lucky to get a command at all. And as for recognition, Jones himself seldom uttered a word of praise for those subordinate to him, while at the same time he was very free with criticism of both juniors and superiors alike.

Nor was he free of the very fault of which he had accused Saltonstall. Complaints by those who served under Jones were frequent, and while obviously not the man to suffer fools gladly, he seems to have gone to the other extreme. There were few officers who sailed with him who did not feel the lash of his tongue—and occasionally the toe of his boot.

His seamen did not exactly adore him either. They were used to being commanded by fellow townsmen, men they knew and who were inclined to treat them with some degree of leniency. To be under the command of a little "furriner," and a hard-driving, no-nonsense disciplinarian at that, was a hard pill for the democratic-minded New Englanders to swallow.

As was to be expected, Jones's complaints to the Marine Committee and others in authority were loud and long. John Hancock admired "the spirited conduct of little Jones" and urged Robert Morris, another Jones supporter, to "push him out again." In desperation, perhaps, the Marine Committee placed him in command of an expedition to take St. Kitts, thence to Pensacola, then to harry British merchantmen off the mouth of the Mississippi, cruise off Georgia and the Carolinas, and finally to attempt to disrupt the slave trade between West Africa and the West Indies. For this ambitious undertaking, Jones was to have *Alfred, Columbus, Cabot, Hampden,* and *Providence.* His pleasure at this assignment was short-lived. The ships were either still at sea, undergoing repair, or without crews. All that happened was that Jones became further embroiled with old Commodore Hopkins, then on the verge of being suspended from his command.

Jones was next ordered to France, where he was to have one of the new vessels being purchased there. Fortunately for Jones, this scheme also fell through—fortunately, for at this moment the command of the sloop *Ranger,* newly built at Portsmouth, New Hampshire, fell vacant, and on June 14, 1777, Congress resolved that the command be given to John Paul Jones.

Ranger was square-rigged on all three masts, ninety-seven feet long on the gun deck, nearly twenty-nine feet in beam, and carried eighteen 9-pounders. Her hull, black with a broad yellow stripe, was fine-lined and showed promise of speed. Jones was delighted with her and threw himself into the task of getting her ready for sea. No easy task, for everything was in short supply and there were acrimonious exchanges with those responsible for procuring the necessary stores and equipment before she was finally ready. With the exception of the captain of marines, her officers were all New Hampshire men; none of them were of Jones's choosing, and none had served in the Navy.

Getting a crew was the usual problem. Most of the seamen were already away at sea or prisoners of war in Halifax gaol, and the privateers then fitting out were offering inducements no Navy recruiter could match. However, at last, on November 1, 1777, *Ranger* headed out to sea, bound for France.

The American Commissioners in Paris were to buy, or have built, a new frigate and Jones was to command her, but the deal fell through. There followed many delays, and negotiations with the French (who were still officially neutral). At last on April 10, 1778, Jones was able to leave Brest. His object was to raid one or more English seaports, do as much damage to shipping as he could, and, if possible, capture some important hostage to exchange for American sailors held captive in British gaols.

On April 18, Jones was off the northern tip of the Isle of Man. One ship had been sent into Brest as a prize, another scuttled and sunk. Next day he sank two more coasters and on the night of the twentieth he attempted to board the 20-gun sloop of war H.M.S. *Drake,* at anchor in Belfast Lough. The plan was to anchor just to windward, but the anchor hung up on the cathead and *Ranger* overshot her mark. *Drake,* unsuspecting, took no hostile action, and Jones planned to try again the following night. But weather prevented the attempt, so Jones decided to carry out his projected raid. He chose Whitehaven as his target, the town from which he had first gone to sea seventeen years before.

Ranger's crew had been an undisciplined lot to begin with. After six months away from home, with almost nothing in the way of prize money to show for their trouble, they were

Naval Pistol. Prong on side hooked into sailor's belt or waistband.

pretty disgusted. And now this bad-tempered little Scotsman, who treated honest, patriotic New Englanders like dirt, was talking about attacking towns and burning vessels at anchor all under the very noses of the Royal Navy. There was little profit in that—no more than there had been in sinking coasters. There had already been near mutiny; now, when Jones called for volunteers for the Whitehaven raid, both lieutenants declined to accompany their captain.

The wind failed while *Ranger* was still some miles from the port. With forty men, in two boats, Jones reached the harbor just at daybreak on April 23. Then with some men of his boat's crew he surprised the sleeping guards and set about spiking the guns in the batteries covering the anchorage. The men of the other boat were supposed to have begun the work of destruction by tossing fire bombs of canvas soaked in brimstone into the dozens of small vessels crowding the anchorage. But the lights taken to ignite the fire bombs had blown out. Not one caught fire, nor did Jones's party have any more luck; their candles had all burnt out too. To make matters worse, one of the boat's crew, an Irishman who is said to have enlisted only with the idea of getting home, ran through the town arousing the people, yelling that pirates were about to burn their ships and homes.

The sun rises early along the Scottish border at that time of year, and it was broad daylight by the time Jones succeeded in setting one of the incendiary bombs alight (by borrowing fire from a nearby house) and starting a blaze in a small collier. It was time to go. The townspeople were aroused and buzzing like a swarm of angry bees. The more aggressive were held up on the pierhead at pistol point while the crews hastily reembarked. A few

shots from cannon that Jones and his men had overlooked splashed around the boats as they made their way back to *Ranger,* which had picked up wind enough to sail in to meet them.

Jones must have been an angry and disappointed man at the failure of the landing parties to start the holocaust he had planned. But the bloodless affair had a moral effect out of all proportion to the damage inflicted. An English seaport had not been raided since the Dutch wars, and indignation ran high. Other ports were on the alert, militiamen were mobilized, and newspapers attacked the government for laxness and the Navy for not doing its duty. Nor did later events of the day tend to spread balm on smarting wounds.

One of Jones's pet projects had been the capture of one or more high-ranking Britons, to hold as hostage against the return of American seamen. And such a hostage lay close at hand. To the north, rising out of the familiar waters of Kirkudbright Bay, was the little peninsula of St. Mary's Isle—site of the ancestral home of the Earl of Selkirk. This local potentate must have loomed large in the imagination of the young John Paul, and it is understandable that the mature John Paul Jones should have overestimated the importance of this worthy but relatively minor peer. So *Ranger*'s course was set for Kirkudbright, and a few hours later her cutter, with Jones in command, grounded at the foot of the path leading up to Selkirk Manor.

A statement that the little party of armed seamen was a Royal Navy press gang seeking "recruits" was sufficient to send all the able-bodied men on the estate scurrying for the hills. But the would-be kidnappers were doomed to disappointment. The earl (who might have made history had he been at home)

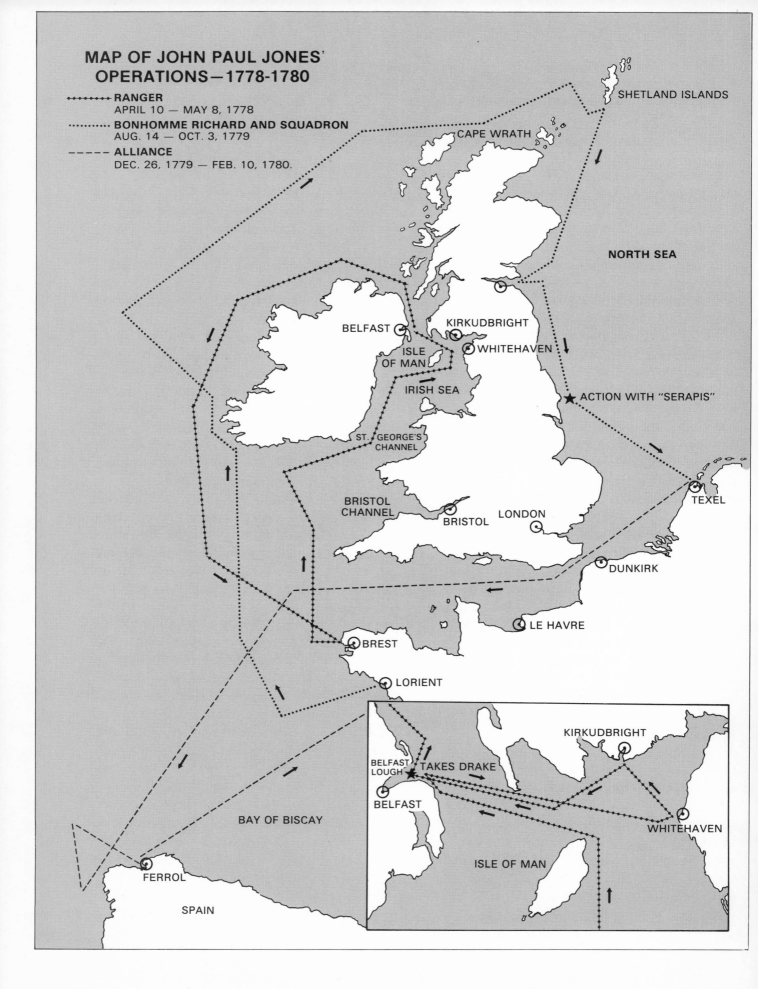

MAP OF JOHN PAUL JONES'
OPERATIONS—1778-1780

•••••• RANGER
APRIL 10 — MAY 8, 1778

•••••••• BONHOMME RICHARD AND SQUADRON
AUG. 14 — OCT. 3, 1779

- - - - - ALLIANCE
DEC. 26, 1779 — FEB. 10, 1780.

SHETLAND ISLANDS

CAPE WRATH

NORTH SEA

BELFAST

KIRKUDBRIGHT

WHITEHAVEN

ISLE
OF MAN

IRISH SEA

ACTION WITH "SERAPIS"

ST. GEORGE'S
CHANNEL

TEXEL

BRISTOL
CHANNEL

LONDON

BRISTOL

DUNKIRK

LE HAVRE

BREST

LORIENT

BELFAST
LOUGH

TAKES DRAKE

KIRKUDBRIGHT

BELFAST

WHITEHAVEN

ISLE OF MAN

BAY OF BISCAY

FERROL

SPAIN

112

was away in England, and Jones, twice disappointed in the space of one day, returned to the cutter. *Ranger*'s boat crew was not to sail empty-handed, however.

The men wanted loot. To be led to the very doors of a British nobleman's house and go tamely away was too much to expect. So Jones, who knew to a hair how far a surly crew could be pushed, reluctantly agreed that the family silver could be taken, but nothing else, nor was anyone to be molested or insulted. The silver was duly removed to the *Ranger* and, so greatly did Jones admire Lady Selkirk's handling of a difficult situation, was returned after the war at the gallant captain's expense.

The raid on Whitehaven had been bloodless, and the affair at Kirkudbright in the nature of an outing. The next twenty-four hours was to see blood flow in plenty. Jones had a score to settle with *Drake* and the morning of the twenty-fourth saw *Ranger* standing into the entrance to Belfast Lough, where she sighted *Drake* working her way out. *Ranger*'s near-mutinous crew brightened up at the prospects of a fight and possible prize money. The capture by a ruse of *Drake*'s gig, sent with a lieutenant to investigate the strange sail, put them in even better humor. For once Jones could count on their whole-hearted cooperation.

The two sloops were fairly even matched. *Ranger* carried eighteen 6-pounders, against *Drake*'s twenty 4's. Jones's crew was smaller, some 135 to 154, but he had undoubtedly trained them into an efficient fighting force, even if rebellious at times, whereas *Drake*'s crew were mostly newly pressed landlubbers and volunteers and lacked a lieutenant, gunner, master's mate, and boatswain. According to Clowes, she had no prepared cartridges aboard, either for the great guns or small arms.

The point is, if she were not ready for action, she should have been. Excuses are of little avail after a defeat, and within two glasses (one hour) of the first broadside, *Drake* was a badly beaten ship. *Ranger*'s gunnery was better, and Jones undoubtedly outmaneuvered his opponent. The Americans, firing to carry away the British ship's spars, soon reduced their opponent to an unmanageable wreck. Her yards cut in the slings, her spanker gaff hanging down alongside the mast, her jib trailing in the water, her rigging cut to pieces, her captain and first lieutenant dead, *Drake* hauled down her colors. Jones's victory had cost him but three killed and five wounded. *Drake*'s loss was four killed and nineteen wounded. If it is true that all the American casualties were caused by fire from the enemy's tops, *Drake*'s shooting must have been very poor. Or perhaps the 4-pounder popguns could not penetrate *Ranger*'s hull. In any event, it was a tidy little victory, and *Ranger*'s entry in Brest on May 8, 1778 followed by Drake, with the American flag flying over the British colors, was a fine tribute to the young Continental Navy.

It might have been expected that a successful cruise, with a couple of fat merchantmen taken, others sunk, a port raided, and a British man-of-war captured, would have brought the victorious commander immediate recognition from his government and a better command. Jones certainly thought so, and the fact that it did not filled him with bitterness. Not only was recognition wanting, but even money and supplies for his crew.

Jones was finally able to obtain both back pay and rations, but the crew did not appreciate their captain's efforts on their behalf and even accused him of withholding prize money, when, in fact, he was doing everything he could to sell the prizes as advantageously as possible. Jones's first lieutenant, Simpson, had previously supported the crew in their insubordination, and Jones finally put him under arrest. This further incensed the majority of the crew, who petitioned Ben Franklin at Paris in behalf of the "Faithful, true and Fatherly Oficer, our First Lieutenant." Simpson, released from arrest, was finally ordered to take *Ranger* back to

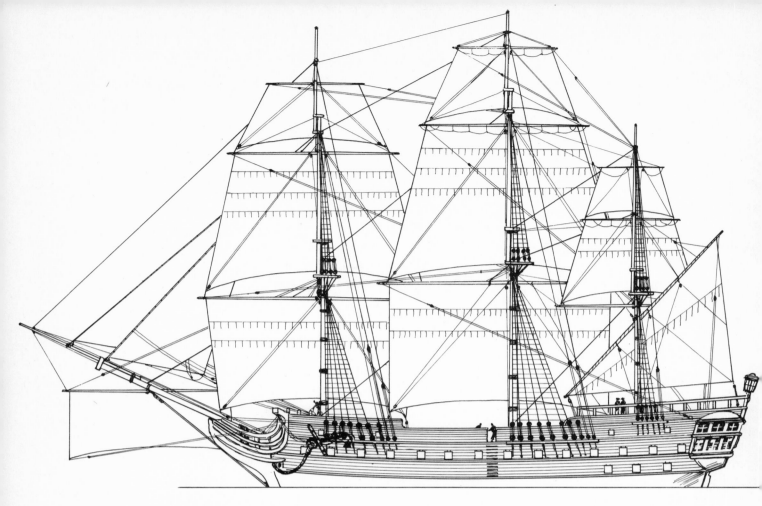

No plans of the BONHOMME RICHARD are known to have survived. She probably looked much like the drawing above. Some models and plans show her with a single-decked stern cabin. As an ex-Indiaman it is more likely she had two, on quarterdeck and gundeck. Ports were cut for the ill-fated 18-pounders below the gundeck aft.

America, where he obtained a captain's commission from Congress.

For Simpson, whom Jones had done his best to have court-martialed, to be rewarded with a promotion seemed to the quick-tempered Scot to add insult to injury. Actually, Jones was lucky to see the last of *Ranger*, her unreliable lieutenant, and her semimutinous crew; although it is doubtful if he saw it in that light at the time.

The ten months which Jones spent in France, from his triumphal entry into Brest to the time (February, 1779) when he was given *Bonhomme Richard*, was a period of frustration and humiliation. There was, primarily, the matter of a ship. He had been promised a new frigate, and had high hopes of getting the fine 40-gun *L'Indien*. She had been built in a

private shipyard in Amsterdam for the Americans, but shortage of money, and the difficulty of persuading the Dutch government to release her had induced Franklin and the Commissioners to sell her to the French. Jones tried his best (and he could be both persuasive and persistent) to get her turned over to him, but the Dutch were not about to risk serious trouble with their English neighbors and *L'Indien* did not get to sea until the summer of 1781, by which time Holland was at war with Britain.

The American Commissioners had many problems and Jones was only one of them. But while making allowance for the difficulties which beset the representatives of a struggling nation with little credit and forced to beg for arms and supplies from a power noted for self-interest, it still seems a great folly to have kept a man of Jones's character unemployed nearly a year—and this almost at the enemy's doorstep.

Finally after many other promises and disappointments, an Irish merchant in Lorient found, not the ideal vessel, but as Jones wrote, "the only ship for sale in France that will answer our purpose." She was a 900-ton East Indiaman, *Duc de Duras*, launched in 1766, and sturdily built, as were all the vessels designed for the dangerous India trade. She was purchased for Jones by the French government, and the King himself bore the expenses of fitting her out. There was great difficulty in finding cannon for her, and when she finally sailed her armament included half a dozen old 18-pounders of questionable worth. Besides these relics, for which ports were cut under the afterpart of the gundeck, she mounted six 9-pounders on forecastle and quarterdeck and twenty-eight 12-pounders on the gundeck. It was a mixed armament, and one which Jones would probably not have chosen, but beggars, as he had long since found out, cannot be choosers, and when she was finally ready to sail, under her new name of *Bonhomme Richard* (or *Bon Homme Richard*, as Jones misspelled it in his log), he was undoubtedly proud of her.

While his ship was being fitted out, there was much discussion as to how she was to be employed. At one time there was talk of an attack on a sizable port, with Jones at the head of a small squadron, and the Marquis de Lafayette—recently returned to France, with his title of Major General in the Continental Army—in command of land forces. Unfortunately this plan fell through, but a squadron was gathered together and readied with the idea of making a cruise in the waters of northern England or Scotland. This cruise was to act as a diversion to draw some of Britain's scanty naval forces away from the intended invasion of southern England.

The invasion itself never came off. The combined fleets of France and Spain—64

ships of the line—failed to bring the British Channel Fleet of 38 sail to action. Riddled with disease, the Allied fleet finally sought its harbors. The French squadrons alone landed 7,000 sick, with hundreds already consigned to the deep. Scurvy, smallpox, and typhus had defeated the invasion attempt as surely as did Trafalgar another, better-planned, assault 26 years later.

Jones's squadron consisted of *Bonhomme Richard*, 40; the new American-built frigate *Alliance*, 36; frigate *La Pallas*, 32; corvette *La Vengeance*, 12; and cutter *Le Cerf*, 18. Two privateers, *Monsieur*, 38, and *Granville*, 10, accompanied the squadron. All government ships were to fly the American flag and sail under Continental Navy regulations. The two privateers were not included in this arrangement. Not that this mattered because, as Jones shrewdly suspected they would, they detached themselves from the squadron not long after sailing.

As commodore of a squadron of his own, Jones might have been well content, but there was a fly in the ointment and one which was to give Jones a great deal of trouble. This particular insect was Pierre Landais, a half-cracked French ex-naval officer, who had wangled a commission out of the American Congress, and an honorary citizenship out of the General Court of Massachusetts. Arrogant, jealous, and incompetent, Landais was the worst possible choice for the captaincy of a fine new frigate, but this was at a period when past service with the army or navy of a European power was an almost sure passport to employment in the American armed forces, and so Landais was given *Alliance*, to the disgust of many American captains—Jones included.

On a shakedown cruise, *Alliance* fouled the flagship in a squall, losing her mizzenmast, while *Richard*'s bowsprit had to be replaced. Finally, all ships were once again in readiness, and on August 14, 1779, the squadron set sail.

For once, Jones could find no fault

with his own ship's officers. They were a mixed group, including Americans, Irishmen from the French Regiment of Marine Artillery of the French Service, and French officers of marines. All were volunteers, some personally known to Jones, and all gave him their loyalty and support. The crew, like most in those days, included men from nearly a dozen nations, including a Swiss, an Italian, and two East Indians. The majority of the petty officers were British, as were the seamen. Accounts vary as to the exact makeup. Morison's *John Paul Jones* gives, out of 187 crewmen, 81 British, 62 Americans, 29 Portuguese, 10 Scandinavians, and 5 others. Besides these there were 36

Uniform of the French Marine Regiment. Dark blue coat with red facings and cuffs and a white turnback. Waistcoat, gaiters and breeches were white.

French landsmen (cooks, stewards, etc.) and a force of 137 French marines. The complement, including officers, totaled 380.

The cruise of *Bonhomme Richard* from Lorient to her last resting place off Flamborough Head can best be followed on the map. The voyage began in good weather and under easy sail. The western approaches and the mouth of the Irish Sea were then, as now, great highways of British trade, and the commodore undoubtedly hoped to pick up some prizes in that well-traveled waterway. *Monsieur* took a vessel on the eighteenth and departed with her prize, having refused to allow Jones to send a prize crew aboard. On the twenty-first, the coastal trader *Mayflower* was taken and sent into Lorient. On the twenty-third, off the southern tip of Ireland the brig *Fortune* was captured, but her name brought no luck to the expedition.

On the evening of the same day, in a flat calm, the current began to set *Richard* dangerously close to the rocky coast. The barge was ordered overside to tow her off, but now the master, Lunt, made a mistake—one which ultimately cost him his life. The barge's coxswain was a man who had been flogged at Lorient, while the crew were Irish to a man. Seeing home so close, they cut the towline and made for shore. The enraged master pursued in the jolly boat, taking with him two officers and nine men, and promptly got lost in a thick fog.

Next day *Cerf* was sent to search for the boats, but, by hoisting English colors, only succeeded in scaring Lunt ashore, where he and his men were captured. The weather now turned nasty, *Cerf* made for Lorient, *Alliance* took herself off and was not seen for several days, and *Granville* went off with a prize and never rejoined. Jones had lost three of his officers, several men, and an 18-gun cutter. Not only that, but the enemy had been warned. The deserters had given the authorities a description of the squadron and such of its plans as had filtered down to the lower deck. British warships went out in search, but

Jones took the stormy route around the west coast of Ireland and they never made contact.

Pallas had parted company earlier to repair a broken tiller, and only *Vengeance* was still with Jones when he made Cape Wrath on September 1. Here Jones took *Union*, bound for Quebec with army stores. Here, too, *Alliance* rejoined (the Cape had been assigned as a rendezvous) with a prize of her own. That night *Pallas* appeared and the squadron—minus *Cerf*, was united once more. Next day *Vengeance* took a brigantine. They were now almost within sight of the Shetlands and the

two colliers, and Jones called his two captains aboard for a council of war. After much delay, which lost him a fair wind, the Commodore persuaded his companions to attack the port of Leith and either ransom it or burn it to the ground. The squadron had of course been sighted and there was great excitement ashore. Leith was practically defenseless,

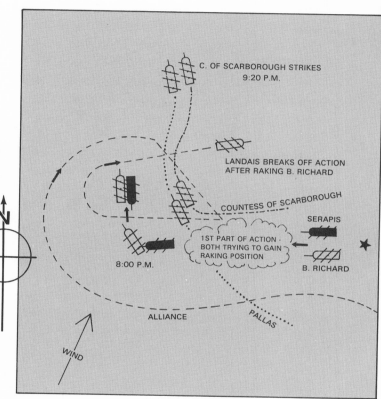

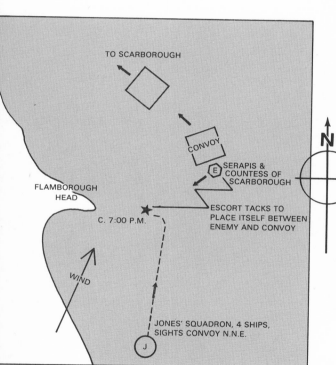

Action between Jones' Squadron and Convoy Escort—Sept. 23, 1779

Commodore ordered course altered to the southward.

Alliance made a couple of small prizes and then, Landais ignoring his orders once more, parted company again. In stormy weather the three vessels made their way south, finally sighting land near Dunbar on September 13. On the fourteenth they took

while the great guns mounted in Edinburgh Castle could not reach out to sea. There was rolling of drums and galloping of messengers ashore, but while Jones's ships were beating up the Firth of Forth a sudden storm came out of the west, which, "being directly contrary obliged me to bear away after having in vain Endeavoured for sometime to Withstand its violence."

Jones next appeared off the coast of Northumberland, but his plan for an attack on Newcastle-on-Tyne was thwarted by the refusal of his French captains to have anything to do with such a scheme. So they sailed south, after taking a couple more colliers. On the morning of the twenty-second they were off the mouth of the Humber, *Pallas* to the north, where the pickings were good. Jones made signal to the British for a pilot. Two, unsuspecting, came out and were taken. That evening the Commodore turned north and at dawn on the twenty-third sighted *Pallas,* and with her, *Alliance.* The four vessels approached Flamborough Head with a failing breeze and at 3:00 P.M., to Jones's delight, a large fleet of merchantmen hove in sight off the Head, standing in their direction. It was a rare prize— a Baltic convoy of over forty sail. Jones knew from the captured pilots that the escort was the 44-gun frigate *Serapis* and sloop of war *Countess of Scarborough,* 20. Captain Richard Pearson of *Serapis,* the convoy commander, was also forewarned; a boat from Scarborough had told him the American squadron had been sighted off the coast. The merchant skippers, as merchant skippers have done since time began, ignored his signals to keep together inshore until they themselves sighted the enemy squadron. They then turned like sheep and ran north for the shelter of Scarborough Castle. The two vessels of the escort steered a course to bring them between the four American ships and the convoy.

Jones, meanwhile, was making all sail to get at the huddled merchantmen, but the light breeze reduced his speed to a crawl. It was not until 6:00 P.M. that the signal for line of battle was flown, although Jones's signalmen might have saved their trouble. *Alliance,* the lead ship, hauled off, as did *Vengeance,* leaving *Bonhomme Richard* to face the British frigate, while *Pallas* engaged the *Countess of Scarborough.*

Jones brought up to windward of *Serapis,* flying British colors. Pearson hailed, "What ship is that?" and *Richard* answered, "*Princess Royal.*" At Pearson's second hail, the two ships being now on parallel courses, Jones hoisted the American flag and fired a broadside. Hardly had the guns flashed before an answering broadside crashed out from *Serapis.* But even as *Richard'*s guns spoke there was a glare from her 18-pounder battery, followed by screams and the smash of timbers. Two of the ancient pieces had exploded, wrecking the battery, killing and wounding many of the gun crews, and shattering part of the gundeck directly above.

It was a bad beginning, for the six 18-pounders were the only heavy guns Jones had, while *Serapis* carried twenty of that caliber on her lower gundeck. Besides that, there were twenty 12-pounders on her upper deck, and ten 6's on the quarterdeck (Clowes gives her her rated 44, but American authorities credit her with 50 guns).

The superior weight of *Serapis's* broadside and the destructiveness of her fire convinced Jones that he must fight at close quarters. In his own words, "every method was practiced on both sides to gain an advantage and rake each other, and I must confess that the enemy's ship, being much more manageable than the *Bon Homme Richard,* gained thereby several times an advantageous situation, in spite of my best endeavors to prevent it. As I had to deal with an enemy of greatly superior force, I was under the necessity of closing with him, to prevent the advantage which he had over me in point of

Fighting Top
Netting or canvas usually rigged around top before action.

Topmast Shrouds

Topmast

Trestle Trees

Platform

Cheek Knees

Lubber's Hole

Crosstrees

Futtock Shrouds

Shrouds

Lower Mast

manoeuvre. It was my intention to lay the *Bon Homme Richard* athwart the enemy's bow, but as that operation required great dexterity in the management of both sails and helm and some of our braces being shot away, it did not exactly succeed to my wishes. The enemy's bowsprit, however, came over the *Bon Homme Richard*'s poop by the mizen mast and I made both ships fast together in that situation, which by the action of the wind on the enemy's sails, forced her stern close to the *Bon Homme Richard*'s bow, so that the ships lay square alongside of each other, the yards being all entangled and the cannon of each ship touching the opponent's side."

It was during the sharp fighting and maneuvering before the two ships came to rest broadside to broadside that Pearson hailed for the first time to ask if Jones had struck. *Serapis* was, at that moment, attempting to cross *Richard*'s bow, but in the light airs she lost her headway and lay for a moment with *Richard*'s bowsprit over her starboard quarter. It was an advantageous position, could Pearson have held it, and the British captain (who did not know his man) may be excused for supposing that surrender might be in Jones's mind. The little captain's magnificent reply, "I have not yet begun to fight," has become history.

So close were the ships that the gunners on *Serapis*'s lower deck, who now found themselves engaged on their starboard side, could not raise their port lids and were forced to blow them open. To use their rammers the gun crews had to thrust them into the enemy's ports, while both ships were set on fire several times by flaming wads and the flashes of the guns.

This was about 8:30 and the ships were now held fast, bow to stern, in a position where the Englishman's heavy battery could do him little good. Several attempts were made to cut the lashings binding the two ships together but the fire from *Bonhomme Richard's* tops foiled each effort. The battle was, in fact, won by the American topmen. Lieutenant Stack, with twenty sailors and marines, held the main top; Midshipman Fanning commanded the fore top, with fourteen men, and Midshipman Coram the mizzen, with nine. The fire of the small arms and swivels from the tops was first directed at the *Serapis's* topmen. When the Britisher's tops were swept clear of men, *Richard's* topmen were able to clamber over the interlocking yards and take possession. From these vantage points a hail of small shot and a rain of smoking grenades were directed at *Serapis's* decks, driving the crews from the quarterdeck 6-pounders, and from those weapons on the upper gundeck exposed to the American topmen's fire.

On the lower decks it was another story. The fire from *Serapis's* battery of 18's cleared *Richard's* gundeck in short order, overturning carriages and reducing the enclosed space to a shambles. Water from several 18-pound shot holes was pouring into the ship and one of the pumps was smashed, while at each discharge the deadly 18's were reducing the old Indiaman's hull to kindling. Despite the fire from the American's tops, the battle was gradually going to the heavier armed ship, when about 10:00 an explosion ripped along *Serapis's* lower deck, killing at least twenty men and terribly injuring many more. A seaman had crawled out along a yard and dropped a grenade squarely down a hatch. Exploding, it ignited some loose powder and spare cartridges and the flash leaped from gun to gun.

But the fight still raged on. *Serapis*, with her upper deck swept clear of men and many of her weapons now silent; *Bonhomme Richard*, with water rising in the hold, her 'tween decks so shattered that there was danger of the upper decks collapsing into the wreckage below. And around the two ships, locked in a death grapple, sailed the crazy Landais. A broadside from his *Alliance* had raked *Richard* early in the engagement; later he slowly crossed his flagship's stern and raked her again. Then, as if he had not done enough mischief, he tacked across her bows and poured in yet another broadside, killing several men on her forecastle, including a chief petty officer. There was no chance of a mistake. The moon was up and despite the smoke the yellow sides of *Serapis* must have been plainly distinguishable from the black topsides of *Richard*.

Pearson was afterwards to claim that he was attacked by two frigates, and undoubtedly he thought he was—a fact which must have influenced his decision to surrender. Perhaps Landais did mean to fire into *Serapis* as well, although Jones claimed she lost only one man to *Alliance's* fire. In the confusion it would be hard to tell, but there is no doubt that the broadsides fired into *Richard* were deliberately aimed. Landais himself is said to have told one of the French marine colonels after the battle that he intended to sink *Richard* and then capture *Serapis* by boarding, thus appearing the hero of the affair. He did, of course, announce that his broadsides had caused Pearson to strike, but there is nothing to substantiate his claim and testimony taken after the battle showed that *Alliance* was not within range during the last half-hour.

Shattered and sinking, and now fired on by one of her own squadron, it is small wonder that some hearts in *Bonhomme Richard* grew faint. The battle had raged for some three hours and still the enemy's guns flashed out. Three petty officers—the carpenter, the master-at-arms, and a chief gunner—decided that the ship must either surrender or sink. The gunner ran aft to haul down the colors but, as Jones wrote, "fortunately for me, a cannon ball had done that before by carrying away the ensign staff." The man then began to yell for quarter but Jones coolly felled him with his pistol butt.

Pearson, pacing his quarterdeck, heard the man's cry and hailed to ask if the American had struck. The only answer was a flash from the 9-pounders on *Richard's* quarterdeck, whose fire Jones was personally directing. These three guns were the only ones left which would bear, and Jones concentrated their fire at the Englishman's mainmast, using double-headed shot.

Meanwhile the master-at-arms had rushed below and released the prisoners. There were over 100 of them, and properly organized, they might have turned the tide. Fortunately for Jones they were nothing but a mob of merchant seamen and fishermen, scared at being confined below while the ship was being pounded to pieces over their heads and the water was rising steadily about their feet. They were told to man the pumps and help save the ship, if they valued their lives. This they did, although one, the master of one of the prizes, clambered through a gunport and told Pearson that there was five feet of water in *Richard's* hold and that if he could only hold on she must surrender or go to the bottom.

It was now a contest of wills between the two commanders. Jones with a sinking, battered wreck, with only three guns in action, nearly half his crew down, and his prisoners loose; Pearson, with some fifty dead and many more wounded, many guns disabled from the explosion, his ship on fire and his mainmast tottering from the effects of Jones's steady pounding.

As a last resort Pearson ordered away boarders. Clutching cutlasses and pikes, they swarmed onto *Richard's* bulwarks; but Jones's men were ready for them, the deadly fire from the tops redoubled, and they fell back. Pearson had had enough. His stubborn opponent obviously had no intention of quitting, *Countess of Scarborough* had surrendered to *Pallas*, *Alliance* had received no damage and could

be expected to fall on him at any moment. With his own hands he tore down the ensign which he had ordered nailed to the staff, and the 3 1/2-hour battle was over.

Hardly had Lieutenant Dale taken possession of *Serapis* than her mainmast went by the board, taking the mizzen topmast with it. She was as badly wrecked aloft as *Richard* was below. The two prizes were jury-rigged and the squadron proceeded slowly eastward. Every effort was made to save the flagship, but by evening of the twenty-fourth it was obvious that she was doomed. Jones reluctantly transferred his flag to *Serapis*, but it was not until 11:00 A.M. on the twenty-fifth that the gallant old ship plunged, bow first, to the bottom of the North Sea.

It had been a notable victory for the American Commodore, and one which made him famous. He had beaten, in fair fight, a more powerful ship and he well deserved any glory that might come his way. It was, although he did not know it, his finest hour. Ahead lay honors in France and in America; command, if temporary, of the Continental Navy's first ship of the line, and flag rank in the service of the Tsarina of all the Russias. Ahead also lay more disappointment, bitterness, controversies, scandal, and intrigue— and ultimately a lonely death. Old *Bonhomme Richard* may not have been the ideal fighting ship, but she had brought him luck. When she slid beneath the cold, gray waters which have swallowed up so many battered hulls she took John Paul Jones's good fortune with her.

Of the other actors in the drama, Landais, after being censured and removed from *Alliance*, intrigued his way back into command and illegally snatched her, with the aid of the anti-Jones party, from under Jones's very nose. The crazed Frenchman's conduct on the return voyage to America was such that he had to be relieved of command en route. He faced a court-martial—after being forcibly carried ashore, kicking and screaming —and was dismissed the service. Even then Jones's old enemy Samuel Adams upheld him as a pitiful victim of "this Jones" and the Franklin party overseas. He later returned to France and was given flag rank in the Navy of the Republic. In 1793 he was retired because of old age, and finally settled in New York, where he died in 1818 at the ripe age of eighty-seven. If the good die young, the reverse is too often true.

Pearson of *Serapis* came out of the affair very well, as he deserved to do. His job was to defend the convoy and this he did, in the face of what must have seemed an overwhelming force. Not one merchantman was lost, and he was honorably acquitted at his court-martial and commended for a gallant defense. He was later knighted by King George, and received a handsome gift from the grateful directors of the Russia Company. Piercy, of *Countess of Scarborough*, was likewise acquitted and commended.

On July 22, 1905, four cruisers of the United States Navy, back from a momentous transatlantic voyage, passed the Capes and entered Chesapeake Bay. Escorting them were seven battleships of the Atlantic Fleet, resplendent in white and buff. At the head of the column of cruisers steamed the armored cruiser *Brooklyn*, and on board she carried the body of John Paul Jones. Amid pomp and circumstance, the shrilling of pipes and the crash of salutes, the little Commodore returned as he would have wished, in glory.

Tactics, Signals, and Maneuvers

Chapter 14

Single-ship actions were won (providing the gun crews were steady and well trained) by the skill, seamanship, and determination of the individual captain. Maneuvering to gain the wind, jockeying for a raking position—the handling of a square-rigged ship in action called for precise ship handling and cool judgement. The handling of squadrons and fleets multiplied the problems of the individual captain and added many new ones. As far back as the days of the Spanish Armada admirals and captains realized that order in battle was vital—that the leader who could concentrate the firepower of the vessels under his command had a crushing advantage over one who let his ships fight as a mob. The best method of exercising such control, and of coordinating the efforts of many vessels scattered over many square miles of water, posed a question which puzzled some of the world's most renowned seamen for the next 250 years—until sail gave way to steam.

The first campaigns in which cannon played an important part took place in the Mediterranean in the sixteenth century, and were fought by galleys. Galley tactics called for line abreast formations, for both the deadly ram and the few cannon the vessel carried could only be used in a straight bows-on attack. But the galleon—and its descendant, the ship of the line—relied on broadside fire, while its fire directly ahead or astern was weak or nonexistent.

Obviously, in a huddle of ships there was danger of vessels blanketing the fire of their colleagues, or worse still, firing into them by mistake. Also, in a mass of ships half hidden from each other by powder smoke, any form of control was almost impossible. So the practice arose of bringing ships into action in line ahead—a line which could follow the movements of the leading ship or perform evolutions by signal from a flagship in the center of the line.

This sounds like a simple solution. In practice it was complicated by a number of factors and in fact was never worked out to perfection as long as sail was the motive power. The first, and most important, factor was the sailing vessel itself. At best the square-rigged ship was unhandy. Tacking or wearing was always a lengthy business, and in a fitful breeze with an adverse swell getting an unwieldy high-sided vessel around on another

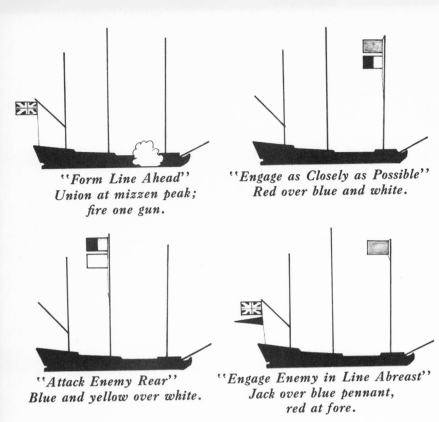

"Form Line Ahead"
Union at mizzen peak;
fire one gun.

"Engage as Closely as Possible"
Red over blue and white.

"Attack Enemy Rear"
Blue and yellow over white.

"Engage Enemy in Line Abreast"
Jack over blue pennant,
red at fore.

Signal Flags Before the Tabular and Numerary Codes
(Flags drawn same scale as ship of the line.)

tack could take half an hour or more. Ships' boats sometimes had to be hoisted out to tow a stubborn craft's head around, and it did not take much damage aloft to make such a vessel unmanageable.

Along with this, no two vessels handled quite alike nor were their rates of sailing the same. One might be a slow sailer through a fault in design; another too much down by head or stern because of bad trim; while another, long at sea, might be trailing a forest of underwater vegetation. When the advantages of coppering ships' bottoms became apparent, it was soon found that not until all the vessels in a squadron were so treated could full advantage of the extra speed be realized. Knowing this, it is easy to see the difficulties of trying to control the movements of a fleet of such vessels, and of the constant sail-handling necessary to keep one ship from lagging behind or another from forereaching on the ship ahead.

And this led to another problem—one which remained only partially solved until the development of the electric signaling light and short-range radio, the T.B.S. (talk between ships) of World War II. Signaling of sorts was known to the ancients—devices such as waving of banners, smoke, a polished shield raised on pole or masthead, and beacon fires at night. Such signals were necessarily simple—"enemy in sight," "attack," "retreat," "council," "chase," etc. But as naval warfare became more complex, the necessity for methods of transmitting an ever increasing variety of messages from ship to ship became pressing.

Signaling as we know it began with codes requiring the hoisting of various flags—national flags or colored signal flags or pennants—in different positions on the masts or in the rigging. Thus in the English fleet in 1645, "a yellow flagge in the uppermost part of the Admiralls Maine Shrowdes" meant that the captains and masters were to convene on board the flagship. "General action" was signaled by the hoisting of a red flag, the "bloody colors," on the poop of the admiral's ship. By 1673, fifteen flags were listed in the Admiralty instructions. These flags had meanings corresponding to the position in which they were displayed in the rigging, thus allowing a number of different signals to be sent.

There were signal books, with colored flags shown in the various places in the rigging and the corresponding signal printed underneath. A French book, dated 1693, is in existence; and the first English pocket volume, for handy use aboard ship, was printed in 1714.

One hundred years later there were 28 flags in use in the Royal Navy and more were added soon after. Some could be flown upside down, bringing the number to about 50. Flown in six or seven different positions, this gave over 300 different signals. But by now the system was getting too complicated. The great variety of flags were too hard to distinguish from one another, especially in battle, where everything was likely to be obscured by smoke. Also, the specified positions were not always the places giving the best visibility, and a signal flag must be distinguishable not only when unfurled in a breeze, but also when hanging limp from the halyard.

A simpler system was urgently needed. In 1740 a brilliant French officer, La Bourdonnais, invented a signal system using numerals, with ten flags denoting the numerals zero through nine. The system was not adopted by the French navy, because of, it is said, the jealousy of fellow officers of nobler birth but inferior talents.

About 1778 three English naval officers —Sir Charles Knowles, Richard Howe, and Richard Kempenfelt—were experimenting with codes based on the numerary system. One, drawn up by Howe, possibly with Kempenfelt's advice, was in tabular form, like a chess board, with sixteen squares a side. A set of sixteen flags was shown across the top of the board and down one side. The top row of flags represented page numbers in the signal book. The vertical row, the numbers of the signals on that page. Number three for instance was a blue cross on yellow, while the fourteenth flag across (and down) was red. So blue cross on yellow over red meant "page 3, signal no. 14." With a simple two-flag hoist 256 messages could be sent.

Flag colors were limited to red, white, blue, yellow, and black and combinations of those five. But while blue on white, for instance, shows up well, blue on red, or vice versa, tends to appear as purple. So, a further advantage was that with fewer flags some color combinations, which could not be clearly defined at a distance, were eliminated. Signal flags were large, the rectangular ones being about 16 1/2 feet deep and 27 feet long.

But this tabular system was unnecessarily complicated, and in 1790 a simple numerical system, using ten flags and repeaters, was adopted with the first nine flags each denoting a common signal: (1) enemy in sight, (4) take and keep stations, (8) anchor, etc. Later (1800) this numerary system was made even more useful by the addition of a "dictionary" of 999 words most useful for naval

purposes. Also, the letters of the alphabet were numbered from 1 to 25 (I and J were the same), so that if a word was not in the dictionary, it could be spelled. Thus in Nelson's famous Trafalgar signal, "England expects that every man will do his duty," the word "duty," not being in the vocabulary list, had to be spelled out. The inventor of this vocabulary signal book, Sir Home Popham, later brought out two more lists: one with additional words and one with sentences applicable to naval and military affairs. A ball or pendant hoisted above or below the last two indicated in which book the signal would be found.

During the war of the American Revolution the older system of numerous flags and pennants, hung in various positions, was still in use in some squadrons, and the system to be used was largely at the discretion of the admiral in command. It will be apparent that the transmission of orders under such conditions was exceedingly difficult, and the plea that the flagship's signals could not be read was often heard at courts-martial.

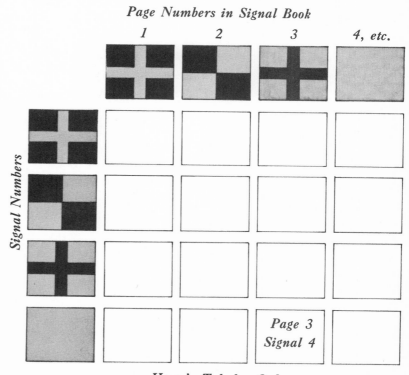

Page Numbers in Signal Book

Howe's Tabular Code

Frigates on the unengaged side relay admiral's signals to van and rear.

Even with the use of frigates as repeaters there was often much confusion— confusion worse confounded by the fact that in a long battle line the van and rear were also under the command of admirals, men who did not always see eye to eye with the commander in chief in the center and who, on occasion, were capable of deliberately misreading or ignoring his signals.

At Ushant, in 1778, Keppel not only signaled to Palliser, commanding the rear division of the fleet, to bear down in the admiral's wake and form line of battle, but, when Palliser ignored the signal, sent a frigate with a message. It was not until the ships with Palliser were summoned individually by their personal pennants, that they came to their admiral's support. Palliser claimed he did not see Keppel's signal, although it was seen by the ship next astern.

The sending of messages by frigates— or, if distances were short, by ships' boats— was by no means uncommon. Nor was the practice of passing commands by speaking trumpet. In the same battle of Ushant, because the French admiral's signal to wear in succession could not be made out, the admiral of the van division went about and hailed the flagship to find out definitely what D'Orvillier's intentions were.

Under such conditions, it was not surprising that signals were as abbreviated as possible. Code books contained only the most necessary signals, and any not contained in the books had to be transmitted by voice or personal contact.

Councils of war aboard the various flagships were common and in fact the only sure means of conveying the commander in chief's intentions. A fleet whose captains and divisional commanders were thoroughly conversant with their chief's overall plans and his general methods of fighting an action were far more likely to act as a team—a "band of brothers"—than those whose knowledge of their leader's purposes was confined to the cryptic contents of the signal code.

Dominating all actions of the eighteenth-century commander were the fighting instructions, issued by admirals and admiralties for the guidance of commanders in battle. The necessity for such instructions stemmed in large part from the difficulties in communications mentioned above. They were also at their inception a guide for the handling of the large fleets, made up of several subdivisions or squadrons, which came into being in the seventeenth century. As time went on, the fighting instructions became, not an aid, a means to an end, but the end itself. Slavishly followed, they inhibited originality and became the refuge of the pedantic and cautious.

A naval battle of the days of sail was in some respects a more complicated affair than an engagement of, say, World War I. Wind and tide were of vastly greater importance, while the maneuvering of groups of vessels at close quarters, attacking from ahead or astern, sometimes doubling on the enemy's line or breaking through it, supporting disabled ships or attempting to cut off damaged enemy vessels, with frequent adjustments of the battle line, called for numerous signals.

The supervision of such an action put far too great a strain on the rudimentary signaling systems then in vogue. The fighting instructions were meant to simplify; instead, they often confused. The following excerpt from Rodney's own additions to the Admiralty instructions puzzled even some of his own officers and, as Admiral Robison wrote in his *History of Naval Tactics*, is today a "mere jumble of words."

If the commander-in-chief would have the squadron when on a wind draw into a line on each other's bow and quarter and keep at the distance directed in the first article (i.e. at one, or two cables, as signaled) those ships which shall happen to be to leeward at the time of making the signal, forming the van of the line, and those to windward the rear, and all the ships from the van to the rear bearing on each other on the point of the compass whereon they will be on the other tack (always taking it from the center) he will hoist a red pennant under the flags mentioned in the said article (i.e. for one cable distance or two) at the mizen peak and fire a gun, and if he should afterwards tack in order to bring the squadron into a line ahead, the ship that becomes the headmost is to continue leading.

It is, perhaps, not a fair sample, but many of the articles in the various instructions and additional instructions were far from clear in their meaning.

In theory, the ordering of a battle line with the aid of code book and book of instructions may have been simple. In practice, due to the factors mentioned above, it was almost unworkable and led to many lost battles and inconclusive actions. Actually, alert and aggressive squadron commanders and captains, properly briefed and unhampered by ironbound rules and regulations, were a far greater insurance of victory than any book, no matter how comprehensive. Nelson realized this when he wrote in his memorandum to Collingwood shortly before Trafalgar, "The second in command will, after my intentions are made known to him, have the entire direction of his line; to make the attack upon the enemy, and to follow up the blow until they are captured or destroyed....Something must be left to chance; nothing is sure in a sea fight beyond all others....But in case signals can neither be seen nor perfectly understood, no captain can do very wrong if he places his ship alongside that of an enemy."

However, at the time of the Revolution the fighting instructions were still rigidly adhered to by most admirals of both French and British navies, which accounts for the rigid formalism of the majority of fleet actions of the war.

From the masthead of a medium-sized vessel (say, 100 feet above the waterline) the topsails of a similar vessel would be visible at about 21 miles. For those who like to work out such things the formula is as follows: 8/7 times square root of height of observer (in feet) above sea level equals distance to horizon in miles.

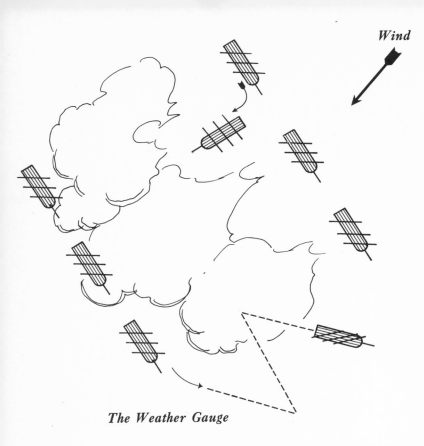

The Weather Gauge

In the preliminary maneuvering before an engagement, an admiral (or captain, if it was a single-ship action) bent on attacking the enemy usually tried to gain a position on the windward side of his adversary. This weather gauge, as it was called, held several advantages. For one thing it gave the attacker considerable freedom of action. He could hold off, keeping his distance, or he could, by sailing with the wind, strike in quickly to close quarters. His adversary, in the leeward position, could only claw his way slowly to windward if he wished to attack.

Another advantage was that the dense powder smoke which belched out at each discharge rolled down on the vessels in the leeward position, masking their signals, making maneuvering difficult, and forcing them to aim blindly in the smother. Also if the breeze was stiff, the hulls of the vessels to leeward were heeled over, exposing their vulnerable underwater planking on the engaged side. Several shot striking here might be enough to force a vessel to remain on that tack until the holes could be plugged. A change of course would immerse them deeply, and perhaps cause her to founder.

As British admirals, in obedience both to naval policy and tradition, usually had as their goal the destruction of the enemy's fleet, they habitually strove to gain this weather gauge. The French, on the other hand, often numerically inferior in total naval strength and thus forced to conserve their forces, often forsook the tactical objective for the strategic. This could sometimes best be attained by an evasive, or at best defensive, action on the part of their fleets. For this reason French admirals often deliberately accepted the lee position, a position from which they were often able to rake and severely damage the British squadrons as they bore down to the attack, and from which they could break off the action when desired.

But the windward position also had its disadvantages. The same breeze which exposed the leeward ship below the waterline often brought the lower tier of gunports of the ships to windward perilously close to the water. In rough weather the gunners might be serving their pieces ankle deep. British ships, generally overgunned for their size, were often forced to close their lower-deck gunports altogether, thus sacrificing the heaviest part

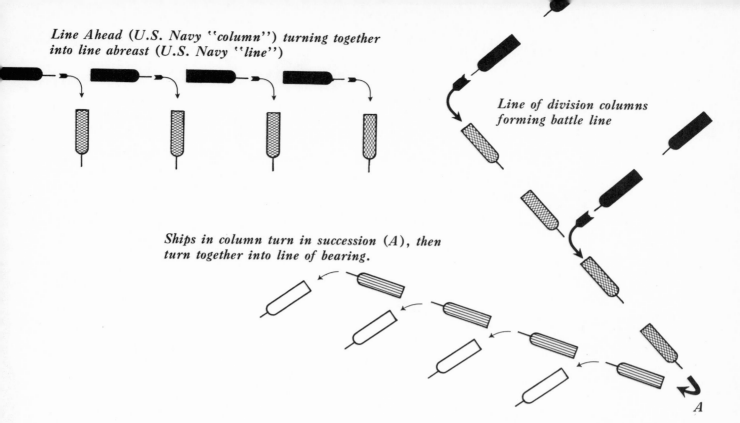

Line Ahead (U.S. Navy "column") turning together into line abreast (U.S. Navy "line")

Line of division columns forming battle line

Ships in column turn in succession (A), then turn together into line of bearing.

of their armament. And a ship of the weather line, crippled aloft, might drift helplessly to leeward, right among her enemies, who could pound her into a wreck unless her friends broke their line and followed.

The formal tactics of the time, restricted as they were by the rigid fighting instructions,

Damage to spars and rigging made approaching line uneven. Foremost ships received concentrated fire before others came up.

called for a battle line parallel to, and matching in formation, that of the enemy. That is, when ranged side by side, van was opposite van, center opposite center, and rear opposite rear. The fleet, which might have been sailing in two or more columns, was brought into line to windward of the enemy. Then, if the enemy were stationary, the signal was given to turn together (each ship at the same time) and the whole array, in a line abreast, put up their helms and came down on the enemy. If the enemy were under way, then the line came down in line of bearing (see diagram).

This had the effect of bringing the enemy to action (unless, of course, he chose to make sail downwind and run for it—but it had serious disadvantages. The ships, as they came down on the enemy line, could only oppose their light bow-chasers, if any were mounted, to the broadsides of the enemy, and stood to suffer considerable damage before they could bring their own broadsides to bear. If certain ships received serious damage aloft, it meant that the line became ragged, as the undamaged ships surged ahead, and these ships arrived in their battle positions before

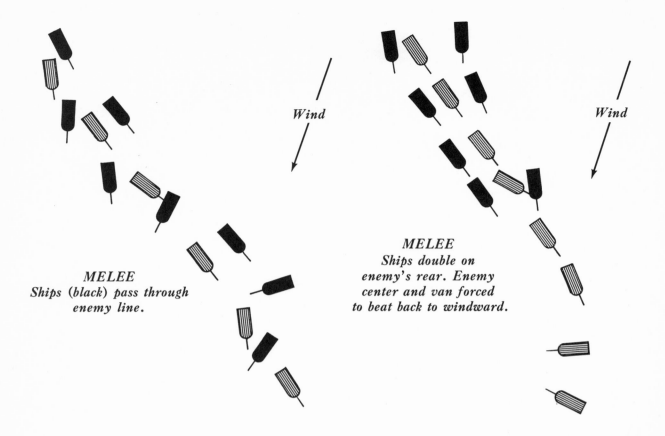

MELEE
*Ships (black) pass through
enemy line.*

MELEE
*Ships double on
enemy's rear. Enemy
center and van forced
to beat back to windward.*

the others and were exposed to concentrated fire. Also, while in theory all ships turned toward the enemy together, in practice, because of the difficulty of reading signals, each ship turned when she saw the next ahead begin to turn, so that the leading ships of the squadron were already on their course downwind before the last ship had put up its helm. In consequence, the line tended to come down at an angle to the enemy, with the leading ships engaged before the others could come into action. The difficulty of maneuvering a large number of vessels was very great, even under peacetime conditions, and it is small wonder that in battle carefully planned evolutions seldom, if ever, could be carried out as ordered.

As French commanders usually played a defensive role, the breaking off of an action was often part of their tactics. In consequence, French gunners were ordered to fire high, with the object of so crippling the British that they would be in no position to give chase. The rigid adherence to the parallel line of battle offered the British commanders no

chance to halt this retrograde movement, and in consequence, a typical engagement ended with the French drawing off, having severely battered those British vessels which had reached their line ahead of the others, and having done sufficient damage to the spars and rigging of the rest so that they could not pursue.

The answer lay in creating a general melee, in which some ships either passed through the enemy line and ranged themselves on the leeward side of the enemy vessels, or doubled on the enemy's van or rear. Either way gave an opportunity of bringing concentrated firepower to bear on part of the enemy's line and prevented the engaged ships from breaking off the action at will.

Adherents of the melee school claimed that their system was the only way in which their ships could come to grips with and hold onto the enemy—traditional bulldog tactics. Proponents of the formal, unbroken line of battle system replied that in such an action the admiral lost all control of his line (which was true), and that the enemy, by bringing the unengaged part of his fleet, van or rear, to assist the threatened part, might, if he were superior in numbers, overwhelm the attackers. The last was only partly true, because it assumed that the enemy line would be compact, with distances between ships of a cable, at most, and the wind conditions were favorable. If, for instance, the enemy line was close-hauled (the wind slightly forward of the beam), then, if the rear were attacked the van and center could wear and come down to its support. But if the wind were abaft the beam the supporting ships would have to beat back, by which time the rear ships, between two fires, might have been taken or put out of action.

The admirals who adhered to the formal manner of fighting seldom lost battles, but neither did they win them. The great victories of the British over the French in the wars of the eighteenth and early nineteenth centuries were won by men with the moral courage to break the rules and risk court-martial and disgrace for the sake of winning a decision. So in the end the melee school won—vindicated as Nelson and Collingwood led their two divisions crashing through the Allied line at Trafalgar.

Rodney breaks de Grasse's line in Battle of the Saints April 12, 1782 British—black

A. Rodney

B. BEDFORD

C. Part of center and van

The double breaking of the French line broke the French into three groups; some vessels of the center were badly damaged. The British van sailed on and was unable to beat back until too late to exploit the victory.

Ships of the line seldom fought under full sail. When ready to engage, canvas was reduced, usually to topsails and jib. Under her fighting sails a vessel was easily managed and required minimum attention (the majority of her crew being employed at the guns).

FIGHTING SAILS
Courses were usually clewed up. Topgallants were sometimes only loosely furled or the yards were lowered to the caps with the sails loose.

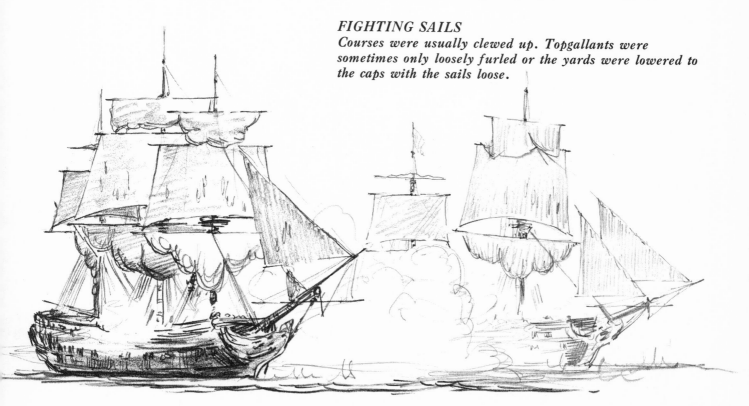

However, in single-ship actions, where a captain had plenty of room for maneuvering, the amount of sail carried might vary considerably.

Running free in an average wind, a ship of the line might make six knots; under fighting canvas, perhaps two. Close-hauled, speed was reduced to a crawl. Even at one knot it only took two minutes for two vessels on opposite tacks to pass each other. During this time only a superbly trained crew, by firing a broadside as the bows overlapped, could hope to get off a second before the enemy passed astern. For this reason it was unusual to engage when on opposite tacks. The average crew would barely have time to fire and reload before the next in line of the enemy squadron would be abreast of them.

In conclusion, while the tactician might gain a momentary advantage, in the long run it was the fighter who won. No strategic victories alone could raise a fleet's morale to the point where adverse odds as high as three to two were automatically discounted. No amount of fancy maneuvering could offset the destruction or capture of major fighting units. That, in the days of sail, could only be accomplished by laying one's own vessels alongside the enemy and pounding him until he struck.

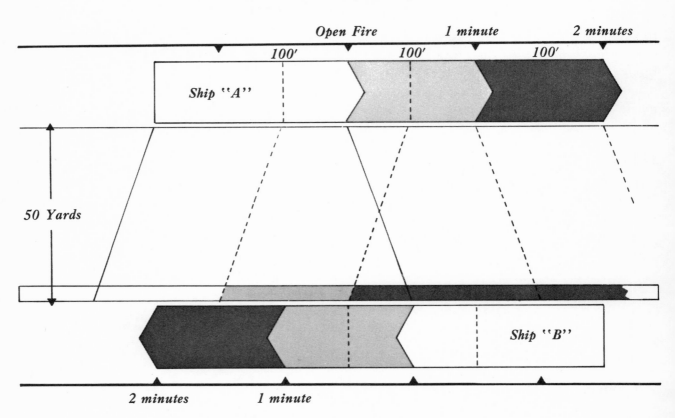

Passing on opposite tacks
Scale—One inch equals 50 feet

If vessels are passing at a distance of 50 yards, then, allowing a training angle of 20° before and abaft the beam, at a speed of 1 knot (approximately 100 feet per minute), ship "B" will be beyond fire zone of ship "A" in 2 minutes.

Rigging and Handling

Chapter 15

Rigging was necessarily complicated, especially when allowing for the numerous light-weather sails, staysails (set on the stays between the masts), etc. The masts and yards were—to a landlubber's eye—festooned with a tangle of cordage of all sizes. For simplification, these miles of rope could be put in two categories. The standing rigging consisted of the stays and shrouds which supported the masts and yards. The network of lines and tackles which hoisted and lowered the yards, trimmed them, and kept them in position, and which controlled the sails themselves was called the running rigging. All the running rigging led down to the deck, which accounted for much of the seeming confusion. To the trained seaman, of course, all this gear was as familiar as the palm of his hand, and on a pitch-black night, with the decks awash, he could unerringly lay his hand on the right rope.

Naturally, this intricate tracery of ropes and spars made a tempting target. Special missiles, such as chain shot and bar shot, were developed specifically to cut up an enemy's rigging. There was some difference of opinion as to whether it was better to cripple an adversary by directing fire on the masts and spars, or to concentrate the full weight of the broadside on the hull and personnel.

Circumstances usually dictated the choice. A weaker vessel—but with aid nearby—might attempt to so damage an enemy's sail power that her subsequent capture was certain. Ships of equal weight might elect to pound each other's hulls, dismounting guns and slaughtering their crews until one was forced to strike her colors.

The fighting tops (the platforms built on the trestletrees where main and topmasts joined) were usually crammed with men. Armed with muskets (in many cases, in American vessels, with rifles) and sometimes small howitzers or swivels, they attempted to clear the enemy's decks. Their fire could be very deadly (the great Nelson was to die by a topman's bullet at Trafalgar), and marines and gunners on the upper decks did their best to counteract this menace by picking off such topmen as they could see. When, as often happened, a ponderous mainmast was so cut through by round shot that it tottered and fell, the luckless topmen were thrown into the sea.

Handling the square-rigged ship, even with the large crews available in a man-of-war, was no easy task. The balancing of one sail with another, and of the sails with the rudder, demanded great experience. To keep station on another ship, or column of ships, meant

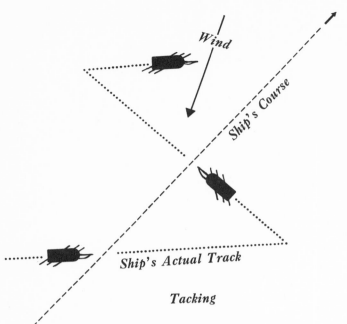

Wind

Ship's Course

Ship's Actual Track

Tacking

The square-rigger was at her best when running free (with the wind astern or on the quarter). But often it was necessary to sail against the wind. No sailboat can go directly into the wind's eye. But it is possible to sail at an angle to it, within four or five points in a well-trimmed boat. So to reach an objective to windward a vessel must sail as close to the wind as possible along a zigzag course. This is called tacking, and each leg of the zigzag is called a board. A vessel sails alternately on the starboard tack (with the wind coming over the starboard bow) and the port tack (when the wind is on the port bow).

constant trimming of sails and yards—now backing some sails against the wind to reduce speed, now showing a little more canvas to regain it. And at any time a flaw in the wind— the slightest change of strength or direction— could throw all the master's calculations off, and necessitate instant readjustments. Those of us who have had trouble sailing a little two-sail sloop to her mooring in a crowded anchorage can hardly imagine the skill needed to handle a vessel carrying at least twenty-four sails, some of them very large.

"In Irons"

A vessel attempting to tack, with the afteryards swung, but with not enough way on her to take her round is said to be "in irons." Head to wind, she gathers sternway and must wear or fall off the wind and try again.

Even in a modern yacht, beating to windward, especially if there is much of a sea running, is a slow business. In a square-rigger of '76, which could not hope to sail closer to the wind than six or seven points, it was slower still—more so because such ships, with their comparatively high sides, tended to drift to leeward.

At the end of each board, the ship had to come about, that is, turn until the wind was coming over the other bow. In a small modern sailboat this is easy. The tiller is put down (away from the wind), the boat shoots into the wind, the headsails flap, then fill as the wind catches them from the other side, and the boat heels over and away on the other tack.

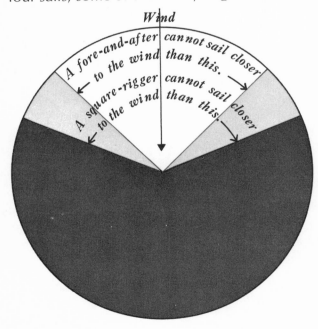

Wind

A fore-and-after cannot sail closer to the wind than this.

A square-rigger cannot sail closer to the wind than this.

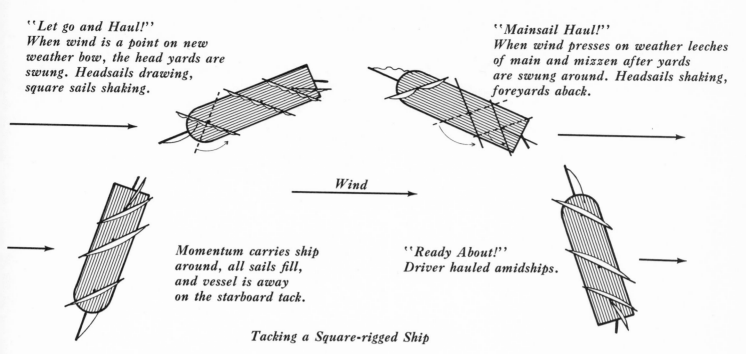

"Let go and Haul!"
When wind is a point on new
weather bow, the head yards are
swung. Headsails drawing,
square sails shaking.

"Mainsail Haul!"
When wind presses on weather leeches
of main and mizzen after yards
are swung around. Headsails shaking,
foreyards aback.

Wind

Momentum carries ship
around, all sails fill,
and vessel is away
on the starboard tack.

"Ready About!"
Driver hauled amidships.

Tacking a Square-rigged Ship

But tacking an old square-rigger meant much pulling and hauling—slackening and tautening of innumerable lines—and might take as much as fifteen minutes before all was sheeted home and belayed and the vessel on her new course. Sometimes she refused to come round altogether, but missed stays and lay helpless, head to wind, "in irons." Then, drifting astern meanwhile, she had to be coaxed back on her original tack until enough way could be got on her for another attempt.

Or, failing in his attempt to tack, the sailing master might decide to wear ship—that is, to sail in a part circle around with the wind, so that, instead of the bow passing across the wind, the stern was brought to it and the yards hauled in on the other side. The diagram makes these maneuvers clear—but fails to give any idea of the commotion aboard, the shouted orders, the thundering of the slatting canvas, or the stamp of hundreds of feet as the sheets and braces were let go and hauled.

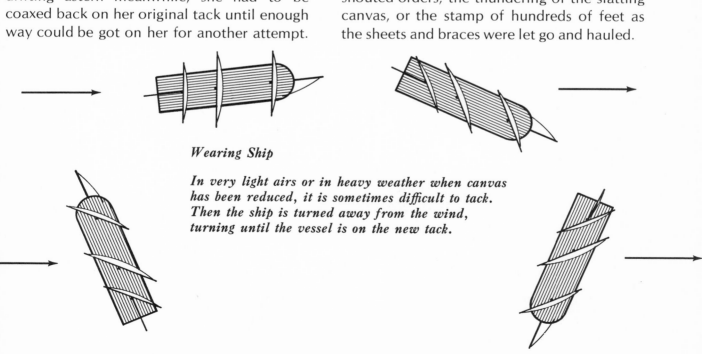

Wearing Ship

In very light airs or in heavy weather when canvas
has been reduced, it is sometimes difficult to tack.
Then the ship is turned away from the wind,
turning until the vessel is on the new tack.

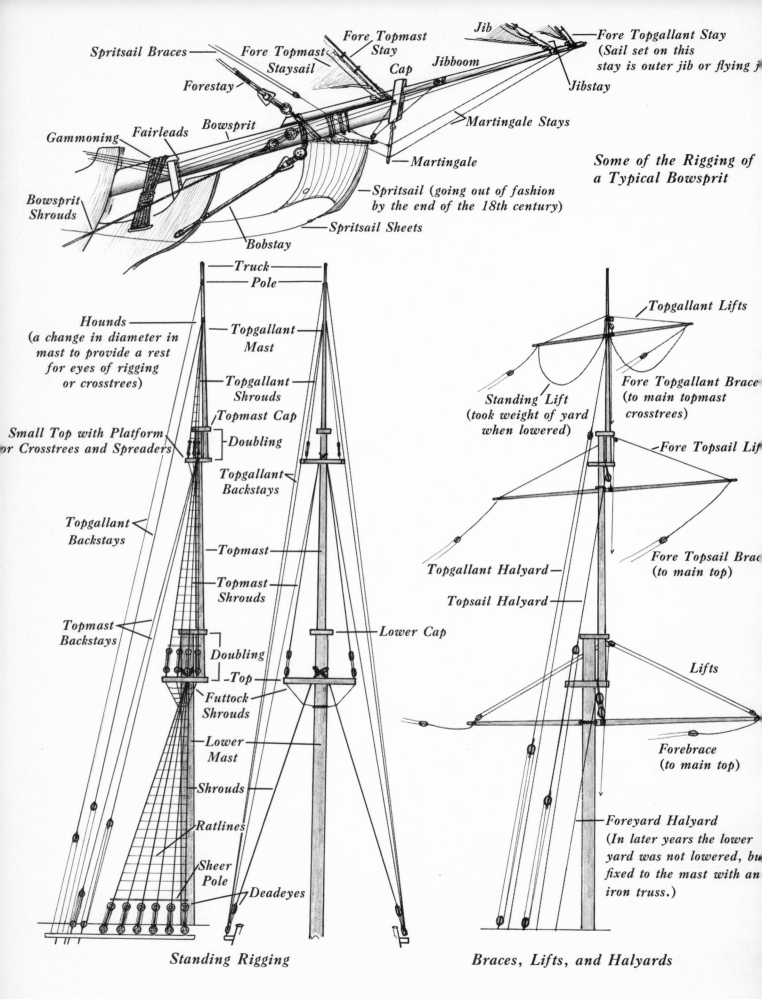

Spritsail Braces

Fore Topmast
Staysail

Fore Topmast
Stay

Jib

Cap

Jibboom

Jib

Fore Topgallant Stay
(Sail set on this
stay is outer jib or flying j

Forestay

Jibstay

Gammoning

Fairleads

Bowsprit

Martingale Stays

Bowsprit
Shrouds

Martingale

Spritsail (going out of fashion
by the end of the 18th century)

Some of the Rigging of
a Typical Bowsprit

Spritsail Sheets

Bobstay

Truck

Pole

Hounds
(a change in diameter in
mast to provide a rest
for eyes of rigging
or crosstrees)

Topgallant
Mast

Topgallant Lifts

Topgallant
Shrouds

Fore Topgallant Brace
(to main topmast
crosstrees)

Topmast Cap

Small Top with Platform
or Crosstrees and Spreaders

Doubling

Standing Lift
(took weight of yard
when lowered)

Fore Topsail Lif

Topgallant
Backstays

Topgallant
Backstays

Topmast

Topmast
Backstays

Topmast
Shrouds

Fore Topsail Brac
(to main top)

Lower Cap

Topgallant Halyard

Topsail Halyard

Doubling

Top

Futtock
Shrouds

Lifts

Lower
Mast

Shrouds

Forebrace
(to main top)

Ratlines

Sheer
Pole

Deadeyes

Foreyard Halyard
(In later years the lower
yard was not lowered, bu
fixed to the mast with an
iron truss.)

Standing Rigging

Braces, Lifts, and Halyards

A. Outer or flying jib
B. Jib
C. Fore topmast staysail
D. Spritsail
E. Fore topgallant sail
F. Fore topsail
G. Foresail or forecourse
H. Main topgallant staysail
I. Middle staysail
J. Main topmast staysail
K. Main staysail
L. Main topgallant sail
M. Main topsail
N. Mainsail or main course
O. Main topgallant studding sails*
P. Main topmast studding sails
Q. Main studding sails
R. Mizzen topmast staysail
S. Mizzen staysail
T. Mizzen topsail†
U. Driver
V. Ringtail

*For clarity the port mainmast studding sails and the studding sails on fore and mizzen yards are omitted.

†Mizzen topgallant sails were often carried, as were royals on all three masts.

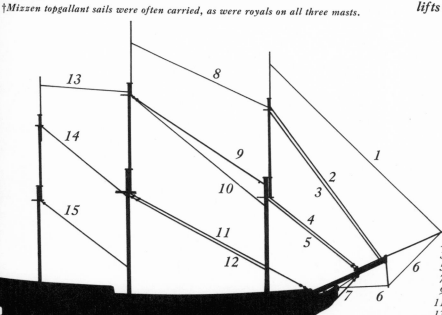

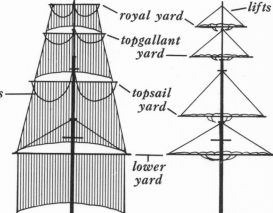

The upper yards lowered onto the hounds or caps. Diagram shows position of yards with sails set and furled.

Diagram at left shows the various stays.

1. Fore topgallant stay
2. Fore topmast stay
3. Fore topmast preventer stay
4. Forestay
5. Fore preventer stay
6. Martingale stay
7. Bobstay
8. Main topgallant stay
9. Main topmast stay
10. Main topmast preventer stay
11. Main stay
12. Main preventer stay
13. Mizzen topgallant stay
14. Mizzen topmast stay
15. Mizzen stay

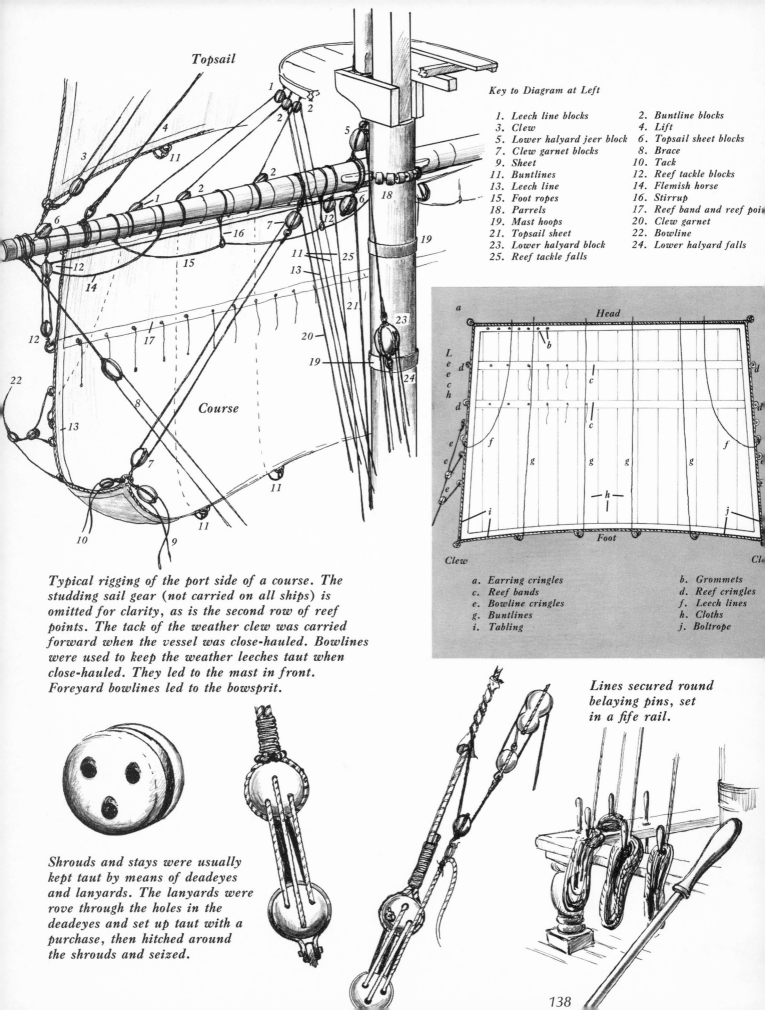

Topsail

Course

Head

Leech

Foot

Clew

Typical rigging of the port side of a course. The studding sail gear (not carried on all ships) is omitted for clarity, as is the second row of reef points. The tack of the weather clew was carried forward when the vessel was close-hauled. Bowlines were used to keep the weather leeches taut when close-hauled. They led to the mast in front. Foreyard bowlines led to the bowsprit.

Lines secured round belaying pins, set in a fife rail.

Shrouds and stays were usually kept taut by means of deadeyes and lanyards. The lanyards were rove through the holes in the deadeyes and set up taut with a purchase, then hitched around the shrouds and seized.

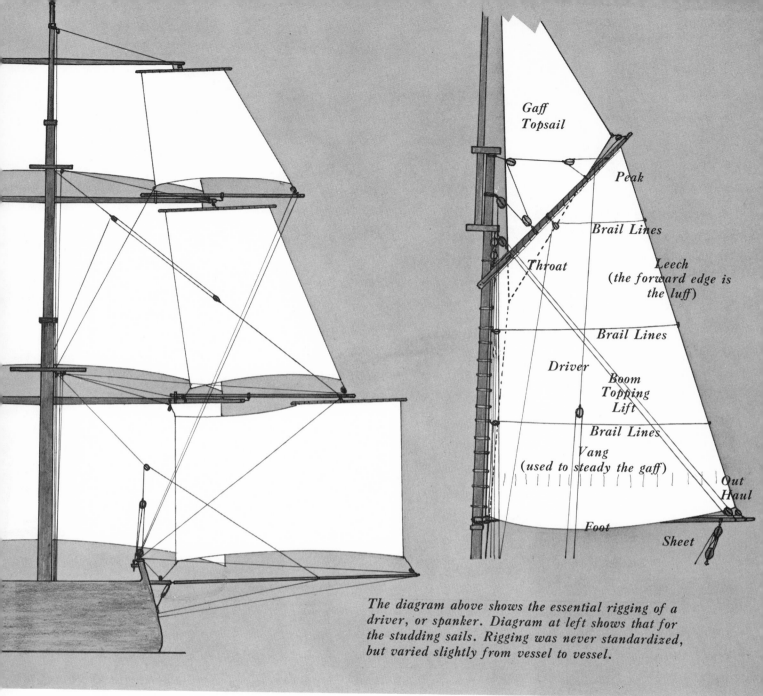

Gaff
Topsail

Peak

Brail Lines

Leech
(the forward edge is
the luff)

Throat

Brail Lines

Driver

Boom
Topping
Lift

Brail Lines

Vang
(used to steady the gaff)

Out
Haul

Foot

Sheet

The diagram above shows the essential rigging of a
driver, or spanker. Diagram at left shows that for
the studding sails. Rigging was never standardized,
but varied slightly from vessel to vessel.

Smart sail-handling was the mark of the competent sailing master and captain. A vessel in irons in a narrow passage might easily mean a wreck, or at least a stranding. In action, clever maneuvering, with a nice judgment of wind power and direction, and an intimate knowledge of the capabilities of his vessel, often enabled a captain to rake his enemy (to place his own vessel ahead or astern so that his own broadsides could bear on his adversary's bow or stern, from which, in turn, only two or three guns could be fired in reply).

And smart sail-handling was also the mark of a competent crew, drilled and re-drilled so that maneuvers could be carried on almost automatically, although round shot and bullets were whistling round their ears and severed tackle snaking down from shattered gear aloft. This was why trained seamen were at a premium—and in the Royal Navy, at least, were often pressed (virtually kidnapped) from their hangouts ashore or from merchantmen afloat.

Navigational aids in the days of the Revolutionary War were much as they had been in the preceding century. The invention of the prototype of the modern sextant (1730) had relegated the old-style backstaff to the rubbish heap, while the successful development by Harrison of a reliable sea-going time-piece (about 1760) had at last taken the guesswork out of determining longitude. But the new chronometers were both expensive and rare, so the time-honored methods of computing a ship's course and speed by compass and log line were still the master mariner's mainstays. There was some slight knowledge of currents and tides and the more-traveled parts of the known world's coasts were fairly accurately charted. Lighthouses and buoys existed, but were few in number, especially in the New World.

Moderns, used to the sophisticated equipment of the present—wireless time signals, echo-sounders, radar, loran and direction-finders, backed by a formidable system of lights, buoys, tide tables, star tables and the like—can only marvel at the skill and courage of the seamen of those days. Equipped with instruments with which most twentieth-century yachtsmen would hesitate to traverse Long Island Sound, they drove their unwieldy square-riggers regardless of storm and fog, rock-studded coasts, and uncharted sea. Great navigators such as Cook and others like him had opened up new seas and put new lands upon the map, but many of the hardy seamen, merchantmen, and privateers who put to sea in the days of '76 sailed, as had their fathers, by guess and by God.

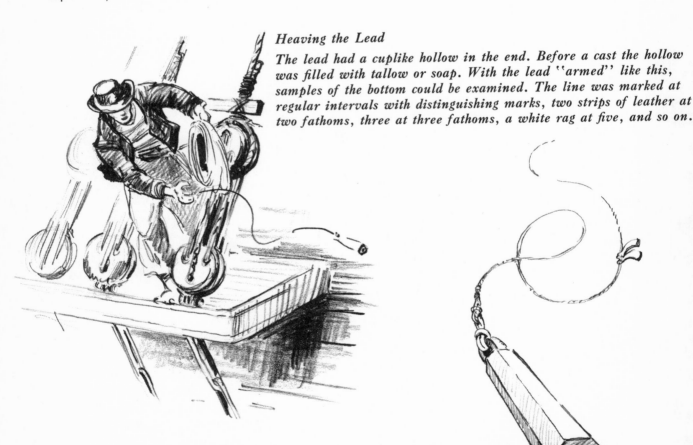

Heaving the Lead

The lead had a cuplike hollow in the end. Before a cast the hollow was filled with tallow or soap. With the lead "armed" like this, samples of the bottom could be examined. The line was marked at regular intervals with distinguishing marks, two strips of leather at two fathoms, three at three fathoms, a white rag at five, and so on.

D'Estaing and Disappointment

Chapter 16

By the end of 1777 the French were sure that the American Revolution had gained enough headway to seriously embarrass Britain in the event of war. On February 6, 1778, therefore, a treaty of friendship and commerce was openly made, while at the same time a secret treaty recognized the Colonists' independence and made a defensive alliance. The open treaty was announced on March 13 and the British ambassador was at once recalled. Preparations for war were pushed in both countries, and a month later a French fleet of twelve ships of the line and eight frigates under Vice Admiral the Comte d'Estaing sailed from Toulon for America.

With the entry of France into the war the whole picture altered. It had been, up to that time, what amounted to a civil war, a war in which British public opinion was sharply divided. But with the armed intervention of France the war became a struggle between England and the Continental powers (Spain and Holland were soon involved) with all its implications. Public opinion in England hardened against the Colonies, now allied with England's traditional enemies, and the war took on the aspects of a struggle for survival.

The Americans could now count on the assistance of a first-class naval power—and it must be remembered that in the seventies the French Navy was far stronger, better manned, and better led than in the preceding war, or afterwards in the long wars of the Revolution under Napoleon. The mismanagement of those officials responsible for England's naval affairs—long deplored and bitterly resented by the British officers in charge of actual operations—now became apparent. Ships "in ordinary" were in bad condition, naval supplies of all sorts were lacking, and the old problem of manning the ships that were actually ready for duty had to be faced once more. The navy, in short, was not prepared for a major war, nor was it equal to the tasks to be imposed upon it. As a result of this unpreparedness Britain would lose, temporarily, that command of the sea on which the control of her possessions overseas depended. And that loss was to have far-reaching effects on world history.

From Washington's point of view, the entry of France into the war was a godsend. Up to that time he had been completely frustrated by British control of the waters off the American coast. While combined operations, as we know them, were still far in the future, the cooperation of the Royal Navy in moving and supplying large bodies of troops had made the task of the Continental forces an increasingly difficult one.

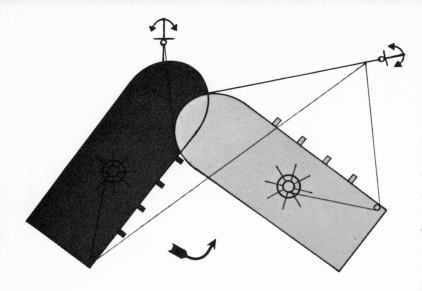

Cable Spring Diagram

Spring was run out through a stern port and made fast to anchor cable. As spring was brought in, stern swung, allowing guns to bear over a wide arc.

Now that control would be challenged. At some future date, when the Congressional armies had grown sufficiently—nourished by French money, arms, and, ultimately, men—it might be possible to box the British forces in, pin them against the coast between a French fleet at sea and strong allied armies on land. The possibilities which became a reality at Yorktown were born when the first French fleet sailed for America.

Unfortunately for Washington and the Congress the effects of French seapower were not immediately apparent. D'Estaing arrived off the Capes of the Delaware on July 6, after a leisurely 85-day cruise from Toulon, to find that the numerically inferior British fleet under Lord Howe had sailed for New York over a week before. "Had," wrote Washington, "a passage of even ordinary length taken place, Lord Howe with the British ships of war and all the transports in the River Delaware must inevitably have fallen." And, he added, Clinton would just as inevitably have met the fate of Burgoyne. Disappointment number one.

The British at New York were readying themselves to repel an assault, and in due course the French fleet was reported approaching the city. On July 11 D'Estaing arrived off Sandy Hook, and Washington promptly sent one of his staff with a view to concerting a land-sea attack. In the meantime, "Black Dick" had anchored his main force of seven vessels—five 64's, one 50, and an armed storeship—with springs on their cables, so that they could swing to rake any ships coming up the channel, or fight them broadside on if they succeeded in forcing a passage. One 50-gun ship and two smaller ones acted as an advance guard, while a 64 and some frigates were in reserve. Four galleys formed a second line, and Clinton had mounted a 5-gun battery on the end of the Hook. Thus prepared, Howe was resolved on a fight to the finish.

D'Estaing's squadron of one 90-gun ship, one 80, six 74's, three 64's, and one 50 was overwhelmingly superior to Howe's, and had the French succeeded in reaching a broadside-to-broadside position, there could have been little doubt as to the outcome. But Howe had the advantage of situation, and greatly in his favor was the fact that normally the depth of water over the bar was only some 23 feet, whereas some of the French ships drew up to 25 feet. A lieutenant from the French flagship reported that he could find nothing deeper than 22 feet, while D'Estaing is said to have vainly offered 50,000 crowns to any pilot who would lead his ships across the bar.

On the twenty-second of July a fresh breeze from the northeast and a spring tide raised the water over the bar to 30 feet. When, therefore, the waiting British saw the French fleet under way they prepared for immediate action. But D'Estaing, a former brigadier general, although personally a brave man, was not seaman enough to override the timidity of the pilots and of his subordinates. To the great surprise of Howe's men, who fully expected to be shortly engaged in a bloody and decisive struggle, the French fleet bore away to the southward and was soon hull down on the horizon. Disappointment number two.

D'Estaing's next target was Newport.

This strategically valuable harbor had been in British hands since the latter part of 1776. The American forces in the area, under General Sullivan, had been reinforced by Washington, and it was hoped that a combined effort by land and sea might crush the British forces in a pincer movement. On July 29 the French fleet was anchored off the Rhode Island coast, waiting an opportunity of forcing the entrance to Narragansett Bay.

The approach of such a greatly superior force caused the British to retire up the bay. Those warships which could not enter the inner harbor—four 32-gun frigates and two sloops, as well as some galleys—were burnt or sunk to obstruct the channels. Also sunk as blockships were five transports. Crews and armament from the sunken ships served to reinforce the garrison of the town.

The French admiral then landed 4,000 soldiers and seamen from his fleet on the island of Conanicut. The American forces surrounding the place numbered some 10,000 men, while the British garrison totaled about 6,000. The garrison's position appeared hopeless, but on August 9 the sails of a British fleet were sighted and before nightfall Howe, his command now swelled to one 74, seven 64's, and five 50's, with attendant smaller craft, anchored off Point Judith.

The French position was strong, their fleet still by far the more powerful, and it is doubtful if Howe would have pressed the attack, vital as it was to relieve the garrison. In the event, the decision was taken out of his hands. As soon as the British squadron was sighted, the men landed only the day before were reembarked and on the tenth, with the wind strong from the northeast, the French put to sea, cutting their cables in their hurry. Howe, with only a faint hope of being able to stand up to D'Estaing in a set-piece battle, very properly retired, hoping to gain some advantage by maneuver. On the morning of the eleventh the French were in position for attack, but rising seas and wind made any decisive action out of the question. By now

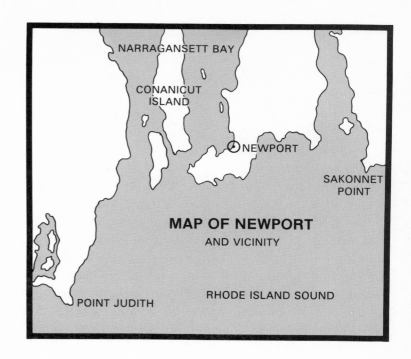

MAP OF NEWPORT
AND VICINITY

NARRAGANSETT BAY

CONANICUT ISLAND

NEWPORT

SAKONNET POINT

RHODE ISLAND SOUND

POINT JUDITH

the wind had increased to gale force, with frequent rain squalls, and D'Estaing's force bore off to the south before the storm.

It was two days before the tempest blew itself out, and by that time both fleets were scattered and many vessels were damaged. The British, who had suffered less, rendezvoused at Sandy Hook to make repairs, while the badly battered French limped back to Newport. A few isolated actions took place as the fleets sought to reassemble, the advantage being with the British.

The siege of Newport had progressed favorably up to this point, and it needed but additional pressure by the French to bring about a victory. But D'Estaing had had enough and despite pleas from Sullivan he ordered his ships to Boston for a thorough refit. One reason for his withdrawal was the report that a British squadron had arrived on the North American station to reinforce Howe's fleet. The French reached Boston on August 28, and on the thirty-first Howe appeared off the port. The three days had given the French time to land guns in sufficient numbers to cover the anchorage, however, and Boston harbor, defended by land batteries, was too tough a nut for even "Black Dick" to crack.

So the naval campaign for 1778 came to an end. The departure of the French was

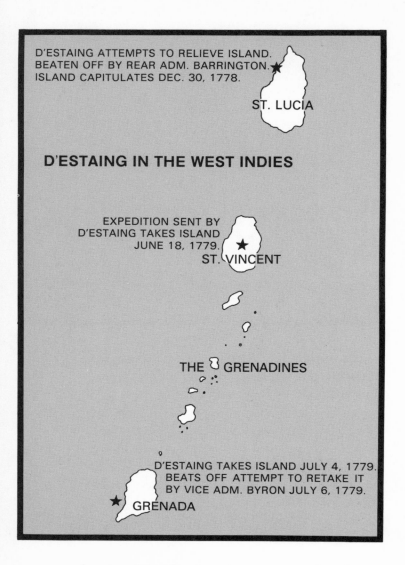

D'ESTAING ATTEMPTS TO RELIEVE ISLAND.
BEATEN OFF BY REAR ADM. BARRINGTON.
ISLAND CAPITULATES DEC. 30, 1778.

ST. LUCIA

D'ESTAING IN THE WEST INDIES

EXPEDITION SENT BY
D'ESTAING TAKES ISLAND
JUNE 18, 1779.

ST. VINCENT

THE GRENADINES

D'ESTAING TAKES ISLAND JULY 4, 1779.
BEATS OFF ATTEMPT TO RETAKE IT
BY VICE ADM. BYRON JULY 6, 1779.

GRENADA

Atlantic gales, and ships were lost or badly damaged. In the West Indies, on the other hand, the danger season was from July to October, when violent hurricanes swept the area. Major naval activity was therefore customarily transferred from one side of the Atlantic to the other—east in summer, west in winter. France still possessed the islands of Martinique, Guadeloupe, St. Lucia, and Haiti; the three former in the Windward Island chain, the latter in the Leeward group. Also among the latter group were Cuba, Puerto Rico, and Santo Domingo, belonging to Spain. The British control of many good bases in the Windward group was a considerable advantage; for in the days of sail to go from, say, Haiti to St. Lucia meant a slow beat to windward against the trades of many hundreds of miles.

In September, 1778, the French took the initiative by seizing Dominica, whereupon the British, under Rear Admiral Barrington, attacked St. Lucia. D'Estaing sailed for the West Indies from Boston in November, and he now attempted to relieve the beleaguered island. But Barrington had anchored his squadron in line across the mouth of the bay (the Grand Cul de Sac) where he had landed his troops, and although in superior force, D'Estaing declined to attack him. Instead he landed 7,000 soldiers nearby and assaulted the British position commanding the anchorage. This attack, led by the doughty D'Estaing himself, was beaten off with the loss of nearly 850 men, and the shaken troops were reembarked. A few days later the baffled relieving force sailed away, upon which the French governor surrendered.

Both British and French fleets were reinforced in the spring of 1779. A French expedition took St. Vincent, and on July 2, D'Estaing appeared with twenty-four of the line and a fleet of transports off Grenada. The island capitulated on July 4. At daybreak of the sixth, Vice Admiral Byron, who had relieved Barrington of command, arrived with twenty-one of the line. Byron attacked in

the signal for the American army to break up. D'Estaing's retreat "struck such panic among the militia and volunteers that they began to desert by shoals." Sullivan was soon almost without an army and withdrew the remnants of his troops, leaving Newport to the British. The angry Sullivan declared that America could win without such allies, D'Estaing was challenged to a duel, a French officer was killed in a brawl, and there was much hard feeling. Disappointment number three.

Anglo-French naval activity in the American theater now centered in the West Indies. This was in great part due to the weather. The maneuvering of large fleets in European or North Atlantic waters was difficult, if not impossible, in the winter. Squadrons were dispersed by the fierce

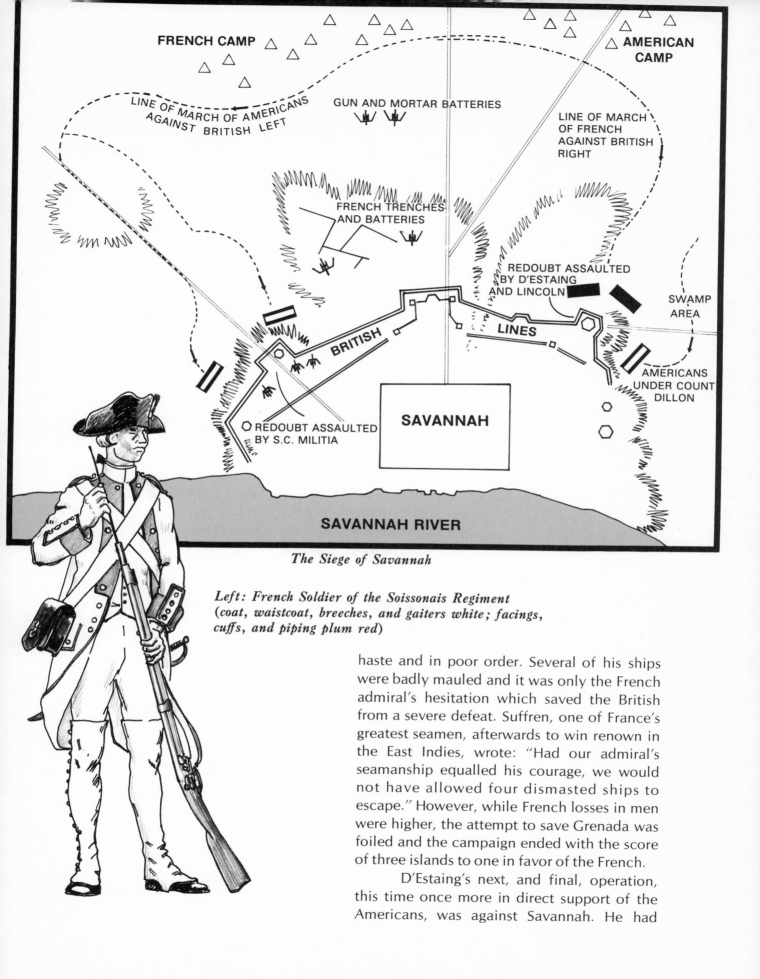

FRENCH CAMP

AMERICAN CAMP

LINE OF MARCH OF AMERICANS AGAINST BRITISH LEFT

GUN AND MORTAR BATTERIES

LINE OF MARCH OF FRENCH AGAINST BRITISH RIGHT

FRENCH TRENCHES AND BATTERIES

REDOUBT ASSAULTED BY D'ESTAING AND LINCOLN

SWAMP AREA

BRITISH

LINES

REDOUBT ASSAULTED BY S.C. MILITIA

SAVANNAH

AMERICANS UNDER COUNT DILLON

SAVANNAH RIVER

The Siege of Savannah

*Left: French Soldier of the Soissonais Regiment
(coat, waistcoat, breeches, and gaiters white; facings,
cuffs, and piping plum red)*

haste and in poor order. Several of his ships were badly mauled and it was only the French admiral's hesitation which saved the British from a severe defeat. Suffren, one of France's greatest seamen, afterwards to win renown in the East Indies, wrote: "Had our admiral's seamanship equalled his courage, we would not have allowed four dismasted ships to escape." However, while French losses in men were higher, the attempt to save Grenada was foiled and the campaign ended with the score of three islands to one in favor of the French.

D'Estaing's next, and final, operation, this time once more in direct support of the Americans, was against Savannah. He had been ordered to bring back to France the ships of the line with which he had sailed in 1778 as soon as the hurricane season had ended operations in the West Indies. On his way home he decided to try to take the town, which had been in British hands since 1778. On August 31, he arrived off the Savannah River with 20 ships of the line and transports carrying more than 3,500 troops.

Washington, who had no previous knowledge of the French admiral's plans, hoped that another effort might be made to take New York, where the British force had, at the moment, been reduced to five ships of the line. In fear of just such an attack Clinton had hurriedly ordered the evacuation of Rhode Island and concentrated his power in New York.

But D'Estaing, still a brigadier at heart, became instead involved in a siege of Savannah. Cannon and mortars were taken ashore, batteries erected and trenches dug. This took time, and the admiral, who had been assured that ten days would see the fall of the town, began to grow impatient. His fleet was exposed both to the storms which might be expected at that season and to Byron's fleet, thought to be on its way from the West Indies. Without waiting for the approach parallels to be driven right up to the enemy's works, on October 8 he gave orders to prepare for an all-out night attack.

In the predawn darkness of the following morning the assaulting columns, French and Americans, formed for the attack. As is so often the case, unforeseen delays held up the hour of the assault and it was daylight before the troops finally moved forward. The leading formations were met with blasts of grape and musketry which cut them to pieces. Despite a hail of lead and iron the assailants tried desperately to make a lodgment in the British lines. Just as desperately the defenders drove them back. The main attack, on the Spring Hill redoubt, was the scene of furious hand-to-hand fighting—the bloodiest encounter since Bunker Hill. At last the attackers retreated, leaving their dead and wounded in heaps in the ditch and on the glacis. D'Estaing himself was wounded and the allies lost over 800 men, among the killed being Count Pulaski. Disappointment number four.

Next day, to the disgust of the Americans, the French troops began to embark. Two squadrons of the fleet, under De Grasse and La Motte-Picquet, left for the West Indies, while D'Estaing prepared to sail for France with the squadron he had brought from Toulon the year before. At that time his arrival in America had been cause for general rejoicing. His return to France, after accomplishing so little in direct support of the Colonists, resulted in a great deal of bitterness and ill will.

Naval Ordnance

Chapter 17

Ship's armament had progressed but little since the beginning of the seventeenth century. Cannon were cast of brass or iron, usually the latter. They were mounted on wooden carriages, made of two sidepieces, or "cheeks," and separated by heavy crosspieces, the whole strongly bolted together. Wooden wheels, or trucks, were fastened to axles with iron pins.

Carriages were varnished or painted, often red. Guns were sometimes painted gray, but were more usually blacked.

The guns were ranged along the ships' sides as close together as would permit the crews to load and train them. This varied from eleven feet on center for the lower deck guns of a ship of the line (32- or even 42-pounders) to eight feet for the 4-pounder popguns of a small schooner or cutter.

The tubes themselves were thicker at the breech, to withstand the shock of the discharge, and ended in a round iron ball called the cascabel. Two projections on either side of the tube, the trunnions, fitted into corresponding depressions cut in the top of the carriage, and were held in place with iron caps. The tube did not balance exactly on the trunnions, but was heavier at the breech. To keep it level, and to elevate or depress it, a thick wooden wedge, or quoin, was inserted between the bottom of the breech and the carriage bed. This quoin was marked, and by lining up a mark on the quoin with a line on the bed the gun could be brought to the required elevation with some accuracy.

Perhaps "accuracy," at least by modern standards, is not a good word. The cast iron cannon balls (which might in themselves vary somewhat in size and weight) were made smaller than the bore of the gun, to allow for inequalities in the bore, and in the shot, for rust and the hard residue left from the discharge of the black powder itself. This difference (windage) not only allowed a considerable amount of the powder gasses to leak out around the ball but was sufficient to give the ball a chance to "bounce" very slightly on its way down the bore. Naturally, the loss of power and the irregular flight of the projectile made precision firing almost impossible. Coupled with this was the difficulty of lining up the target over the tube and the crude methods of training and elevating.

Sights were nonexistent, at most a notch on the breech and on the swell of the muzzle. Continuous aiming (in which the sight is kept on the target regardless of the motion of the hull) was impossible, and the guns were fired when, in the gun captain's judgment, the tube was "on target"—always taking into consideration the not inconsiderable time lag between the order to fire and the actual explosion of the charge. Under such conditions, long-range fire wasted ammunition.

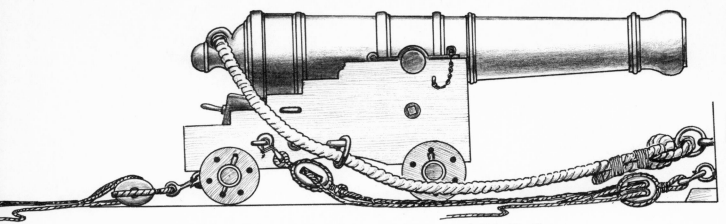

24-Pounder, Showing Breeching, Train Tackle, and Side Tackle

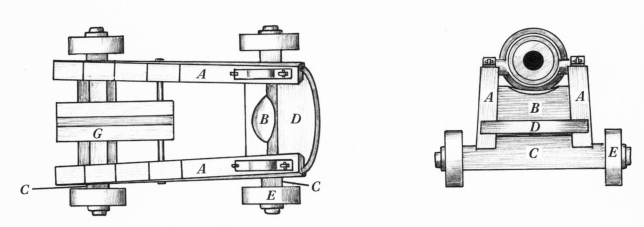

Plan View and Front Elevation of a Typical Truck Carriage

A. Brackets—B. Transom—C. Axletrees—D. Breastpiece—G. Stool—E. Trucks

Dimensions of carriages were usually determined by the size of the shot. Brackets were one diameter in thickness, and the axletrees were the same, square. Height of brackets was one shot diameter × 4.75. The front trucks were diameter × 3.25; rear, × 2.88. Both were one diameter thick.

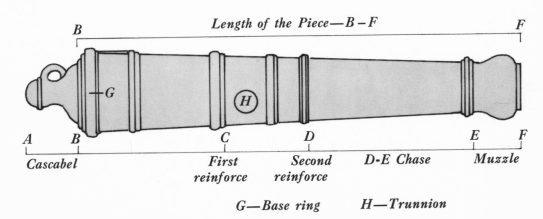

Length of the Piece—B – F

A   B   C   D   E   F

Cascabel   *First reinforce*   *Second reinforce*   *D-E Chase*   *Muzzle*

G—Base ring   *H—Trunnion*

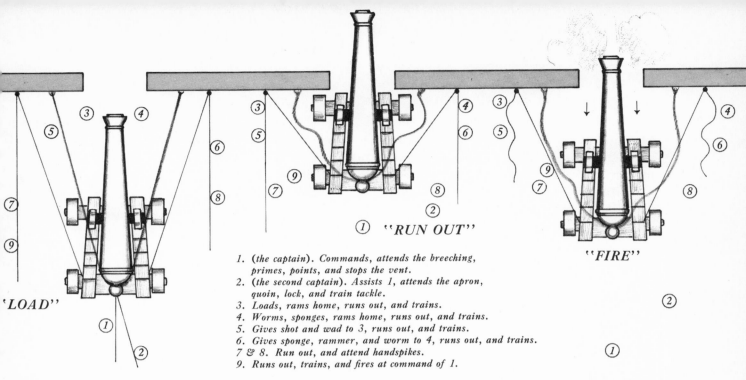

'LOAD"

① "RUN OUT"

"FIRE"

1. (*the captain*). Commands, attends the breeching, primes, points, and stops the vent.
2. (*the second captain*). Assists 1, attends the apron, quoin, lock, and train tackle.
3. Loads, rams home, runs out, and trains.
4. Worms, sponges, rams home, runs out, and trains.
5. Gives shot and wad to 3, runs out, and trains.
6. Gives sponge, rammer, and worm to 4, runs out, and trains.
7 & 8. Run out, and attend handspikes.
9. Runs out, trains, and fires at command of 1.

Working an Upper-Deck Gun with a Nine-Man Crew.
(*from an old British naval gunnery manual*)

A stationary powderman, positioned well to the rear, served two guns. He was supplied from the magazine by an extra powderman, who served four guns.

The carriage was secured to the ship's side by a heavy rope called the breeching. This rope was firmly fastened to large rings bolted to the ship's side, and ran through rings on either side of the carriage and through a ring lashed to, or actually cast as part of, the cascabel. This breeching was of sufficient length so that when the gun was run in for loading, the muzzle was just inside the gun port. The breeching not only held the gun in position against the roll of the ship, but checked the piece as it recoiled after firing. The gun was run out after loading by side tackles, hooked to rings on either side of the carriage and to the ship's sides. By hooking one end of the side tackle to rings on deck on either side of the gun, the rear of the carriage could be hauled from one side to the other. This was done when the gun was to be fired far forward or aft of the beam. Ordinarily, small adjustments were made with large wooden levers called handspikes. A preventer tackle, or train tackle, hooked to the back of the carriage, was used to stop the gun from running out with the motion of the ship, and to run the gun in.

The sequence of firing was as follows. On being called to quarters (action stations) by beat of drum or bugle call, the gun crew first cast off the lashings with which the guns were always securely fastened to the ship's side when not in use. (A gun which broke

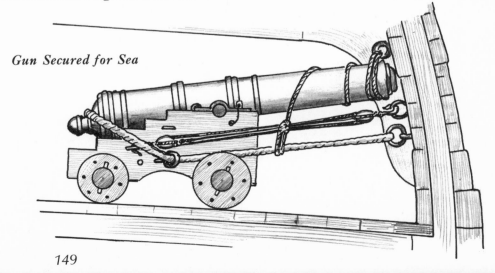

Gun Secured for Sea

loose from its fastenings in a rough sea was a terrible menace and might, by crashing through the side, actually endanger the ship.) The gun was run in and the tampion, or wooden plug used to keep out spray and moisture, was taken out of the muzzle. A cartridge—a cylindrical bag of powder, often made of flannel—was brought up to the gun from the magazine below decks by a young "powder monkey," whose duty it was to keep one or more guns supplied. The cartridge was rammed all the way down the bore, and a ball was taken from the shot racks which lined the bulwarks and hatchways and rammed down on the charge. A wad made of rope yarn was then rammed on top of the ball, to keep it from rolling out as the ship heeled. Then a small sheet of lead, called the apron, was untied from the breech, revealing the touchhole, or vent. The gun captain took a small iron skewer called a priming iron and thrust it down the touchhole and into the cartridge. From a box at his belt he next took a priming tube, usually a length of quill filled with fine powder mixed with spirits of wine, and inserted it in the vent. If no priming tubes were furnished, the gun captain primed the vent with powder from a horn. A lighted slow match, made of cotton wick soaked in lye, or some other substance, was twisted about a forked stick some three feet long (the linstock). Tubs half full of wet sand or water were placed at intervals along the decks. Spare slow match was coiled beside them, held in notches in the rim of each tub so that the smoldering ends overhung the sand.

To elevate the gun to the required range a handspike was inserted under the breech. Using one of the steps of the side of the carriage as a fulcrum, one of the gun crew levered up the heavy mass of metal while the gun captain adjusted the quoin. Adjustments in train (sideways or in azimuth) were made with handspike or side tackle.

When the gun captain thought his piece was well and truly laid on the target he sidestepped smartly to avoid the backward rush of the cannon in recoil and ordered the glowing end of the match brought down on the vent. There was a poof of flame and smoke from the vent, followed almost instantaneously by the flash and roar of the gun, which ran back until checked by the breeching. Before reloading, any sparks or smoldering pieces of cartridge were extinguished by swabbing out the bore with a wet sponge, usually made of sheepskin fixed to the end of a wooden staff. The other end of the staff was strengthened to serve as a rammer. Flexible rammers and sponges, made of heavy rope stiffened by wrapping with twine, were often used. They could be bent, and the swabbers and loaders did not have to lean out of the port (which exposed them to the fire of the enemy sharpshooters). Once swabbed, the gun was loaded and fired as before. In training, the gun would be served "by the numbers," the gun captain or the midshipman in charge of the section shouting out the commands. In action a well-trained crew worked like a machine, automatically performing the operations as fast as humanly possible.

The opening broadside of an engagement was fired by command, either all guns together or in rapid succession as they bore. As the action got hotter guns were usually fired as rapidly as they could be swabbed, loaded, and aimed (if the gun captains could by then see their targets through the smoke). As some crews would be naturally faster, while others might be weakened by casualties, the firing became increasingly ragged.

The largest guns afloat were those throwing a 42-pound shot; but the weight, and consequent difficulty of handling, plus the added strain on the ships' frames, had caused these to lose favor in the British navy, and the largest gun in general use was the 32-pounder. Most calibers were cast in two sizes, long and short. The long gun was more accurate and had a longer range. It was also heavier. A long 32-pounder weighed about 5,500 pounds, while the shorter tube weighed some 4,900 pounds.

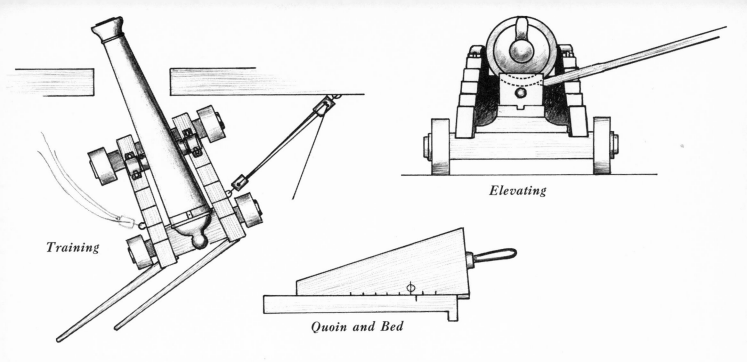

Training

Elevating

Quoin and Bed

In training the handspikes were placed under the ends (horns) of the carriage and the gun levered around, helped by the side tackles. In extreme training the side tackle to be used was hooked to the bolt of the next port.

To elevate or depress the piece, the handspike was placed on one of the steps of the carriage and the breech of the gun levered up.

The quoin was then moved in or out until the desired elevation was attained.

The quoin moved on the bed, which in turn rested on the stool. Quoins were sometimes marked. The marks when lined up with a mark on the bed represented certain ranges; i.e., extreme range, point-blank, and extreme depression.

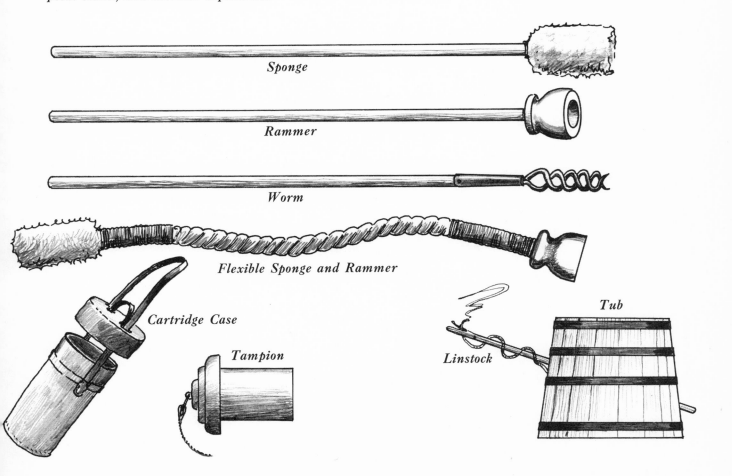

Sponge

Rammer

Worm

Flexible Sponge and Rammer

Cartridge Case

Tampion

Linstock

Tub

Class	Length (in feet)	Weight (in pounds)	Caliber (in inches)	Charge (in pounds)	Windage (in inches)
42-pdr	10	6500	7.03	17	.35
32-pdr (long)	9.50	5500	6.43	14	.33
32-pdr (short)	8	4900	6.43	11	.33
24-pdr (long)	9.50	5000	5.84	11	.30
24-pdr (short)	7.50	4000	5.84	8.50	.30
18-pdr (long)	9	4200	5.30	9	.27
18-pdr (short)	6	2700	5.30	6.25	.27
12-pdr (long)	9	3200	4.64	6	.24
12-pdr (short)	7.50	2900	4.64	6	.24
9-pdr (long)	9	2850	4.22	4.50	.22
9-pdr (short)	7.50	2600	4.22	4	.22
6-pdr (long)	9	2450	3.67	3	.19
6-pdr (short)	7	1900	3.67	3	.19
4-pdr	6	1200	3.22	2	.18
3-pdr	4.50	700	2.91	1.50	.14
½-pdr (swivel)	3.50	150	1.69	.25	—

The table above, from British naval sources, shows the characteristics of the naval weapons of the period.

Most of the figures in the table date from the mid-eighteenth century and are representative of the naval guns of the Revolutionary War period. There were more classes than are listed in the table; there were, for instance, six types of 24-pounders, three 18's, three 12's, five 9's, and six 6's. The allowance for windage in the older guns was very large. In later years this was reduced, with a corresponding reduction of the powder charge. In the first half of the nineteenth century, although the gun was approximately the same,

the windage of the long 32 had been reduced by some two-tenths of an inch, and the charge reduced to 10 pounds.

Extreme range for a long 32-pounder, at 10 degrees elevation, was about 2,900 yards. Point blank, the distance at which a shot would hit the water when fired from a gun with zero elevation, was some 350 yards. Little serious shooting was done at extreme range, and half a mile would have been considered a good distance. Smaller guns ranged considerably less. A 12-pounder could reach out about a mile, with a point-blank range of some 300 yards.

Grapeshot was seldom used at any

Sights, as we know them, were nonexistent. Lining up a notch filed on the top of the base ring and on the swell of the muzzle was the usual method. This "line of metal" sighting gave some elevation, corresponding in some guns to 1½°, or a range, for a 24-pounder, of about 900 yards. A dispart sight, rarely used, was merely a metal foresight on the muzzle which provided a line of sight (C-D) parallel to the axis of the bore (E-F).

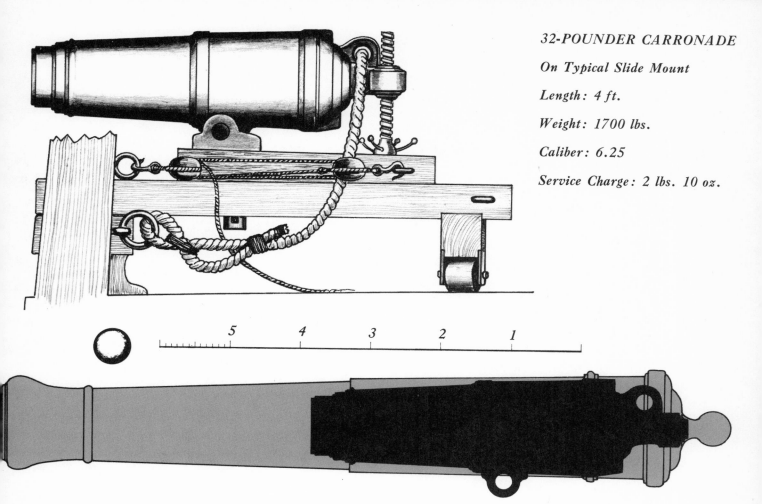

32-POUNDER CARRONADE

On Typical Slide Mount

Length: 4 ft.

Weight: 1700 lbs.

Caliber: 6.25

Service Charge: 2 lbs. 10 oz.

5   4   3   2   1

Outline of carronade superimposed on a long 32-pdr. Length of gun: 9.5 ft. Weight: 5500 lbs. Caliber: 6.43. Charge: 14 lbs.

Carronades were cast with a lug under the gun, instead of trunnions. A heavy pin fastened the lug to a slide, which was held in a slotted carriage, or bed, by a thick bolt. The carriage was pivoted to the ship's side and usually traversed on two small trucks. Elevation was commonly by means of a screw, although quoins were sometimes used. Recoil of the slide along the bed was checked by the customary breeching.

great distance because of the increased spread of the shot and its rapid loss of velocity. However, grape from the larger guns could range upward of three-quarters of a mile. In a test firing, three rounds of grape were fired from a long 32-pounder at a target vessel 750 yards away. Of the 27 balls, 10 hit (in a space about 100 feet by 8 feet), one of them with force enough to penetrate four inches of oak.

Case shot, on the other hand, did not have much carrying power and was of little or no value above a couple of hundred yards.

An important addition to the naval armament of the late eighteenth century was the carronade, named for the Carron Iron Foundry in Scotland, where it was first cast. The carronade was a very short, light weapon, firing a much heavier ball than was possible from a conventional weapon of comparable weight. The original model, though throwing a 68-pound ball, was shorter than the standard naval 4-pounder and weighed less (3,100 pounds) than the long 12. By reducing windage very fair accuracy was attained, while reduction of the charge enabled the gun to be cast much lighter. Reduced charges also meant less recoil; hence a lighter carriage which, with the lighter tube, meant that the crews required to work the weapon could be halved. And as many actions were decided within pistol shot, loss of range did not much matter.

Naval men had long known that the impact of one large projectile, even at comparatively low velocity, would do far more damage to the timbers of a vessel's hull than that of several smaller ones. The small, high-velocity ball would often go right through, leaving a neat round hole which could be easily plugged. The large projectile shattered strakes and frames alike and left a great ragged hole difficult if not impossible to plug. It was not for nothing that the 68-pounder carronade was nicknamed "The Smasher."

The advantages of the new type of gun were so obvious that smaller models were soon in demand by merchant captains, privateers, and naval officers. Armed with the new weapons, British merchantmen had a fair chance of beating off attacks by privateers. British privateers could outgun a larger opponent, while the lightness of the pieces enabled the navy to add substantial firepower to the existing armament of all classes of ships.

The prototype was cast in the early part of 1779, and by July the carronade was adopted by the Admiralty. By January 1781 they were in service in 492 vessels of the Royal Navy. For some reason carronades were never officially listed as part of a naval vessel's armament. Thus a 74, which carried eight of the new weapons on poop and forecastle, actually mounted 82 guns, while a 32-gun frigate had an actual broadside of 20 guns.

The greatly increased hitting power of the vessels mounting the carronade is shown by the comparison between the old and new armament of Rainbow. This ex-East Indiaman had been armed with twenty 18's, twenty-two 12's, and two 6's mounted on the forecastle. Weight of broadside: 318 pounds. Rearmed solely with carronades, she carried twenty 68-pounders, twenty-two 42's, and six 32's. Total weight of broadside: 1,238 pounds.

Some months after rearming, Rainbow fell in with a large French frigate. A few projectiles from Rainbow's forecastle 32-pounder carronades landed on board the enemy; whereupon the Frenchman, wisely figuring that if the Britisher mounted guns of such caliber on her forecastle the weapons on her main deck would be heavier yet, fired a broadside "for the honor of the flag" and surrendered.

How many carronades fell into American hands and were mounted in private or Continental vessels is impossible to say. Certainly American captains would have been quick to see the merits of the weapon, but many were no doubt satisfied with the accurate fire of their longer-ranged long 18's and 12's.

Lightweight, portable mortars called coehorns, which could throw small bombs or carcasses, were often carried aboard ship. They were sometimes used in the fighting tops, to toss their projectiles on the enemy's deck below. Small-caliber guns firing balls of about one-half pound, or charges of small shot, were carried in brackets on the bulwarks and in the tops. These were called swivel guns or swivels and took their name from the way in which they were mounted. They were the descendants of the numerous "murthering pieces" of Elizabethan days and resembled them closely.

Shot was invariably of cast iron. Besides the rigging-cutting chain and bar shot, there was grapeshot—clusters of nine iron balls packed and lashed tightly in cylindrical canvas bags made to fit the bore. The weight of these balls varied with the caliber of the gun. Those for a 32-pounder weighed three pounds apiece; for a 24, two pounds; for a 12, one pound, and for a 6-pounder each ball weighed eight ounces. They had fair range and penetration and were used against ships' boats, lightly built vessels, rigging, and to sweep an adversary's deck. Also used against rigging, but more exclusively as an antiperson-

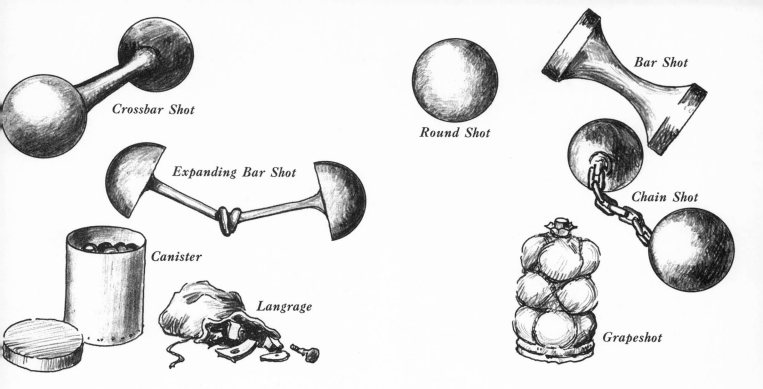

Crossbar Shot

Expanding Bar Shot

Canister

Langrage

Round Shot

Bar Shot

Chain Shot

Grapeshot

nel weapon, was canister, also called case shot (although technically this included grapeshot as well). This consisted of tins or bags of leaden musket balls, and gave the effect of a large shotgun blast. It was a short-range projectile; after some 200 yards the shot spread so widely that it lost its effect. Another similar projectile was langridge, or langrage— small iron scrap (bolts, bits of chain, bars, anything) bagged and tied and used mainly against rigging.

Shell was seldom used, except by the great mortars in the bomb-ketches. These were specially built vessels, easily recognizable by the position of their masts, which were stepped far aft to allow for the working of the pieces in their foreholds. To lessen the shock of the recoil, mortars were often bedded on piles of cut rope. They were not used in a general engagement, but for bombarding fortifications. Mortar shells, or bombs, were made hollow and filled with powder. A time fuze was lit just before the piece was fired. The bomb was flung in a high arc and smashed down with considerable force, but the bursting charge was small, and compared to a modern shell, it did little damage.

Carcasses, hollow projectiles filled with combustibles, were sometimes used against forts or suitable targets. Hot shot—round shot heated red in a furnace and carried to the guns in special stretcherlike ladles—were occasionally used, but the difficulty of heating the shot aboard ship, and the ever present danger of fire made this primarily a weapon used against ships by shore defenses.

Because the weapons were so inaccurate, most captains attempted to place their ships as close alongside an enemy as circumstances permitted. In many cases vessels fought literally yardarm to yardarm; and in more than one instance hulls were so close that the lower deck ports could not be raised, and had to be blown open by the first discharge. At such ranges there could be no question of missing. Every shot was a hit, and at each broadside a storm of projectiles crashed into the enemy's hull. There was little need to aim. Speed in loading was what counted. A ship which could get off three broadsides to her opponent's two was in a fair way to winning. Brawny arms and cool heads and, above all, training were what won battles such as these. Constant exercising, until clockwork precision was attained was the key to success. It is said that during the Napoleonic Wars, Collingwood's *Dreadnaught* could fire three broadsides in three and one-half

Gunport

Note tricing tackle and port wriggle (the molding above the port to carry water off either side of the porthole).

minutes. Three in six minutes was considered good, but gun crews could not keep up this exhausting rate for very long.

Given such close ranges and a fair rate of fire, one might expect that ships exposed to such a blast of round shot would have speedily gone to the bottom. Actually, the heavily built hulls could only be vitally damaged by hits at or close to the waterline. As the largest shot made only a comparatively small hole (shell was not used in those days) and as these could often be plugged from the inside during the action, it took a number of such hits to batter a ship of the line into a sinking condition. Hulls might be badly shattered and decks run red with blood, but for a ship to go down in battle was a rare occurrence indeed.

It might be argued that at very close range a high percentage of waterline hits might be expected. Such was not the case. Because of the motion of the hull and the crude method of elevating and depressing the guns (and it must be remembered that after each shot the quoin was usually displaced and had to be readjusted), elevation was a far greater problem to the gunner than deflection. Added to this was the fact that unless the action was fought in a high wind, dense clouds of smoke blanketed the target, making the gun captain's task even more difficult. Another

factor—and this one dealt largely with the human equation—was the natural desire to first beat down the fire of the enemy gunners, whose smoking gun muzzles pointed threateningly only a few yards away.

In the heat of action, amidst the smash of enemy shot, the howl of splinters, shouts, shrieks, blinding flashes, and choking clouds of smoke, it was a cool gun captain indeed who could attempt to aim shot after shot, not at the opposing battery, but at a narrow and often partially obscured target.

Nevertheless, ships occasionally did sink, though not as a rule until long after an action, when the incoming water gradually gained over exhausted and depleted crews manning such pumps as remained undamaged.

Fire was a greater hazard, and one dreaded by friend and foe alike. Blazing gun wads often set an enemy's hull alight, while the canvas and tarred rigging which often festooned the sides of a vessel after a short time in action were particularly susceptible. This wreckage was not only endangered by burning wads but was frequently set afire by the flashes of the guns themselves. Explosions also took their toll. And in every case it was far more probable that the blast was accidental than that it was caused by an enemy shot. Red-hot shot were seldom, if ever, used in action between fleets at sea, and the chances of a solid shot directly causing an explosion were few and far between. The cause of such explosions in action, and they were rare, was more likely to be the accidental ignition of spilled powder (from faulty cartridges, or ones torn open by enemy shot) flashing in some way into the magazine, perhaps set off by a smashed battle lantern, or a smoldering slow match. Black powder is itself a tricky substance, and can be set off by the grinding of a leather heel or a spark from a shoe-nail striking metal. Not until the general adoption of shell in the 1830's and '40's was there acute danger of fire and explosion due to enemy gun action alone.

Navigational hazards and accidents took as great a toll as did the broadsides of the enemy. During the war of 1775-1783, 203 British government vessels were lost from all causes (the figures are from Clowes's *The Royal Navy*). Of these, 90 were taken or destroyed due to enemy action (including those sunk to avoid capture), 18 were taken, but recaptured later, five were deliberately destroyed, as block ships, or condemned, while 90 more were wrecked, foundered at sea, or were accidentally burned. Out of the 108 lost to enemy action, only seven were larger than 32-gun frigates, and of those seven, two were retaken. Vessels mounting some 1,788 guns were actually taken or destroyed in action, while the total of guns mounted on those lost by accident came to 2,444. In almost every instance ships lost in action were surrendered, not destroyed. If too badly battered they were sometimes sunk by their captors, but in most cases the captured ship was taken into the victor's service, in many instances to be retaken at a later date.

Warships today seldom surrender. A tradition of fighting a ship until she sinks has grown up in the last two great naval wars. Even vessels hopelessly outclassed usually go down with colors flying and guns blazing. Not so in the days of the old sailing navies. If a ship had well and truly done her best, there was no stigma attached to an honorable surrender, and the subsequent court-martial invariably found her commander not guilty. Vessels rendered unmanageable because of loss of masts and spars and in positions where they could not bring their own guns to bear while being raked by the enemy, almost always hauled down their flags. Senseless slaughter of a helpless crew was frowned on in those days. It was left for a more modern, and, in some ways less civilized, age to demand a battle to the death.

But if ships rarely sank, they occasionally absorbed a terrific amount of punishment. Shot from the heavier guns could penetrate even the stoutest oak sides, and while the hole which a missile made on entrance was small, the damage on exit was often devastating. Splinters flew in clouds, and were a prime source of the most terrible wounds. Ship's sides were sometimes so shattered that the decks above were in danger of collapsing. Bows and sterns were most vulnerable, both from the construction of the ships, and because few ships could bring any guns to bear dead ahead or right aft. Raking broadsides from bow or stern swept the decks from end to end, nor was an attempt ever made to reinforce the hulls with stout bulkheads forward and aft to obviate this deadly fire. A ship thus raked might have half the fight knocked out of her at one broadside.

When *Victory* broke the line at Trafalgar, she passed astern of *Bucentaure* at a range of 30 feet. As each double-shotted gun bore, it was discharged into the Frenchman's stern. This one broadside swept her decks, killed or wounded 400 men, and dismounted 20 guns. Casualties in this kind of infighting were often appalling. In the same battle the French *Redoubtable,* ably commanded by Captain Lucas, fought until "our whole poop was stove in, helm, rudder, and sternpost all shattered to splinters, all the stern frame and decks shot through." All her 74 guns were dismounted and of her crew of 634, 300 were killed and 222 wounded. Twenty-two out of

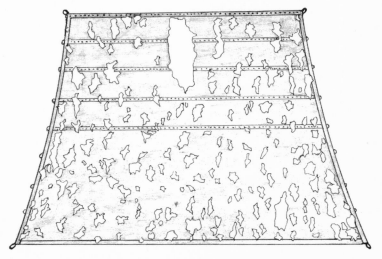

As an example of how the iron flew in an old-time engagement, above is a sketch made from a contemporary drawing of one of Victory's topsails after Trafalgar. (The sail, by the way, was made by Ratsey.)

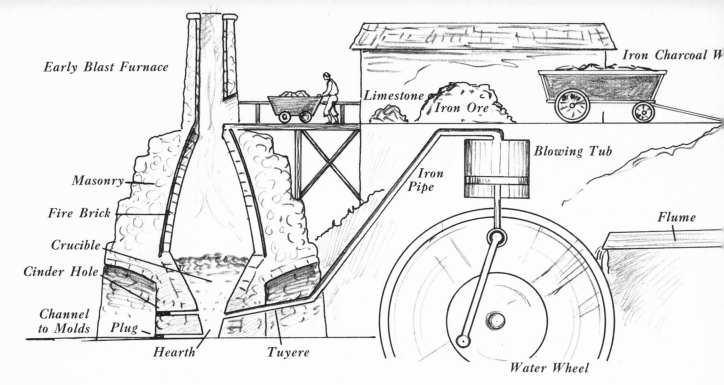

Early Blast Furnace

Masonry

Fire Brick

Crucible

Cinder Hole

Channel to Molds Plug

Hearth Tuyere

Limestone Iron Ore

Iron Charcoal W

Iron Pipe

Blowing Tub

Flume

Water Wheel

A blast furnace such as this could produce about 500 tons of iron a year. The ore was mostly taken from or near the surface, seldom more than 40 feet deep. The fuel used was charcoal, and huge quantities of wood (mostly hickory, chestnut, and black oak) were cut and charred in great stacks, some as much as 50 feet in diameter. A good-sized furnace used about 800 bushels of charcoal every 24 hours. To make this required some 50 cords of timber, of at least 20-year growth—perhaps close to the yield of an acre of forest—every day. At the furnace the charcoal was kept in long sheds. The furnace was charged through an opening in the stack with alternate layers of charcoal, iron ore, and a small amount of limestone. A blast of air from the waterpower-operated blower was forced through one or more tuyeres. As the charcoal grew white-hot, the ore melted and dropped down to the hearth. Impurities floated to the top and were drained off through the cinder hole. The furnace was tapped periodically. The fire clay plug was driven in and the molten ore ran into sand molds, a main channel with side gutters. The pattern reminded someone of a sow and her litter; so the small cast billets were called ''pigs,'' hence pig iron.

29 officers were casualties.

These were ships of the line, but frigate actions could be obstinate and bloody, too. In 1779, *Surveillante*, 32, fought the British 32-gun *Quebec* in an epic battle, which left the heavier armed Frenchman dismasted, leaking, and badly battered, with 115 men out of a crew of 255 casualties. *Quebec,* also dismasted, took fire, the flashes of her guns igniting her tattered sails as they hung overside. She blew up and went down with the loss of all but 65 of her 195-man crew.

But *Quebec's* loss could be termed an accident, and for every such encounter there were scores where the combatants, after expending hundreds of rounds of ammunition, broke off the action to patch their shot holes, splice their rigging, send up spare spars, and bend new sails. Ships were remarkably self-sufficient in those days, and many a disabled vessel was made serviceable again within hours of her coming out of action.

When the Revolution began, the only cannon of any size available were those mounted in the various forts and batteries taken from the British. (A list of cannon in Rhode Island as of June 30, 1775 shows six 24-pounders, eighteen 18-pounders, two 9-pounders, two 6-pounders, and ten 4's.) Foundries there were—in Pennsylvania, Rhode Island, Connecticut, Massachusetts, Maryland, and even South Carolina—but the manufacture of cannon had always been a British prerogative, and Colonial ironmasters lacked both the techniques and technicians to produce the necessary weapons in any quantity.

George Washington's little navy was armed with cannon bought, begged, borrowed, or captured. Those ship owners who possessed cannon were not always eager to risk them, and we find one Captain John Derby insisting on the immediate return of his six weapons, loaned to schooner *Lee*. He got them, too, and *Lee* had to borrow four 4-pounders and haggle for a pair of 2's before she could again put to sea.

The armament for the newly authorized frigates was originally to have come from Pennsylvania, the largest producer of iron. (In 1760 there were twelve furnaces in Pennsylvania, producing an estimated 5,000 tons annually.) It was intended to standardize the frigates' armament—the 24-gun ships to have twenty-four 9-pounders, the 28-gun ones twenty-six 12-pounders, and two 6-pounders, and the 32-gun vessels, twenty-six 12-pounders and six 6's. It was soon found, however, that because of technical difficulties the Pennsylvania foundries, such as Reading, Warwick, Cornwall, and Hopewell, were not equal to the task of turning out the required armament, either in the quantity needed or the time allowed. In a letter from R. T. Paine, in Philadelphia, dated September 18, 1776, to Colonel Peter Grubb of Cornwall Furnace, Mr. Paine complains: "Sir, by Capt. Joy I understand you have at last made some 12-pounders, but I fear they are heavier than they ought to be. Those made by Col. Bird [of Hopewell Furnace] weigh but 27 C and some under.... The Cannon must be proved with two shott, or they will never be put on board the ships."

Other foundries received orders; the guns for *Alliance* and *Confederacy*, for instance, were contracted for at Salisbury Furnace in Connecticut. But they failed to deliver and the order was transferred to a Massachusetts iron works, which also was unable to complete the order in full.

So the frigates mostly received a mixed armament; *Boston*, for instance, went to sea with a hodgepodge of weaponry—five 12-pounders, nineteen 9-pounders, two 6-pounders, four 4's, and sixteen swivels.

It was finally realized that Americans could not at that time produce even enough cannon to arm a few frigates, let alone a ship of the line (the largest naval gun cast during the war was an 18-pounder). So, besides captured and salvaged British weapons, cannon were procured in France, although that country was seemingly hard put at times, as witness the ancient relics which exploded so disastrously between decks in *Bonhomme Richard*.

Benedict Arnold seems to have armed his fleet on Lake Champlain, at least in part, with weapons from Ticonderoga and Crown Point. A letter from Arnold to the Massachusetts Committee of Safety lists 111 taken at Crown Point—ranging from 24-pounders to 13-inch mortars—of which 48 were classed as "useless." Of 86 at Ticonderoga only two were termed "useless," although 27 were classed as "bad."

Arnold closed his list by writing, "I shall send to Cambridge the 24-pounders, 12 and 6 pounders, howitzers, etc." If he did so, there remained fifteen 18-pounders, thirty-three 9-pounders, nine 4-pounders, nineteen swivels, and a couple of wall guns—all classed as "good." There were, however, 12-pounders and 6-pounders on board his vessels at the battle of Valcour Island. There are no records to show whether these were new weapons brought in from the coast or were the old pieces, many of them French, classed as "bad" or "useless." Or whether Arnold did not send all the guns of those calibers to Cambridge, as he stated he would do.

Cannon were cast in molds. First a model or pattern was made. This was usually built up around a wooden spindle, around which rope or straw plait was wound until the approximate shape of the gun was attained. The pattern was then covered with a mixture of clay, sand, and horse dung (the latter ingredient helped bind the mixture together and later made it easier to crumble the pattern out of the mold). A modeling board, the edge of which was contoured to the exact form of the finished gun, was then brought up against the pattern. The wooden spindle was then revolved and the modeling board pared the wet clay mixture to the correct shape. Wooden trunnions were fastened into place with an iron pin. The cascabel was often made separately.

The mold was made with a clay and sand mixture, usually with a binder such as cow hair. After the pattern was coated with some composition to prevent the mold from sticking to it, the mold material was applied to the pattern, generally in several coats. Thin rope was sometimes wound around the first coat to strengthen it, and the finished mold was barred and hooped with iron to further strengthen it. An extension of the muzzle-end of the mold, called a deadhead, was also made. This allowed extra metal to be poured, ensuring that the mold was completely filled.

The pattern was then removed from the mold. First the pin holding the trunnions in place was withdrawn. The wooden spindle was struck several times with a mallet and then drawn out, pieces of the clay pattern adhering to it. The trunnions could then be dislodged and withdrawn and the remainder of the pattern (dried, if necessary, by inserting some combustible material) was then crumbled out by hand. The mold was then baked in a pit until completely dry. (As many an amateur potter has found out, the too sudden application of great heat to damp clay can cause an explosion of no mean proportions.)

The casting pit (or pits) was situated a short distance from the "gate" of the furnace. First the mold of the cascabel was positioned in the bottom of the pit and bedded in earth, then the mold for the cannon was lowered into place on top of it, and earth rammed around it, the ends of the trunnions being plated over (to cover the holes where the pin was pulled out). The deadhead was put in place and wired into position and the whole pit around the molds packed with earth. A clay-lined channel led from the furnace to the mold. Usually there was more than one mold pit. In that case the main channel had branches, plugged with clay, leading to the various molds. It was customary to fill two molds at a time. When time came for the pour, a plug in the furnace was driven in with an iron bar, and the molten metal rushed out and into the molds.

After cooling for two or three days the molds were lifted out of the pits, the iron reinforcing removed, and the molds broken up with hammers. The deadhead was then cut off and the gun was then ready for boring and turning. Boring was done with a solid iron boring bar, steel-tipped and securely mounted. The gun was chucked and revolved by horse or waterpower, the muzzle resting in a brass ring. The cutting tool was advanced against the work by means of a rack and pinion or some such device. The tube was usually started small, and larger cutting heads fitted until the desired caliber was reached.

While the gun was being bored, it was also turned (castings were fairly rough). The space between the trunnions was finished by chiseling and filing. Boring was a slow process—three or four days, or more.

Sometimes the bore was formed by the gun being cast around a central core. However, there was difficulty in keeping the core in position, and the metal around it tended to be poor in texture. In any case the cast bore had to be reamed out to the proper size, to true it up and eliminate the imperfections of the casting.

The trunnions were also turned, and one method was to position the gun so that the trunnions were vertical. A hollow cylinder, heavily weighted and holding a cutting tool, was suspended from above and revolved around the trunnion by hand.

In some cannon the touchhole, or vent, was simply drilled in the top of the breech end of the tube. In others the gun was bouched. The vent hole was bored out to about an inch in diameter and a bushing of

Rough pattern of straw plait and
rope around spindle.

Pattern was then covered with clay mixture.

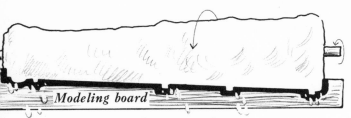

True pattern then cut with
metal-edged modeling board.

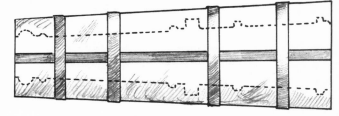

Mold material applied to pattern, and hooped
and bound. When dry, pattern was broken out.

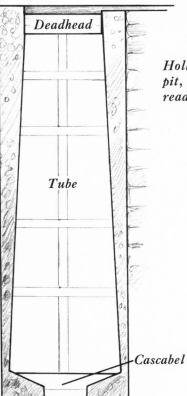

Channel to furnace

Deadhead

Tube

Cascabel

Hollow molds in casting
pit, packed with earth
ready for pouring

Steps in the Manufacture of a Cannon

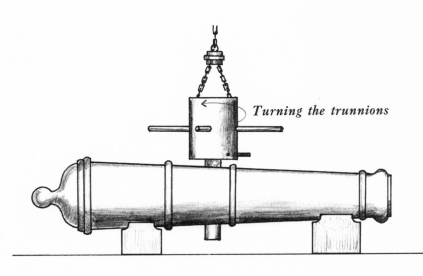

Turning the trunnions

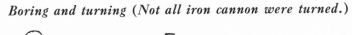

Boring and turning (Not all iron cannon were turned.)

161

some metal, sometimes copper, was inserted. This bushing, which had the vent hole drilled through it, was either fastened in the gun by tapping and threading or the hole was enlarged at the bottom and a tapered bushing inserted from inside. Succeeding firings forced the bushing further into place. The rush of powder gases through the vent tended to erode it, with subsequent loss of power, so that bouching was often used to restore a gun whose vent had become enlarged.

Some weapons were cast with thicker walls. These "double fortified" cannon were considerably heavier than regular weapons of the same caliber but could stand larger charges of powder, and thus gained somewhat in range and accuracy.

Before being put in service, guns were always proved by test-firing with extra heavy charges and usually two or three shot.

In Colonial days the main supply of gunpowder had come from Great Britain. Consequently, powder was often very scarce, especially at the beginning of the war. Much was later imported from France, but though great efforts were made to manufacture an adequate supply in America, there was often a shortage. Powder and its ingredients were so much in demand that in July, 1775, the Continental Congress "resolved, that for the better furnishing of these colonies with the necessary means of defending their rights, every vessel importing Gun powder, Salt petre, Sulphur, providing they bring with the sulphur four times as much salt petre, brass field-pieces, or good muskets furnished with Bayonets, within nine Months from the date of this resolution, shall be permitted to load and export the produce of these colonies, to the value of such powder and stores aforesd the non-exportation agreement notwithstand-ing..."

Gunpowder is composed of three ingredients in varying proportion, the usual being saltpeter, 75 percent, sulphur, 10 percent, and charcoal, 15 percent. Saltpeter (potassium nitrate) is found in natural deposits in some parts of the world. The natural conditions can be simulated by exposing heaps of decaying organic matter mixed with alkalies, such as lime, to atmospheric action. The saltpeter was extracted from these "niter beds" by leaching out with water, to which was added wood ashes or potassium carbonate. The liquid was then filtered and crystallized, and purified by repeated boilings, skimmings, and filterings.

Sulphur deposits occur in many places, notably Sicily and Spain. There are sizable deposits in North America, but unfortunately for the Colonists, not in areas (with the exception of Louisiana) then inhabited by white settlers. Sulphur rated high on the list of priority imports. However, ships running the British blockade could also bring the finished article, gunpowder.

Charcoal there was in plenty but large-scale mills for grinding and preparing the ingredients of gunpowder in quantity were lacking. The materials were ground separately, then mixed in their proper proportions and ground again into a fine powder (or rather paste, as water was added) by stamping mills or wheel mills, in which latter two large, heavy wheels revolved freely around a pan, on the end of a horizontal shaft, turned by rotation of a vertical spindle. The resulting paste was pressed into a thin cake and on drying was broken up and passed through sieves, the finer grains being used for small arms and the largest for cannon.

Peril on the Penobscot

Chapter 18

Some 170 miles north and east of Boston, the mouth of the Penobscot River, with its many islands and deepwater inlets, afforded the British an ideal base for operations against the coasts of Massachusetts and New Hampshire. On June 10, 1779, a fleet of transports from Halifax, escorted by the sloops of war *Nautilus*, 16; *Albany*, 14; and *North*, 14, landed 450 men of the Seventy-fourth and 200 of the Eighty-second regiments, under Colonels Campbell and MacLean, on the little peninsula of Bagaduce (part of present-day Castine).

The British wasted no time. Soon the stillness of the Maine woods was broken by the clink of picks and shovels and the crash of falling timber. A small fort swiftly took shape, and just as swiftly news spread to the towns of Portsmouth and Boston that the redcoats were entrenching themselves on the shores of Penobscot Bay. A well-established base within two days' sail of Boston Harbor was a threat that the New Englanders could not ignore. Massachusetts rose to the occasion, and organized the greatest naval effort that the Colonies put forth during the whole war. Three Massachusetts state cruisers—the 14-gun brigs *Tyrannicide*, *Hazard*, and *Active*—were assigned to the expedition (all figures on armament are approximate, there being almost as many estimates as there are historians).

Besides the state vessels there were numerous Massachusetts-owned privateers, while an estimated 2,500 troops, many of them Massachusetts men, were embarked on some 22 transports.

Generals Solomon Lovell and Peleg Wadsworth were in command, and Paul Revere, of midnight ride fame, was in charge of the artillery.

New Hampshire was represented by the brig *Hampden*, 20, while the Continental Navy supplied the expedition's most powerful vessel, the 32-gun frigate *Warren*, Captain Dudley Saltonstall; the sloop *Providence*, 12 (John Paul Jones's first command) commanded by Hoysted Hacker, and brig *Diligent*, 14, Moses Brown.

Man does not live by ships alone, and supplies were voted by the General Court: "Nine tons of Flour or Bread, Nine Tons of Rice, Eighteen Tons of Salt Beef, six hundred Gallons of Rum, six hundred Gallons of Molasses, Five hundred stand of Fire Arms."

Instructions to the leader of the expedition ordered him to "Captivate, Kill or destroy the Enemies whole Force both by Sea & Land, & the more effectually to answer that purpose, you are to Consult measures & preserve the greatest harmony with the Commander of the Land Forces, that the navy & army may Co-operate & assist each other."

But cooperation depended on a perfect understanding between the commanders of the land and sea forces—an understanding as rare as it was necessary. All through history land-sea expeditions have been imperiled or met with disaster because the leaders of the naval and military contingents did not see eye to eye. The expedition to drive the British from the Penobscot was to prove no exception.

As captain of a Continental frigate Dudley Saltonstall was the obvious, if perhaps not the most popular choice for commander. Saltonstall, who had been Esek Hopkins's flag captain, was not universally admired in the American service. Jones had been Saltonstall's executive officer in *Alfred,* and bore that "Sensible, indefatigable Morose man" no love. Saltonstall's distant and condescending manner grated on his second-in-command, who described him as being of "Rude Unhappy Temper." On another occasion the peppery Jones called him "the well-intended and narrow-minded Saltonstall."

Rude and narrow-minded or not, Salton-

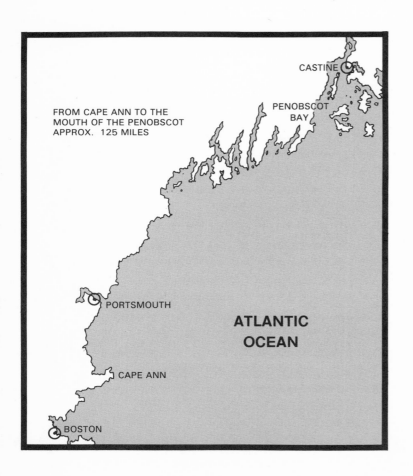

FROM CAPE ANN TO THE MOUTH OF THE PENOBSCOT APPROX. 125 MILES

CASTINE

PENOBSCOT BAY

ATLANTIC OCEAN

PORTSMOUTH

CAPE ANN

BOSTON

stall ranked high on the Continental Navy list, and it was as Commodore Saltonstall that he led his fleet north—seven warships, twelve privateers, and twenty-two transports.

While New England was thus girding herself to throw out the invaders, the redcoats were working steadily on their fortifications. Still the redoubts were only half finished when, on July 25, their labors were interrupted by the sight of an enemy squadron coming up the bay. Drums rolled as the garrison hastily exchanged picks and shovels for muskets, while in the little bay on the north side of the promontory the three sloops anchored in front of the transports, prepared to offer what resistance they could to the overwhelming force now almost within gunshot.

As the American squadron, *Warren* leading, came within range, the shore batteries opened fire. In reply, gray smoke spurted from the sides of the American vessels, and soon a long smear of powder smoke hung over the upper reaches of the bay. Though attacked by nine ships, in three divisions, the British sloops suffered little damage. A two-hour bombardment of the fort proved equally disappointing. The banks on which the work stood were steep, and the place, though only partly completed, was in a commanding position.

An attempt to land on Bagaduce that same evening was foiled by high winds, but on the twenty-sixth a council of war held in *Warren* decided that each ship should provide marines to make up a landing party to capture a small island off the south side of the promontory. This island, Nautilus, or Banks, Island, mounted a battery of two guns. Led by Captain Welsh, of *Warren,* the marines took the islet, supported by fire from the sloop *Providence* and the brigs *Pallas* and *Defense.* Two 18's and one 12-pounder were mounted, and as the island commanded the mouth of the harbor, the British sloops were forced to fall back to a new anchorage to the north of the fort.

The following day was spent in reconnoitering the British positions—time wasted, in the opinion of some of Saltonstall's naval

officers, who urged him to get on with his job, "that the most speedy Exertions should be used to accomplish the design we came upon."

The captains wished "to go immediately into the Harbor & Attack the Enemy's Ships" and it is difficult to see why this was not done. An all-out attack must have proved successful, and the destruction or capture of the three sloops, as well as of the transports and supply vessels, would have seriously affected the garrison's chances of survival. However, plans were made for a landing on Bagaduce at daybreak, under cover of a bombardment by two ships and three brigs who were "to fire into the Woods with an intent to scower them of the Enemy," while *Warren* and the battery on Nautilus Island engaged the sloops at long range.

First light found the American supporting vessels in position, and the waiting boats crammed with men. At the signal cannon balls and grapeshot smashed into the woods, sending saplings, branches and splinters of rock flying, turning the patch of forest into an inferno of shrieking iron and splintered wood. Not until the laden boats touched shore did the fire slacken and die away.

The Americans landed in three divisions: marines on the right, Colonel Mitchell's troops on the left, and the volunteers and artillery in the center. The latter, under Revere, were landed with small arms only; the steep, 100-foot-high banks made it impossible to bring field pieces into action. So steep was the bank that the men had to clamber up it with the aid of the trees and bushes which covered it.

The strongest resistance was encountered by the marines, but after a sharp skirmish the defenders retired hastily, leaving twelve dead, eight wounded, and some ten prisoners. They also abandoned a battery of three 6-pounders. American losses were about ten killed and twenty wounded.

Although established within 600 yards of the fort, Lovell refused to order an assault until Saltonstall had eliminated the three sloops, whose fire supported the defenders. Saltonstall, in his turn, refused to attack the sloops until Lovell had reduced the fort. In this he was upheld by most, if not all, the privateer captains—men not noted for risking their ships and crews where little but glory and hard knocks were to be gained. In the meantime the garrison was busy throwing up gun emplacements and strengthening the works.

On August 6, Lovell wrote to Saltonstall to find out "whether he wou'd or whether he wou'd not go in with his Ships & destroy the Shipping of the Enemy, which consist only of three Sloops of war, when he returned for answer, if I wou'd storm the fort he wou'd go in with his Ships, upon which I called a Council,

the result of which was that in our present situation it was impractible, with any prospect of success."

Reports of the Commodore's lack of activity had meanwhile reached Boston, and a letter from the Navy Board of the Eastern District to Saltonstall asked why the sloops had not been attacked, although "it is agreed on all hands that they are at all times in your power." They went on to remind him that "our apprehensions for your danger have ever been from a reinforcement to the enemy" and finished by directing him "to attack and take or destroy them without delay, in doing which no time is to be lost, as a reinforcement are probably on their passage at this time. It is therefore our orders that as soon as you receive this you take the most effectual measures for the capture or destruction of the enemy's ships, and with the greatest dispatch the nature and situation of things will admit of."

Apprehensions about reinforcements for the enemy were not confined to the Navy Board. The failure of the troops to assault and carry the fort at one blow, and the subsequent resolve to undertake siege operations, must have worried many of the seamen. Several were noted privateersmen, men whose safety depended on fast ships and plenty of open ocean. To be cooped up at the head of a bay, with no sea-room and every possibility of an enemy squadron appearing from the southward, was a privateer's nightmare. Yet the prospect of sailing tamely away, leaving the fort still flaunting the Union colors, was even worse.

So for two weeks the siege went forward. Earthworks were dug and the American guns pounded the fort and exchanged long-range shots with the British sloops. But news of the beleaguered garrison's plight had had time to reach New York. There Vice Admiral Sir George Collier got together a relieving force and prepared to sail for the Penobscot. On August 3, the squadron set sail: *Raisonnable*, 64, flagship; *Blonde* and *Virginia*, 32's; *Greyhound*, *Camilla* and *Galatea*, 20's, and *Otter*, 14.

Wooden-stocked anchor, showing usual method of bending on cable

A — *Shackle*
B — *Stock*
C — *Shank*
D — *Arm*
E — *Fluke or Palm*
F — *Bill*
G — *Crown*

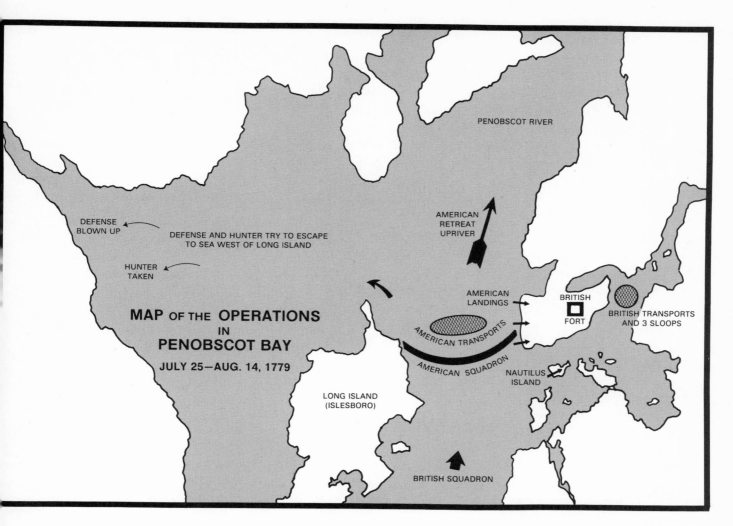

MAP OF THE **OPERATIONS**
IN
PENOBSCOT BAY

JULY 25—AUG. 14, 1779

A British map, frequently published, "by an officer present," is hard to reconcile with the chart or with contemporary accounts. It is more probable that the action occurred somewhat as shown above, with the seventeen vessels of the American squadron in crescent formation to the west of Castine, between that little promontory and the northern end of Long Island, or Islesboro, as it is now called. Also that they retired up the Penobscot River proper and not the Bagaduce, as shown in the officer's map.

Fog slowed the admiral's progress and scattered his force, but by the evening of August 13, all his command except *Otter* had rendezvoused off the entrance to the bay. Without further delay, Sir George led his little fleet up the bay, and early on the fourteenth the American squadron was sighted.

The Americans, according to an old plan of the battle mapped by a British officer present, had drawn their ships up in a crescent formation, the storeships and transports, with the hastily reembarked troops aboard, behind them. The American vessels mounted some 316 guns, the British about 190. To offset the numerical advantage, some of the British guns were heavier, and the 64, with her great size and stout timbers, could withstand considerably more punishment than any of Saltonstall's squadron. All the same, the Americans could have put up a fight, and if they had been able to do enough damage to the enemy's spars and rigging some at least might have got away to sea. Instead, after firing a few ineffectual broadsides, Saltonstall's squadron disintegrated into a fleeing mass of vessels with the British in hot pursuit.

As the men of the garrison cheered, the three sloops which had helped defend the anchorage sailed boldly out and joined in the action. The pursuit became a rout. Bottled up in the upper reaches of the bay, the Americans had no way of escape. *Hampden* and *Hunter* were boarded and taken, and the forested shores of the Penobscot echoed with the crash of guns as the exultant British pressed on after the flying Yankees.

Saltonstall's only thought seems to have been to destroy his vessels to prevent their capture; and soon to the haze of powder fumes was added volumes of black smoke as vessel after vessel went up in flames and grounded, or drifted blazing down the bay. *Defense* exploded with a shattering roar as the fire set by her crew reached her magazine, and the cannonade was punctuated by more loud crashes as flames reached the powder stores of other ships.

The destruction was complete. The Continental frigate *Warren,* the state ships, transports, storeships—all were flaring wrecks. The swift privateers, dangerous and destructive as so many wolves on the open ocean, drifted helplessly ashore belching smoke and flame, their slender spars sending up clouds of sparks as they crashed down through the burning decks. Of 41 ships, two armed vessels and a transport were taken, the rest destroyed. American losses were close to 500 men. Those who escaped faced a terrible march back to the settlements. The Penobscot area was a wilderness in those days, and it was a ragged, footsore mob of half-starved, dispirited men who finally reached Portsmouth.

British losses were light. Fifteen were killed or wounded aboard the three sloops during the siege. Sir George's squadron suffered no losses or damage at all. Of the garrison, seventy men of the Seventy-fourth and Eighty-second were casualties. It was a major disaster for the Colonies (one usually made light of in history books), and there was both dismay and anger in New England when the facts became known.

Saltonstall was court-martialed and dismissed the service. Other officers were also tried, among them Paul Revere. He was aquitted, as was Lovell. But Saltonstall's head on a platter, pleasing as it might be to some in the service, could not bring back nineteen lost warships. All in all, it was a sorry chapter in America's naval history.

Ships carried several anchors, of various weights, depending on the tonnage of the vessel. Bower anchors, the two main working anchors, were carried at each side of the stem. A rough rule was that, in warships, the bowers each weighed 100 lbs. for every gun carried. There was usually also a spare bower. Abaft the bowers were the sheet anchors. There were usually two, of the same weight as the bowers. They were let go in an emergency, when the bowers had dragged or carried away. Carried astern was a stream anchor, perhaps one-third the weight of the bowers. Also carried were two or more kedge anchors, each about half the weight of the stream. These were used to move the ship by laying out the kedge and hauling the vessel up to it (see diagram).

Kedging: By alternately laying out one anchor while the other was being hauled in, a vessel could be moved against wind or tide.

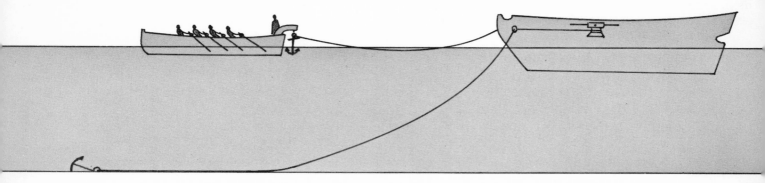

Life Aboard Ship

Chapter 19

Ships and guns were no use without the seamen to sail and fight them. What sort of men were they who manned the fleets in the days of the Revolution. Patriots? Some of them, perhaps. Adventurers? That term suits many more; for every man who could be coaxed to serve in the Continental Navy or the British service, there were dozens who would cheerfully go to sea in a privateer.

Jolly tars? Well, sometimes, but to judge from the descriptions that have come down to us, the ships' crews were often a sorry lot of discontented farm boys, hijacked ne'er-do-wells, paroled prisoners, and runaway apprentices—signed on under the influence of much cheap rum, and hustled aboard in a half-drunken stupor. But whatever their reasons—enlisted from the highest motives, or slugged on the streets of an English port and forcibly signed on for the war's duration—they were the raw material upon which the navies of both countries had to depend.

Both the Congressional and the Royal navies were perennially short of men, but with this difference: American warships lacking crews stayed in port, while British ships had to go to sea; the safety of Britain depended on it. And go to sea they did, although perhaps only one man of every four in their crews was aboard of his own free will.

Because of the harsh discipline, poor food, and miserable pay (19 shillings a month for ordinary seamen, a rate unchanged for some 125 years), most seamen looked on service in a King's ship with horror. Life in the merchant marine—no picnic either, in those days—was infinitely to be preferred. Wages were higher, discipline was less rigid, and there was the chance for a fling ashore at the end of each voyage. In the Royal Navy, on the other hand, pay (often long overdue) was generally in the form of a "ticket," not coin—a ticket which could only be cashed by application at Tower Hill in London. In practice seamen often transferred their tickets (at an outrageous discount) to some enterprising shark in the nearest home port.

Then, too, a seaman could not leave his ship until her commission (which might be for years) was over and she was paid off. And—a favorite trick when men were scarce—there was always the chance that the sailors of a vessel returning after a long cruise might be transferred wholesale to one newly commissioned and only awaiting a crew to join the fleet.

So sailors shunned the Navy like the plague, but by law they were liable for duty if caught, and catching them was the job of the press gang. Seafaring men were rounded up in every port and fishing village, and if a landsman or two got caught in the net, so much

the worse for them. Merchant seamen, homeward bound after a long voyage, were forcibly taken from their ships, often within sight of home. Drunken seamen were seized in their favorite grog shops, and sober fishermen taken from the doorsteps of their cottages. It was brutal; it was unjust; but it was necessary. Much has been written about the horrors of impressment, but perhaps it was the manner in which it was done and the rigors of the life into which its victims were forced which arouses pity, more than the fact that men were made to serve against their will. The draftee or the reservist suddenly called back to duty, leaving family and business, has little choice, either. When governments need men, men must be provided.

But even the press could not supply sufficient men. So to the pressed seamen were added quotas from the jails (debtors, petty offenders and such), who, despite Dr. Johnson's remark, "I wonder why people go to sea, when there are jails on shore," preferred a life afloat to one behind bars.

Foreigners were also to be found among the crews of His Britannic Majesty's ships. Some were swept up by the press in the ports;

some few were prisoners of war, who elected to fight for Britain (sometimes against their own countrymen) rather than rot in a prison hulk or cell.

Out of an average Royal Navy crew of 300 men there might be some 70 volunteers, of whom over 75 percent were seamen. Half of the whole crew had probably been pressed, and of these all but a tenth likely had been to sea before. Some 35 might be foreigners—all seamen, and mostly pressed. The remaining 45 would have been taken from the jails— debtors and petty offenders of various kinds— landlubbers all.

Seamen were usually so scarce in American ports that often ships could only be manned by the employment of British sailors—deserters or prisoners of war. While the former could be expected to carry out their duties reasonably well and fight like cornered rats if necessary (the fate of a recaptured deserter from the Royal Navy was not a pleasant one), the latter were always an uncertain quantity. There was also a considerable percentage of landsmen in every crew.

Makeup of an Average Crew of a Royal Naval Vessel in Wartime

Total Crew (100%)	% Seamen in Total Crew 75	Total Crew			
		% Pressed 50	% Volunteers 23	% from Jails 15	% of Foreigners 12

The force which bound these motley arrays together was discipline, spelled with a capital "D." By our standards it was unbelievably harsh. But life everywhere was hard in those days, and so perhaps life afloat was not quite so terrible as our rereading of contemporary accounts would indicate. But it was grim enough. Once afloat, the captain's word was law. He had complete and absolute power over his subjects and could order them flogged or punished in various ways. And his vast powers were delegated to his officers. A twelve-year-old midshipman could strike a seaman old enough to be his grandfather. Petty officers made free use of the cane and the knotted rope's end (called a "colt," or a "starter"), and a first lieutenant could, subject to the captain's approval, see to it that a man was flogged with the dreaded cat-o'-nine-tails every day in the week, if it pleased him.

The seaman, the man before the mast, had no enforceable rights. Nor, to compensate for the rigid discipline, did he have either comfortable quarters, good food, adequate pay, or even decent clothing. On the contrary, living conditions aboard ship were usually miserable. Scores or hundreds of men were jammed together, in damp, dirty quarters so crowded that there was scarcely room to swing a hammock. Health precautions were as lacking as hygiene. The ship's surgeon, if she had one, was too often a drunken good-for-nothing, who could not have made a living ashore. The food was usually almost uneatable—moldy ship's biscuit, hard as rocks and alive with weevils; rancid salt pork (but who was to know what beast the blackened, shiny, evil-smelling hunk of meat fished out of the brine tub really came from?); dried peas like little brown bullets, and water so bad that it made the dirtiest farm pond look like a mountain spring.

The skimpy pay was often in arrears, and when it arrived at the end of the voyage, the luckless sailor often found that the cheap clothing doled out to him from the ship's slop chest had cost him so much that he had little left. Small wonder that the brightest part of the day for most seamen was the issuing of the daily rum ration; or that sailors were notorious for finding, and drinking, any liquor not kept securely under lock and key.

Yet these men—cooped up for months on end in a sort of floating prison, and in constant dread of punishment, deserved or not—would perform their duties in the dirtiest weather. Turning out from their sodden hammocks in the dripping 'tween decks at all hours of the night to man sheets and braces, or edging out on an ice-covered foot rope 150 feet above a black, roaring, foam-streaked ocean, while the swaying yards all but dipped their ends in the sea, was part of their job.

It would certainly be untrue to say that they did it uncomplainingly. Sailors are noted grumblers, and no man can be routed out of even the semiwarmth of a damp blanket to pull and haul for hours waist deep in icy water without feeling a little bitter. But they did it, just as they fought their guns, cheering each shot, with a few extra cheers for captain and Congress, or King and country.

Life aboard a privateer was a little easier. Living conditions were just as bad (they remained as bad for the common seaman until toward the end of the nineteenth century), but discipline was not as rigid, and men usually signed on for only one voyage, after which they could count on a spell in some port. Also, there was always the chance of prize money if they made a good cruise. Navy crews received prize money, too, although not on such a lavish scale. Nor was there the same opportunity. A navy seaman was more likely to receive hard knocks than gold pieces. It was his ship's primary duty to find and fight enemy warships, not snap up fat merchantmen.

But there were lighter sides to life afloat. Despite the hardships, the seamen of the period seem on the whole to have been a jolly crowd, quick to forget the dangers and privations of sea duty, and to look forward instead to a frolic ashore or a fight. Nor were all captains monsters who delighted in hounding their crews with unnecessarily harsh discipline and too frequent use of the "cat." There were many who had a genuine interest in the welfare of the men under their command. Discipline had to be asserted and maintained (and a ship's officer then had to deal with some very tough characters indeed), but beyond that, some did their best to make life at least bearable for those under them. The cleverest commanders, and usually the most successful, were those who realized that most men will do more for a just and humane leader than for one who ruled with the lash alone.

Ships' officers varied as much as their men. Some were accomplished seamen and navigators; some were incompetents who owed their promotions to influence (and this was as true in the American service as in the British). Some were brutal, some stupid, some

Lieutenant, Royal Navy
White facings and cuffs.

Captain, Royal Navy
(Three years' seniority— 12 buttons on lapels in threes. Under three years' —12 buttons by twos.) Facings, cuffs, and collar, blue. Waistcoat, breeches, and stockings, white.

both; while others appear as kindly souls. But even the kindliest captain was, by reason of his authority, something of a despot. He dwelled aboard in solitary splendor, even though his cabin might be but little bigger than the average hall closet. He lived alone, ate alone, walked his quarterdeck alone, and did his planning alone. His was the ultimate responsibility for any blunders on the part of his subordinates. It was a lonely life, and it was only natural that it should give some men a sense of power which, in an age more brutal than ours, they took out in abuse and ill treatment of their men.

Next in the chain of command were the lieutenants. A ship of the line might carry as many as eight; smaller vessels, one or more.

Master and Midshipman, Royal Navy. Master's coat same as Captain's, but buttons evenly spaced. Midshipman has white tabs on collar and white cuffs.

The senior, or first lieutenant, was responsible to the captain for the running of the ship. He did most, or all, the executive work (some captains spent nine-tenths of their time at sea in their cabins). The second lieutenant was generally in charge of the ship's gunnery, while the others, if any, shared the watch-keeping duties.

Midshipmen can best be described as officer-cadets, who joined the navy at a very early age, sometimes ten or twelve. It was from their ranks that most of the officers of the Royal Navy came. This did not, of course, apply to the young Continental Navy, whose officers came mostly from the merchant marine (although Nicholas Biddle had once been a midshipman in the Royal Navy). Midshipmen were employed in minor posts of command, according to their age and ex-

perience. The youngsters were also schooled in navigation and seamanship. After a few years at sea they were ready to be examined (at nineteen years of age in the Royal Navy) for their fitness for the post of lieutenant. This did not mean that they immediately assumed this rank. Promotion, especially in time of peace, could be painfully slow, particularly if no influence could be brought to bear in their behalf. Some hopefuls, with more brawn than brain, might flunk their examination year after year, and midshipmen of thirty or more were not uncommon.

Besides the captain and lieutenants there were subordinates—men who usually held their rank by warrant rather than by commission. Highest ranking of these was the sailing master. All commissioned officers had to know some navigation, but the master was

British Seaman

There was no regulation uniform. Loose-fitting trousers, about knee length, were common, and over these was often worn a canvas petticoat. Shirts, jerseys, waistcoats, and jackets were of various patterns.

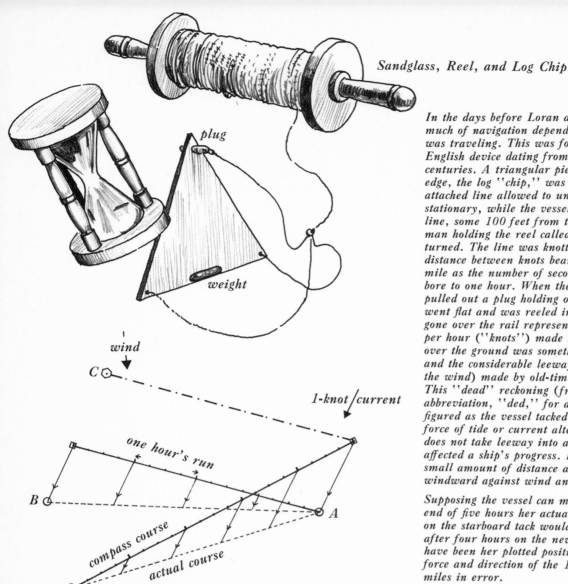

Sandglass, Reel, and Log Chip

In the days before Loran and radio direction finders, much of navigation depended on knowing how fast a vessel was traveling. This was found by the log and line, an English device dating from the late 15th or early 16th centuries. A triangular piece of wood, weighted on one edge, the log "chip," was dropped over the stern and the attached line allowed to unreel, the chip remaining stationary, while the vessel moved ahead. When a mark on line, some 100 feet from the chip, flew over the rail, the man holding the reel called "Mark," and the glass was turned. The line was knotted at regular intervals, the distance between knots bearing the same relation to a nautical mile as the number of seconds it took the sand to run out bore to one hour. When the sand ran out, a jerk of the line pulled out a plug holding one leg of the bridle, and the chip went flat and was reeled in. The number of knots which had gone over the rail represented the number of nautical miles per hour ("knots") made through the water. Distance made over the ground was something else. The action of currents, and the considerable leeway (sideward motion imparted by the wind) made by old-time vessels, had to be reckoned. This "dead" reckoning (from an old misspelling of the abbreviation, "ded," for deduced,) had constantly to be figured as the vessel tacked, the wind changed, and/or the force of tide or current altered. The diagram at left (which does not take leeway into account) shows how these factors affected a ship's progress. It also shows the heartbreakingly small amount of distance actually gained when beating to windward against wind and tide.

Supposing the vessel can make four knots on each leg, at the end of five hours her actual position when she went about on the starboard tack would be at A. Her actual position after four hours on the new tack would be at B. C would have been her plotted position without reckoning in the force and direction of the 1-knot current—or some nine miles in error.

responsible, under the captain, for the safe conduct of the ship from port to port. He sailed the ship, ordered the trimming of the sails, and took her into battle. In foreign waters he did such survey work as was practical, carefully noting his findings on the charts. He was also expected to teach the midshipmen the business of ship handling and navigation. Among numerous other duties connected with the running of the ship, he supervised the writing up of the ship's log. Aiding him were one or more master's mates.

Then there was the surgeon, who had charge of the ship's hygiene, of doctoring the sick (of which there were often all too many), and of the bloody business of tending the wounded in action. In battle his place was

in the cockpit. If it boasted a table, this was where he operated. If not, the midshipmen's chests were used. The low, cramped room was lit by candles. A small stove was sometimes lighted, for warming oils and the saws and knives used for cutting and amputating (not for sterilization—no one had realized the necessity for this in 1776, nor would for nearly a century—but because a warm saw caused less agony than a cold one). There were also a couple of tubs of water for washing wounds, instruments, compresses and bandages, and the surgeon's hands. Another, empty, awaited its load of amputated limbs.

The wounded were brought down by their shipmates and laid in rows in and near the cockpit, on the deck. Aiding the surgeon and his assistants (if the ship was large enough for him to rate any) were such noncombatants as the purser, chaplain, the stewards, and the captain's clerk. Surgery was without anesthetic, other than a stiff tot of rum, and infections from dirty instruments, sponges, and bandages killed more men than the enemy's shot.

Scurvy, caused by lack of fresh fruit and vegetables, always threatened a ship's crew on a long voyage, and one of the surgeon's duties was to see that a small amount of fruit juice, usually lime, was handed out to those suspected of the disease.

Not all vessels carried a surgeon (small ones seldom did), but few went to sea without a boatswain. Usually an old sailor who knew his business from A to Z, the boatswain was to a ship what a top sergeant is to a company. He had charge of sails, rigging, anchors, cables, boats, and everything else pertaining to the working of the ship. His assistants, the boatswain's mates, were picked from the best seamen aboard. Among other things, the boatswain and his mates saw to it, with cane and ropes' ends, that commands were properly obeyed. The mates also had the unpleasant duty of flogging offenders.

The purser was the warrant officer in charge of the ship's provisions. It was his duty to see that the vessel sailed with her full quota of food, spirits, water, candles, coal (for the galley fires), etc. He also had charge of the "slops," the supply of sailors' clothes and bedding issued by the authorities. Men who came aboard in rags, as many did, were able to purchase outfits, the money being deducted from their pay. There were many opportunities for graft, and while there were honest pursers, they seem to have been scarce.

Just as the boatswain had charge of the working gear of the ship, the gunner was responsible for her armament. He and his mates saw to it that the guns were properly secured at their respective ports, with all the tackle and tools—handspikes, rammers, sponges,

etc.—needed to work them. The gunner had charge of the magazines, the manufacture of the cartridges, and the care of the shot. He also instructed the gun captains and their crews.

In the days of the all-wooden ship the post of ship's carpenter was a most important one. He had to be a competent craftsman who could do almost anything, from building a ship's boat to shaping a new mast. He was in charge of all repairs and kept the captain informed of the state of the ship's hull, masts, yards, and decks. He also sounded the ship's well at regular intervals, to see how fast she was making water (all ships leak to some degree), and saw to it that the pumps were clear and in good working order. In action he and his mates plugged the shot holes and made such temporary repairs as they could.

It was the carpenter's job to keep the ship afloat, and the sailmaker's to keep her moving. He repaired damaged canvas and made new sails from the spare canvas carried aboard. On naval vessels he was appointed by warrant. So was the ship's cook who, in the Royal Navy, was often a one-legged pensioner from the naval hospital at Greenwich. His position did not require him to have any knowledge of the art of cooking. Boiling water for pea soup and for cooking salt "junk," as the beef, pork, horse, or what-have-you was

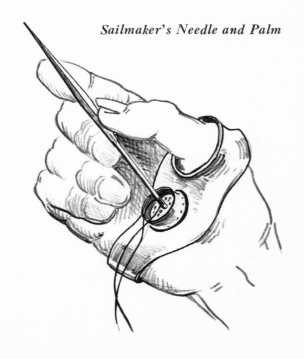

Sailmaker's Needle and Palm

called, and keeping his pots and galley reasonably clean was about the extent of his duties.

Policing the ship was the job of the master-at-arms and his assistants. He ferreted out all wrong-doers, saw to it that there was no illicit drinking, gambling, smoking (outside of the galley), or fighting, and kept a sharp look-out for all unauthorized lights below decks— an important point in a wooden ship. As his labors often resulted in one or more of his shipmates being triced up to a grating and flogged, he was usually the most hated man aboard, and masters-at-arms sometimes disappeared over the side in mysterious circumstances.

Besides these holders of office by warrant, there were numerous petty officers— quartermasters, master's mates, boatswain's mates, quarter gunners (in charge of sections of guns), etc. Their pay and privileges varied with the size of the vessel in which they served. Like noncommissioned officers in the army, they could be reduced to the ranks (disrated is the naval term) at the discretion of a superior officer. And, like the army's N.C.O.'s, it was mainly upon their efficiency and loyalty that the ship's officers relied for the smooth

functioning of the vessel as a fighting unit.

The ship's company was divided into groups, each one selected according to ability. The youngest and most active of the experienced seamen (able seamen) were assigned as "topmen." Their duty, the most dangerous and exacting aboard ship, was to work the three masts above the lower yards. They were the ones who had to race aloft and lay out on the yards to reef, furl, or loose the canvas. The navy demanded that this be done at top speed; some captains flogged the last man up or down. For practice, the upper masts and yards were often unshipped, sent down to the deck, sent up again, rerigged and sail set. This difficult work was done against a stopwatch, one ship against another, and it was an ill day for the topmen who lagged behind. Stoppage of their precious rum ration and a drubbing with cane or colt was the least they could expect. Good topmen were scarce, and much sought after when a ship's company was being recruited.

The topmen were grouped in divisions, one for each mast, and the best of division had the title of captain of the top, whether fore, main, or mizzen.

The more elderly of the able seamen were stationed on the forecastle, to work about the anchors, foreyard, and bowsprit. These anchor-men, or forecastle men, were some of the finest, most experienced in the ship. The afterguard, composed of ordinary seamen, took care of the afterbraces, mainsail, lower staysails, and the spanker. In action they manned some of the guns on the quarterdeck, or were stationed as sail trimmers.

The largest division was made up of the "waisters," recruited from the poorest seamen and the newly joined landsmen. They hauled on the sheets, kept the decks clean, and did all the deck jobs beneath the dignity of real sailormen. In action they provided the gun crews for the lower decks.

These divisions were split into two "watches", starboard and larboard (known today as port). These watches were usually for

Catting and Fishing the Anchor

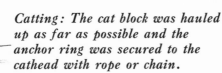

A. *Cathead*   C. *Cat block*

B. *Catfall*   D. *Cat hook*

Catting: The cat block was hauled up as far as possible and the anchor ring was secured to the cathead with rope or chain.

Fishing: A tackle (the fish tackle)—one end of which was secured aloft to a yardarm or foretop—was hooked to the arm of the anchor, which was raised and secured, often to the channel.

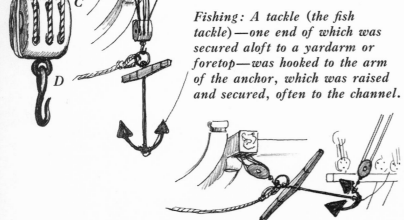

periods (also called watches) of four hours each. They were named as follows—

12 P.M. - 4 A.M.	Midwatch
4 A.M. - 8 A.M.	Morning watch
8 A.M. - 12 M.	Forenoon watch
12 M. - 4 P.M.	Afternoon watch
4 P.M. - 8 P.M.	Dog watch
8 P.M. - 12 P.M.	First watch

In order that the same group should not have the same hours of duty, day after day, the dog watch was usually divided into two parts, the first and second dog watch. (Dog watch is a corruption of "docked," or shortened, watch.)

Four hours on and four hours off—the "off" taken up partly by the ship's routine work—was a considerable hardship. "All hands up hammocks" was piped by the boatswain's mates about 7:30 A.M., and from then until 8 P.M. those off watch got little chance for an extra snooze. This meant that the men had less than four hours' sleep one night and some seven and a half the next.

"All hands on deck" might be called at any time during the night, sometimes timed so that a watch, wet and weary, might be called from their hammocks ten minutes after climbing into them—to spend their remaining sleep period pulling and hauling on a gale-swept deck, until it was time for "up hammocks" and a new day.

Besides the starboard and larboard watches there were the "idlers," those whose duties kept them busy during the working day: clerks, carpenters, cooks, sailmakers, etc. These hands—along with the captain, first lieutenant, surgeon, purser, boatswain, gunner, and other "technicians"—stood no watches, and had all night in, although the cry "all hands" would bring them tumbling up, too.

The day's work aboard a man-of-war began just before eight bells in the midwatch, or 4 A.M. The watch, larboard or starboard, whichever was below, were roused by the shrilling of the boatswain's pipes and the crack of starters on slow-moving backs, while the men of the midwatch went below to their hammocks. The idlers were roused up, too. The cook and his helpers lit the galley fires and began preparing breakfast, which usually consisted, in British ships, of poor-quality oatmeal boiled in the thick, greenish ship's water.

The watch on deck began the daily task of holystoning the decks. After pumps had been manned and hoses rigged, the decks were wet down and sprinkled with sand. Then rows of men, on their knees, scrubbed the planks with blocks of stone (called holystones because of their resemblance to Bibles), bringing them to gleaming whiteness. Broom and bucket men came next, to remove the sand, followed by the swabbers. By 7 A.M., when the first lieutenant usually made his appearance, the decks were spotless, ropes neatly coiled, and the bright work polished.

The call "all hands up hammocks" brought out the watch below. Hammocks were unslung and with the blankets were rolled and lashed tightly and stowed in the hammock nettings. These nettings, supported by iron posts, ran along the ship's side, on top of the bulwarks. This arrangement served two purposes; it provided stowage space for the crews'

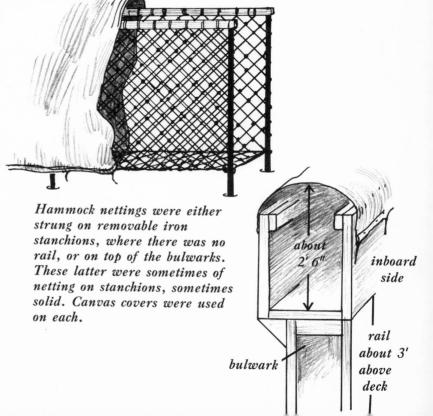

Hammock nettings were either strung on removable iron stanchions, where there was no rail, or on top of the bulwarks. These latter were sometimes of netting on stanchions, sometimes solid. Canvas covers were used on each.

about 2' 6"

inboard side

bulwark

rail about 3' above deck

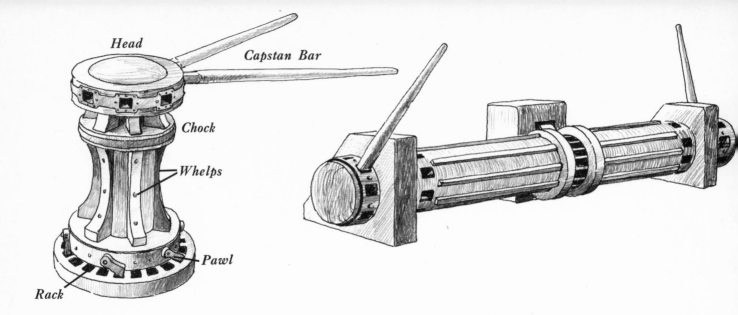

Head

Capstan Bar

Chock

Whelps

Pawl

Rack

While the windlass (right) was often found in small vessels, the capstan was standard equipment for larger ships and men of war. On large vessels there were usually two, and often one or both were double capstans, one on one deck and the other directly below, built around the same spindle, so that twice as much manpower could be used. Square, tapered socket holes were provided for the capstan bars, which might be some six feet long for a small capstan, longer for larger ones. Fifty seamen, with the ship's fiddler on top of the capstan head—and a little encouragement from the boatswain's mates' starters—could usually heave up the heaviest anchor. When this failed, the anchor cable was hove in short ("up and down"), some sail put on, and the hook broken out of the ground.

bedding (an important item where space was at a premium) and gave extra protection against enemy musketry.

At 8 A.M. the hands were piped to breakfast, after which the watch below brought up the seabags and chests in which the sailors kept their spare clothes, personal gear, etc. Then the lower decks were holystoned. Those off watch could sometimes catch a little sleep curled up in some corner on deck, mend

clothes, or amuse themselves as they pleased. More often they would be drilled at the guns, or in the use of cutlass or musket.

Dinner was at noon, and at 12:30 the rum ration was served out. At 1:30 the watch on deck was called to duty and the day's routine proceeded. Supper was at 4 P.M. Afterwards the drums beat "to quarters" and all hands went to their battle stations. The guns were cast loose, pumps rigged, and the

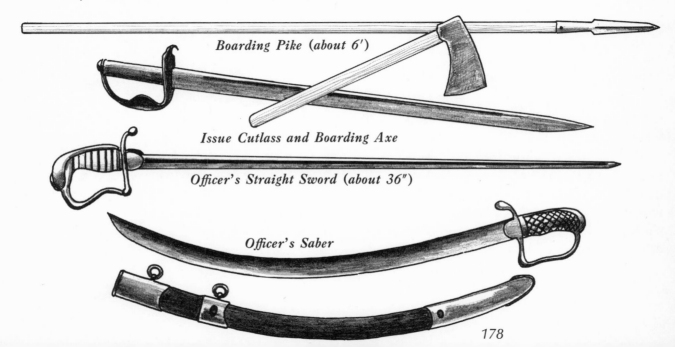

Boarding Pike (about 6')

Issue Cutlass and Boarding Axe

Officer's Straight Sword (about 36")

Officer's Saber

178

ship prepared for action. After an inspection the guns were secured, and hammocks were taken down from the nettings and slung. At 8 P.M. the first night watch was set, all unnecessary lights were extinguished, the idlers and the watch below took to their hammocks, and the ship settled down for the night.

The monotony of the daily routine was broken when a strange sail was sighted. If private signals showed her to be a friend, a boat might be lowered and news and messages exchanged. But if the stranger appeared to be an enemy, the marine drummers beat "to

extinguished, as a precaution against fire.

Topmen made all secure aloft, slung the lower yards in chains (as being less likely to be shot away), and readied weapons in the tops. Nettings were sometimes hung, to catch falling gear. Boarding nettings were often rigged, to prevent or delay boarders from swarming over the rails when ships were brought alongside each other. Pumps were got ready, fire buckets filled, and the decks, which might soon become slippery with blood, sprinkled with sand. Buckets of water were put beside the guns and the match tubs half filled

The Ship's Bell

Hung usually at the break of the forecastle, sometimes in a simple bracket, in large ships often in an ornate four-posted belfry, the ship's bell sounded out the time, one stroke every half-hour of a 4-hour watch.

Just as today, the first bell of the new day was at 12:30 A.M. 4:00 A.M. was 8 bells; 4:30 A.M., 1 bell. 6:30 A.M., 5 bells. 8:00 A.M., 12:00 Noon, 4:00 P.M., 8:00 P.M., and midnight—8 bells. As well as giving the time, the bell sounded a warning in thick weather.

quarters," and the ship cleared for action. Each man knew exactly what he was supposed to do (innumerable drills had seen to that) and went at it on the double.

The light bulkheads which partitioned off the various officers' quarters were unshipped and struck into the hold, as were the few bits of furniture, sea chests, etc. Even the captain's quarters were not exempt, and tarry seamen invaded the sacred precincts and stowed away his few belongings, to make way for working the pair or more of cannon included in his cabin space. The galley fires were

with water or wet sand.

At the same time the guns were being cast loose, tackles rigged, and the sponges, rammers, and handspikes made ready. The gun captains saw to it that the slow matches were lighted and checked their pouches of priming quills and their powder horns. Battle lanterns were often lit on the lower gun decks, where little daylight penetrated and where dense powder smoke filled the low, cramped spaces in choking clouds. When night actions were fought, lanterns were also hung on the upper decks. The men were taught to go about

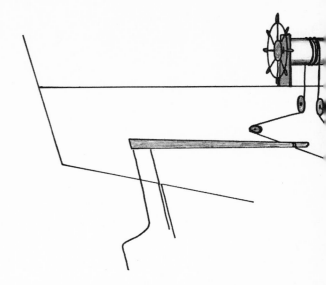

their business in silence, so that the orders of the officers and petty officers could be heard. Despite all the bustle and seeming confusion, a ship with a well-trained crew could be cleared for action in a very few minutes.

Flying the colors of neutral or enemy powers was a ruse almost as old as naval warfare itself. In the days of sail, the general similarity of ship design, the use of vessels previously captured from an enemy, and the difficulty of reading signals made practical the employment of this ancient stratagem. Frequently ships could be lured within effective gun range by such means, while at night, in answer to the hail, "What ship is that?", false names and nationalities were often given to gain a momentary advantage. A

British Marine

Coat red; facings, collar, cuffs—buff. Waistcoat and breeches white.

captain usually took good care, however, to hoist his own colors before opening fire. Failure to do so was a breach of the rules of war, and in a case involving neutrals there might be serious consequences.

A ship could usually identify itself by hoisting its private signal (making its number), and the lack of such identification was often enough to warrant a warning shot, if not a broadside. But signals, even national ensigns, were sometimes hard to make out, and by the time a ship had drawn close enough for positive recognition, action, perhaps at a disadvantage, might have become inevitable.

Last, but certainly not least, in the roster of the ship's company were the marines. The use of soldiers aboard ship dates back to ancient times. Then the division between those who worked the ship and those who did the actual fighting was well defined. But with the coming of the gun—and of the seaman-cannoneer—the distinction became less marked. However, small contingents of troops were often embarked for special purposes. The advantages of having such troops familiar with ships and small boats were obvious, and at the end of the seventeenth century a regiment of sea-soldiers was formed in England. These marines became a regular part of each ship's complement—often about one marine to every four sailors and idlers.

The marine detachments of 200 years ago were as much an armed guard as a fighting force. The presence aboard of a body of strictly

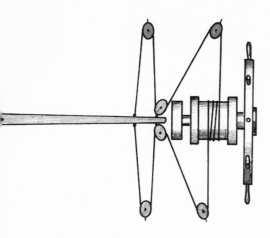

Small vessels could be steered by a tiller, but in larger ships the tiller became unmanageable in heavy weather, even when held by two men. So by means of various block and tackle combinations the tiller was worked by a wheel, sometimes a double one so that, if necessary, four helmsmen could be used.

disciplined men, with their own officers, served as a check to the seamen. With crews composed of tough characters, liberally mixed with hardened criminals and often treated with calculated brutality, there was an ever present threat of mutiny. The smartly uniformed marine sentry on guard outside the captain's cabin was not there just to make a show. The traditional rivalry between sailor and marine undoubtedly dates from those days, and this rivalry was carefully promoted by those in command so as to permit as little chance of collusion as possible.

In addition to their duties of helping to police the ship and furnishing guards and sentries, the marines also helped the after-guard on deck, tailing onto sheets and braces and hauling along with the crew. In action they furnished men for the fighting tops, while detachments drawn up on poop and quarter-deck helped sweep the decks and tops of the enemy.

In operations ashore their training as soldiers and their superior discipline were invaluable. Seamen were also used in landing operations, but their duties were likely to be confined to the landing of guns and supplies and the throwing up and manning of batteries

for siege operations. Where opposition from regular forces was expected, it was usually the marines who led the way.

The marines of the Continental Navy, ancestors of the United States Marine Corps of today, were brought into being by a resolution of the Continental Congress, dated November 10, 1775.

Resolved, that two Battalions of marines be raised consisting of one Colonel two lieutenant Colonels, two Majors & Officers as usual in other regiments, that they consist of an equal number of privates with other battalions; that particular care be taken that no person be appointed to office or enlisted into said Battalions, but such as are good seamen, or so acquainted with maritime affairs as to be able to serve

American Marine
Coat green; facings and cuffs, red.

American Uniforms. From left to right: officer of marines, captain in the Continental Navy (coat and breeches blue; facings, cuffs, and waistcoat—red), and seamen.

with advantage by sea, when required. That they be enlisted and commissioned for and during the present war between Great Britain and the colonies, unless dismissed by order of Congress. That they be distinguished by the names of the first & second battalions of American Marines, and that they be considered as part of the number, which the continental Army before Boston is ordered to consist of.

It is perhaps appropriate that such a hard-fisted, hard-drinking corps should have had a tavern as its birthplace. The first marine officer, Captain Samuel Nicholas, whose commission was dated November 28, 1775, began recruiting for the new corps at the Tun Tavern on the Philadelphia waterfront.

Of the actual organization, training,

and equipment of these first marines we know practically nothing. We do know that marines took part in Hopkins's expedition to the Bahamas in March of 1776. Some 220, under Captain Nicholas, made the corps' first landing on foreign soil on the island of New Providence. Marines were present in almost all actions involving Continental vessels throughout the war, and in many land operations as well.

There was little uniformity about the dress of seamen until the beginning of the nineteenth century. The typical sailor of the Revolution wore loose-fitting trousers, wide bottomed and quite short, a shirt or vest and over this perhaps a short coat or waistcoat; a handkerchief was often worn around the neck. Headgear came in a number of shapes and sizes: the common round felt hat, cocked up or not; stocking caps; handkerchiefs; flat,

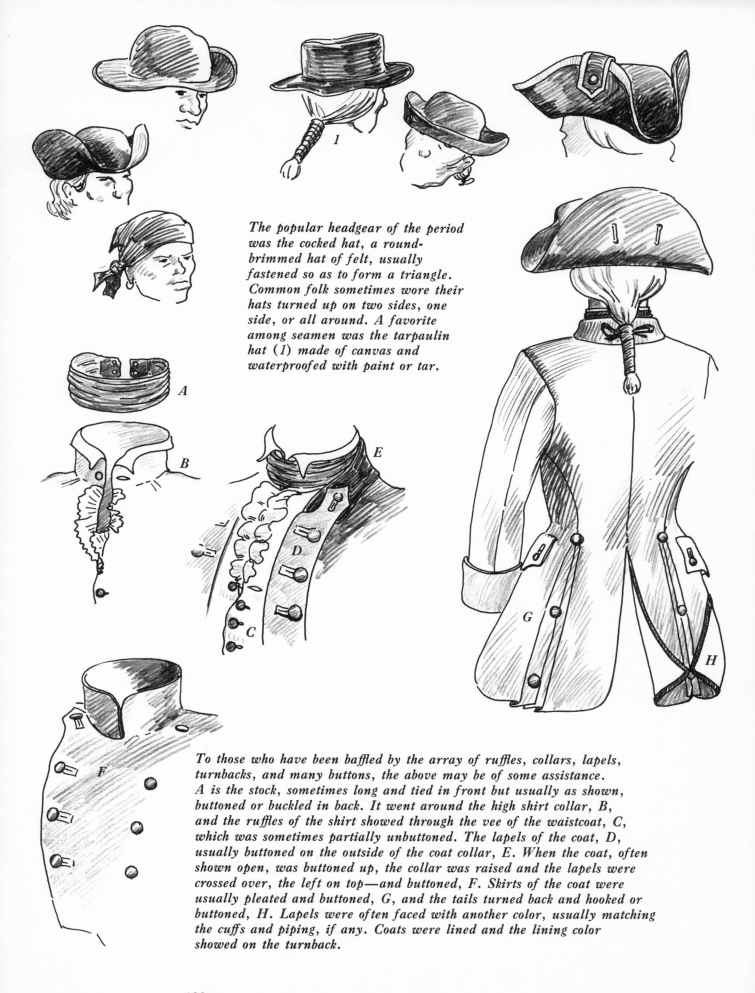

The popular headgear of the period was the cocked hat, a round-brimmed hat of felt, usually fastened so as to form a triangle. Common folk sometimes wore their hats turned up on two sides, one side, or all around. A favorite among seamen was the tarpaulin hat (1) made of canvas and waterproofed with paint or tar.

To those who have been baffled by the array of ruffles, collars, lapels, turnbacks, and many buttons, the above may be of some assistance. A is the stock, sometimes long and tied in front but usually as shown, buttoned or buckled in back. It went around the high shirt collar, B, and the ruffles of the shirt showed through the vee of the waistcoat, C, which was sometimes partially unbuttoned. The lapels of the coat, D, usually buttoned on the outside of the coat collar, E. When the coat, often shown open, was buttoned up, the collar was raised and the lapels were crossed over, the left on top—and buttoned, F. Skirts of the coat were usually pleated and buttoned, G, and the tails turned back and hooked or buttoned, H. Lapels were often faced with another color, usually matching the cuffs and piping, if any. Coats were lined and the lining color showed on the turnback.

narrow-brimmed round hats of straw or canvas, often painted or tarred.

Official uniforms for officers had been adopted in the Royal Navy only as late as 1748. The coats were blue with white lapels, with gold buttons, and considerable gold lace (the more rank the more gold). White knee breeches and stockings, a white waistcoat, a tricorn hat, and black shoes with large silver or pewter buckles completed the outfit.

The Marine Committee of the Continental Congress issued the first regulations for uniforms for the officers of the Continental Navy in September, 1776. These called for a blue coat with red lapels and cuffs and yellow metal buttons, a red waistcoat, blue breeches, white stockings, and the usual tricorn hat. The majority of senior naval officers did not approve of this uniform, and in March,

1777, proposed one with a blue coat lined with white, with gold lace and gold buttons, and waistcoat, breeches, and stockings in white. Among others, John Paul Jones wore this uniform, although it was never officially recognized.

Officially at least, the marines of the Continental Navy were attired in green uniforms with red facings, knee breeches, and small-brimmed felt hats, turned up on the left side with a big cockade. It is doubtful if many men were ever issued these snappy uniforms, and the "leatherneck" of those days probably went to sea in whatever clothes he enlisted in. His counterpart in the British service wore a red coat with buff facings, collar, and cuffs; white waistcoat and breeches; black gaiters to below the knee, and the usual tricorn hat.

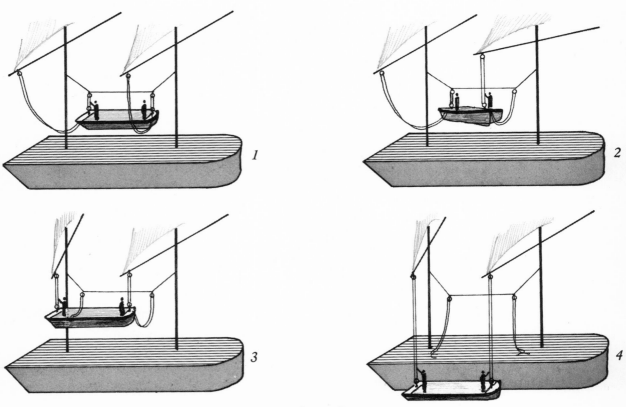

Hoisting Out a Boat

While a few vessels carried a whale boat at the stern, side davits were almost unknown, and the larger boats, usually carried amidships, were hoisted out with tackles on stays and yardarms, as on the vessel above. 1. Boat raised on stay tackles, yard tackles hooked on.
2. Foreyard swung back, yard tackle takes strain, forward stay tackle slacked off.
3. Afteryard tackle takes strain, afterstay tackle slacked off, boat is now outboard.
4. Stay tackles cast off, boat is lowered alongside.

The Spoyle of Mariners

Chapter 20

Medical and surgical science at the time of the American Revolution was in a peculiar state. There was considerable knowledge of the structure of the human body, less of the way in which it functioned, and very little of correction and cure. Surgeons might be clever with scalpel and saw (a skilled man could amputate an arm at the shoulder in less than forty seconds), but the complete lack of any comprehension of asepsis doomed many who went under the surgeon's knife to death by infection.

Gangrene often set in following the simplest operations, and wounded men died who today would have been returned to duty in a few weeks. Scalpels might be razor-sharp, but too often they were contaminated as well. Instruments, sponges, bandages—a quick dip in a water bucket already stained deep red and they were ready for the next victim.

There were no anesthetics as we know them. Laudanum and opium were used, when they could be had. More often the sufferers were given a stiff tot of rum and a gag or a bullet to bite on, and then forcibly held down by attendants while the surgeon went about his gory business. Many died from shock, and it usually took a strong and healthy man to

survive such rough and ready treatment.

Medical men could sometimes diagnose correctly; they could seldom cure. Ignorance as to the cause of many diseases, lack of proper drugs, and reliance on time-worn remedies—some of which were as dangerous as the ills they were supposed to combat—spelled death for many. Excessive blood-letting (the lancet was generally looked upon as a cure-all for practically everything) and massive doses of purgatives were the average doctor's stock in trade.

Far more dangerous to the military patient was the fact that the surgeon usually employed ashore or afloat was far from being a shining example of his profession. Too often he was a drunken incompetent, unable to make a decent living in civilian life even when judged by the easy standards of those days. An American ship's surgeon of the war years—always provided the vessel was large enough to warrant one—was likely to be a mere apprentice whose knowledge of medicine came from helping mix his master's drugs. His surgery he might have got from a book. There were exceptions, but as a general rule the level of ability of the surgeon of the average small government vessel or privateer must have been low indeed.

The overall effect on naval warfare of the various diseases which were rampant in the navies of the world before 1800 is almost impossible to assess. It is known that it was very great, and must have been a considerable, if indefinable, factor in the planning of any naval operation. No admiral could count on the continued health of the crews under his command on a cruise of even moderate duration. A prolonged expedition, especially if it were in tropical waters, usually meant sickness, if not death, for a considerable percentage of the manpower of the fleet. That such losses were accepted as inevitable did not make their occurrence any less a misfortune. And there was always the chance that the outbreak in a squadron of a serious epidemic might change misfortune into complete disaster.

It is perhaps hard to imagine a period when a diet deficiency could alter the course of a naval campaign or shatter a fleet without even a gun being fired. Yet scurvy, which is caused by the lack of Vitamin C, did just that, and not once but many times. Tens of thousands of seamen died; hundreds of ships, their crews too feeble to carry out their duties, were lost. Not for nothing was scurvy called "the Scourge of the Sea and the Spoyle of Mariners." Yet the remedy had been discovered, lost, found, and lost again scores of years before. More astounding, the ignorance of the true causes of scurvy persisted as late as the beginning of the twentieth century, and in 1900 a paper read before the Royal Society stated that neither lime juice nor fresh vegetables could prevent or cure the disease because it was caused by tainted food! It was not until the publishing of Sir Frederick Gowland Hopkins's work on vitamins in 1912 that a full understanding of the effects of diseases due to dietary deficiencies became possible. The antiscorbutic compound, ascorbic acid, was finally isolated in 1932.

The symptoms of scurvy are varied, but usually begin with failing strength and mental depression. Sallow complexion, swollen legs, aching muscles, tender swollen gums, and bad breath follow and in a matter of weeks the teeth may fall out. Skin eruptions and puffy yellow flesh are common. In the final stages the victim is extremely weak, with a tendency to diarrhea and kidney or pulmonary trouble. In many cases those who escape death from scurvy are so weakened that they fall easy victims to other diseases. However, the disease is easily treated by the addition of fresh vegetables or fruit to the diet, and usually by this means complete cures are effected.

The lowly potato, introduced into Europe from the Americas, saved many lives. Onions were also a preventative, but green vegetables and fruit, which was of little value unless served in quantity, did not keep aboard ship, while fresh meat, with the exception of the small amount of livestock which could be housed aboard, was usually unobtainable. Lemon juice could be preserved, and was only needed in comparatively small amounts, which made it very suitable for use aboard ship. Unfortunately, it was believed that limes were as efficacious in the prevention and cure of the disease as lemons. Actually, the West Indian lime has only about one-fourth of the antiscorbutic value of the lemon, and when lime juice was substituted for that of the lemon there was a recurrence of the disease in some ships. The advent of steam (which meant shorter voyages), the discovery of the art of canning and preserving meats and vegetables, and finally, refrigeration, has eliminated the disease from shipboard except in the most extraordinary circumstances.

Scurvy was known to the ancients but it was not a menace to the mariners of their world. Their cruises were short; in many cases, after a day's run, ships were beached for the night. But when in the late fifteenth and sixteenth centuries men began the long voyages to the Indies and the Americas, scurvy became a major problem. Vasco da Gama, on his exploration round the Cape of Good Hope,

1497-1498, lost 100 out of 160 men. (Those who escaped, it is said, owed their lives to eating fresh meat—the ship's rats, which sold for half a gold ducat apiece!) Magellan fell victim to native spears and swords, but the majority of his men died of scurvy. Only eighteen weakened survivors, out of the crews of five ships, reached home in the little *Vittoria*.

Jacques Cartier reached Canada in 1534, with 100 out of 106 of his men down with scurvy. Kindly Indians cured them with a tea of sassafras leaves and bark. Sir Richard Hawkins said in 1593 that in his 20 years at sea 10,000 English sailors had died of the disease. It has been estimated that scurvy killed 1,000,000 British seamen alone. Yet in 1593 one Salomon Albertus wrote that oranges cured scurvy, and in 1600, when Sir James Lancaster sailed to the East, he took "certain bottles of the juice of lemons." The voyage was singularly healthy, but no concrete conclusion seems to have been drawn, although Hawkins extolled "the virtue of this fruit, to be certain remedy for this infirmity."

John Woodall in his *The Surgeon's Mate*, published in 1617, perhaps the first book on naval medicine, stated that lemon juice "is a precious medicine and well tried." Yet well over 100 years later, during Commodore George Anson's voyage around the world (1740-1744), 1,051 out of 1,955 men of his seven ships died, mostly from scurvy. Many cures were suggested, including burying victims up to the neck in sand or earth. But it was not until 1747 that James Lind, a surgeon in the Royal Navy, gave what should have been incontrovertible proof that lemon juice was the best remedy for the dread disease. While serving aboard H.M.S. *Salisbury* he made a controlled experiment, using as guinea pigs twelve men suffering from scurvy, as nearly alike in physical condition as possible and with nearly the same symptoms. Dividing the twelve into six groups, he gave each man of one group a quart of cider a day; a second group, twenty-five drops of elixir of dilute sulphuric acid three times a day (all the treatments were in common use) and a mouthwash of the same; a third group, two teaspoonsful of vinegar three times a day, and diluted vinegar as a mouthwash; a fourth group, a quart of seawater apiece every day; a fifth group, a pill containing garlic, mustard seed, radish, balsam of Peru, and gum myrrh; and a sixth group, a lemon and two oranges daily. In six days the last group were cured, one man returning to duty while the other nursed the remaining ten.

One would have thought that this test should have convinced the Admiralty, but, while some individual admirals and captains recognized the value of Lind's experiment and acted on it, others chose to ignore it, with unfortunate results. In 1780 a British fleet, after a ten-week cruise in the Channel, landed 2,400 scurvy cases at Portsmouth. Out of the 12,000 men of the British forces in the West Indies, one in seven died of scurvy. Yet at the same time, due to the influence of Fleet Surgeon Blane, not one case of scurvy occurred on board Rodney's flagship *Formidable*, out of a crew of 900. This so impressed Rodney that he wholeheartedly supported Blane's attempts to combat the disease. Even so, it was not until 1795 that orders went out, requiring all vessels of the Royal Navy to issue lemon juice (one ounce per day per man) as a preventative. Two years later, in 1797, there were no cases of scurvy reported at the Royal Naval Hospital at Haslar, where before 1795 the wards were often crowded with victims.

The general use of an effective antiscorbutic greatly influenced the campaigns of the wars of 1793-1815. Without this preventative the blockade of the great French naval bases of Toulon and Brest, with ships at sea for months on end, would have been impossible. "Those far-distant, storm-beaten ships, upon which the Grand Army never looked" could not have remained at sea if scurvy and disease had been allowed to riddle their crews.

Scurvy was by no means the only disease which took a frightful toll of the seamen of pre-nineteenth-century days. Typhus, dysentery, smallpox, yellow fever, cholera—all contributed. Large groups of men, confined in small spaces, unwashed, ill-fed, and often suffering from cold and exposure were prone to any communicable diseases which might be brought aboard. As seamen were usually picked up wherever they could be found, sometimes from the pestilential jails, with no regard to their general health or cleanliness, it is small wonder that sickness ran through ships like wildfire.

Scurvy, once it was recognized, was, as we have seen, easily curable and as easily prevented. But the earliest voyagers to the West Indies encountered a mysterious killer whose identity remained unknown, though guessed at, until 1900. The skins of the victims of this disease turned an intense yellow, and they vomited quantities of black fluid. And then, very often, they died. Yellow fever, vomito negro, yellow jack—under these and other names, the disease had killed hundreds of thousands, and is capable of killing hundreds of thousands more. It struck ships' crews, armies, and the inhabitants of cities with equal ferocity and with equally deadly results. And as was the case with so many diseases which plagued our ancestors, the horror of an epidemic was heightened by the fact that nobody knew what caused it, how it spread, or how, if at all, its victims could be cured.

We know today that the yellow fever virus is transmitted by the bite of the female mosquito of a number of species (not just *Aëdes aegypti,* as was thought at first) which has previously fed on the blood of a yellow fever victim. The virus (so small that it will pass through a fine porcelain filter) needs some twelve days to become established in the insect's salivary glands, and infects the mosquito permanently. Unfortunately, the victim from which the female draws blood does not have to be human. Over two dozen species of monkeys, including the common rhesus monkey, squirrels, and other small mammals are susceptible to the disease, which makes eradication difficult, if not impossible. Yellow fever exists in vast areas of tropical and subtropical Africa and South America, and during World War I cases occurred in Mesopotamia and Iraq. Recovered victims are permanently immune. Mortality varies; in an epidemic in Rio de Janeiro in 1927-28 it was 59 per cent.

In the past epidemics have occurred in many places, including Barcelona, Spain; New York City; Philadelphia; New Orleans, and Buenos Aires. The disease was always prevalent in the West Indies and has invaded the United States scores of times.

Any operations in the West Indies ran the risk of serious losses among both soldiers and sailors alike. The garrison of St. Lucia, for example, in one year lost 1,411 men out of a total of 1,500. Cuba was always a danger spot, and losses among the Spanish garrison and naval squadrons were often severe. The sporadic, though often severe, epidemics which ravaged the ports of North America were presumably due to victims being brought in by ship and bitten by the local mosquitoes, or the unwitting importation of infected mosquitoes from Caribbean ports.

The Great Fleets

Chapter 21

The naval war was not confined to American and West Indian waters. While French and British squadrons were maneuvering and occasionally meeting in inconclusive engagements off the American coast and in the West Indies, the main fleets of both powers were engaged in similar fashion nearer home. But if such actions had no direct bearing on the American war, their indirect results were very great. Warships taken or badly damaged in European waters meant less vessels available for the western Atlantic and Caribbean. A great convoy captured or driven back to port might mean the abandoning of a campaign in Virginia or the loss of a strategic West Indian island. The threat of an invasion of England, and the Spanish attempts to retake Gibraltar, tied down considerable forces whose presence might have been vital in the Chesapeake or off Martinique.

While D'Estaing was en route from the Delaware Capes to New York, the Channel Fleet, of thirty ships of the line—Admiral the Honorable Augustus Keppel—and the fleet from Brest of 29 ships—under Admiral the Comte d'Orvilliers—put to sea. On July 23, 1778, the two fleets sighted each other some 100 miles west of Ushant. The Frenchman was hampered by his instructions, of the ambiguous "don't fight unless you are sure of winning" sort, which crop up so often in naval history.

Keppel, on the other hand, sought an engagement, but until July 27 d'Orvilliers succeeded in baffling all the British Admiral's attempts to force an action. On the morning of the twenty-seventh, shifts in the wind brought the leading British ships within range. Keppel, considering that if he delayed to order a formal battle line he might lose the enemy altogether, ordered the signal for a general chase, followed by that for battle. Rather than have the enemy overtake and engage the ships in the rear of his column, the French Admiral signaled for his line to turn together, each ship going about at the same time. The hostile fleets were now approaching each other on opposite tacks, and as the irregular lines of vessels surged past each other the action began. And ended, for after one pass, in which the French, firing high, did much damage to British masts and rigging, the fleets were not again in close contact. Keppel signaled for the formation of his battle line, but owing to damage, misread signals, and the reluctance of Admiral Sir Hugh Palliser, who led the British rear division, to engage once more, efforts to form a line of battle failed. D'Orvilliers got his line about on the other tack but, although his ships were in fairly good order, declined to renew the engagement. By the time Keppel had finally formed his line it was very late in the day, and he decided to put off further action until

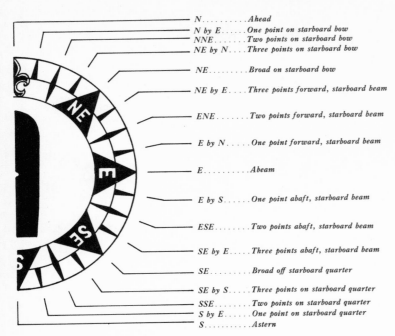

N	Ahead
N by E	One point on starboard bow
NNE	Two points on starboard bow
NE by N	Three points on starboard bow
NE	Broad on starboard bow
NE by E	Three points forward, starboard beam
ENE	Two points forward, starboard beam
E by N	One point forward, starboard beam
E	Abeam
E by S	One point abaft, starboard beam
ESE	Two points abaft, starboard beam
SE by E	Three points abaft, starboard beam
SE	Broad off starboard quarter
SE by S	Three points on starboard quarter
SSE	Two points on starboard quarter
S by E	One point on starboard quarter
S	Astern

The old mariner's compass was not marked in degrees, the 32 points, 17 of which are shown above, was accurate enough. Relative bearings of an object from a vessel were given, irrespective of the compass heading, as on the right, from bow to stern, port and starboard.

morning. During the night the French fleet made sail for home, and when dawn broke they were well on their way to Brest. Keppel in turn ordered his fleet back to Plymouth to repair damage. For a French fleet to escape without loss of a single ship, even if its casualties were the greater, did not sit well with the British public. The controversy finally came to a head when Palliser's charges brought on Keppel's court-martial. He was cleared on all counts, a victory pleasing to most naval officers and to public opinion. The London mob celebrated his acquittal with bonfires, while Palliser's house was wrecked and the Admiral nearly killed.

To those accustomed to the "Nelson touch" of twenty years later the indecisive affair off Ushant makes sorry reading. The dead hand of the fighting instructions still lay heavy on many officers. Nor was there any of the "band of brothers" concept which bound Nelson and his captains into an integrated unit. Far from it. Politics loomed large in the Services in Britain in those days. Keppel was a Whig—and one who felt so strongly about the American war that he had refused to serve against the revolted Colonies. Palliser was a Tory, and was probably not adverse to seeing Keppel in difficulty, even to the point of not cooperating fully against a life-long enemy such as the French. And those who wonder that party politics could play so large and dangerous a part in the nation's affairs at a time when there was a very real threat of invasion from across the Channel, should remember that at the time of the Revolutionary War there were many who could recall the troubled days of the '45. For it was scarcely thirty years since England had been threatened with invasion and civil war—when Charles Stuart, Bonnie Prince Charlie, had marched his Highlanders as far as Derby in the Midlands. And there were still gentlemen in England who drank secret toasts to the "King across the water."

Invasion was once more on Englishmen's minds in 1779. In June, d'Orvilliers sailed from Brest with 28 ships of the line to rendezvous with the navy of Spain. While he was at sea, Madrid, in accordance with a prearranged plan, forced a declaration of war with England. In August, after many delays, the combined fleets of 67 ships appeared off Plymouth. Fifty thousand troops were camped at Le Havre and St.-Malo, waiting the word to enter 400 transports. To oppose this armada, 35 ships of the Channel Fleet, under Admiral Sir Charles Hardy, were cruising in the vicinity. The original French intent was for a landing on the Isle of Wight and the use of Spithead as an anchorage. A sudden change of plan by the French government then called for the invasion to take place in Cornwall, near Falmouth. Here was no safe anchorage, and the Allied fleets, already hard hit by sickness and a shortage of supplies, would have had no suitable base of operations. As if to point up the French admiral's remonstrances, an easterly gale drove the Allies out of the Channel. It was then decided that the best plan would be to seek out and destroy the Channel Fleet. Hardy succeeded in evading action, and the Allies took their fever-riddled ships into Brest.

The threat of invasion was over, but England could find small cause for elation. For a month a superior enemy force had dominated the Channel. A British admiral had shown skill in evading an enemy in waters where traditionally no enemy dared show his flag. It was a humiliating reminder that sovereignty of the seas was not a God-given right but, like liberty, called for eternal vigilance—and eternal taxes.

Like most alliances the Franco-Spanish alliance suffered from divergence of interests. They were both bent on doing as much damage to Britain as they could, providing that such efforts worked to their own advantage. Basically, France found her interests to lie in the West Indies; Spain in Europe, to regain Minorca and Gibraltar.

This latter design—perhaps it were better to call it a hope—was to have considerable impact on the naval war, absorbing at different times sizable forces on both sides. Its first effects were felt in the fall of 1779, when Spain recalled her ships from Brest so that she might more effectively threaten the approaches to Gibraltar. The actual blockade, which began the moment that war was declared, was carried on by vessels cruising in the entrance to the bay and by some ships of the line and lighter vessels at Algeciras, across the bay from the fortress. The whole was supported by a strong force at Cadiz.

The blockade soon forced the garrison of the Rock to tighten their belts. By the end of the year flour was selling for more than £14 a barrel. The British Mediterranean squadron of one 64-gun ship, three frigates, and a sloop was obviously unable to effect any relief. It was equally obvious that if the Rock were to be held that relief in the form of supplies and reinforcements for the garrison must be thrown into the place as soon as possible. Admiral George Rodney had been ordered to the West Indies to command the Leeward Island station. En route he was to escort a huge convoy of transport and store-ships of all kinds to Gibraltar. The squadron

he was taking to the West Indies (a few ships of the line) had been reinforced by a large detachment from the Channel Fleet, and it was with twenty-two ships of the line and fourteen frigates and smaller craft that Rodney approached the Spanish coast.

On January 8, a Spanish squadron of twenty-two sail was sighted, chased, and taken. The prizes included seven warships, one of them a 64. A dozen of the Spanish merchantmen, laden with naval stores for Cadiz, and the 64, now with a British crew, joined the convoy for Gibraltar. This was a tidy little haul, but there was more to come. On the sixteenth, a Spanish fleet of eleven of the line and two frigates was sighted. The Spanish ships maneuvered to escape, but although superior in design to the British vessels, they were uncoppered and so were outsailed—an example of the advantages of clean bottoms over foul. Rodney made signal for "general chase," and the British ships, under all the sail they could carry, engaged as they came up. The action began just before evening and continued until 2 A.M. One Spanish 70-gun ship blew up and six other ships of the line were taken, one of them the flagship. A gale made up during the action, and two of the captured vessels afterwards drove ashore and were wrecked.

So the hungry garrison of Gibraltar was treated not only to the sight of a vast armada of British shipping, with bulging storeships and crowded transports, but also to five enemy ships of the line, flying British colors over the red and gold of Spain. It was a handsome victory, even if won with overwhelming force, and started Rodney on his rise to fame and fortune.

Rodney arrived at St. Lucia in the West Indies on March 27, 1780. About the same time Rear Admiral Comte de Guichen took over the French command in place of d'Estaing. Almost at once Rodney was engaged in a battle which, in his words, was "a glorious opportunity (perhaps never to be recovered) of terminating the naval contest in these seas."

And had the same spirit animated all his captains as fired the commanders who followed Nelson there is no doubt he might have won a decisive victory. As it was, due to inattention to, or misinterpretation of his signals by several of his captains, including that of the leading ship, the action was as indecisive as Keppel's off Ushant.

The maneuvers on both sides were characteristic of the formal unbroken battle-line technique of earlier days. Even so, had Rodney's intentions been clearly understood and acted upon, the British position would have been a strong one. The French battle line stretched in a long column for about 12 miles. Rodney, to windward—his ships at intervals of some two cables (a cable in those days was reckoned as 120 fathoms, or 720 feet)—kept his line more compact. His intention was to bear down on the enemy in line abreast, thus ultimately concentrating massed fire-power on a comparatively small section of the enemy's line. Unfortunately for Rodney, the captain of his leading ship understood Rodney's signals to mean that he was to attack the ship leading the French line, not the one actually opposite to him when the signal was made. The diagrams show what the British admiral had intended—and what actually happened.

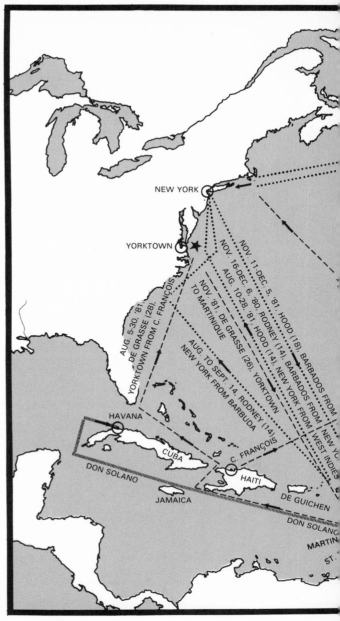

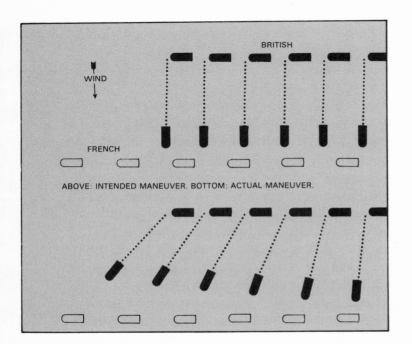

ABOVE: INTENDED MANEUVER. BOTTOM: ACTUAL MANEUVER.

The center and rear of the British line therefore engaged before the van and at closer range. *Sandwich,* 90, Rodney's flagship, pressed the fight so closely that at one point she passed through the French line. She took 80 shot in her hull and lost her foremast, while the guns on her engaged broadside fired an average of 73 rounds apiece, or a total of 3,288. Had the rest of the fleet followed her example, de Guichen would have taken a drubbing. As it was, the French bore away and the action ended. As usual, from the French practice of firing high, the British suffered more aloft

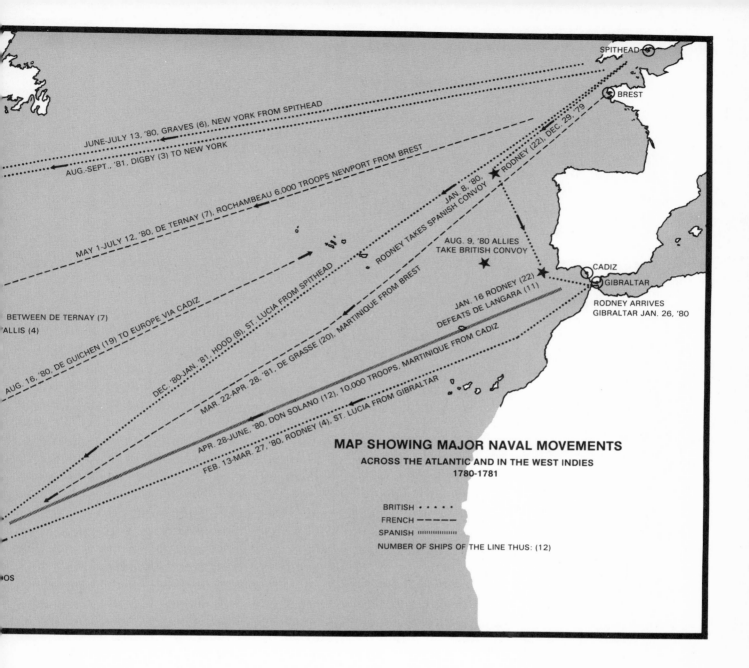

JUNE-JULY 13, '80, GRAVES (6), NEW YORK FROM SPITHEAD

AUG.-SEPT., '81, DIGBY (3) TO NEW YORK

MAY 1-JULY 12, '80, DE TERNAY (7), ROCHAMBEAU 6,000 TROOPS NEWPORT FROM BREST

SPITHEAD

BREST

RODNEY (22), DEC. 29, '79

JAN. 8, '80, RODNEY TAKES SPANISH CONVOY

AUG. 9, '80 ALLIES TAKE BRITISH CONVOY

CADIZ

GIBRALTAR

RODNEY ARRIVES GIBRALTAR JAN. 26, '80

BETWEEN DE TERNAY (7)
'ALLIS (4)

AUG. 16, '80, DE GUICHEN (19) TO EUROPE VIA CADIZ

DEC. '80-JAN. '81, HOOD (8), ST. LUCIA FROM SPITHEAD

RODNEY TAKES SPANISH CONVOY

MARTINIQUE FROM BREST

JAN. 16 RODNEY (22) DEFEATS DE LANGARA (11)

MAR. 22-APR. 28, '81, DE GRASSE (20), MARTINIQUE FROM BREST

APR. 28-JUNE, '80, DON SOLANO (12), 10,000 TROOPS, MARTINIQUE FROM CADIZ

FEB. 13-MAR. 27, '80, RODNEY (4), ST. LUCIA FROM GIBRALTAR

MAP SHOWING MAJOR NAVAL MOVEMENTS
ACROSS THE ATLANTIC AND IN THE WEST INDIES
1780-1781

BRITISH · · · · ·
FRENCH — — —
SPANISH |||||||||||||
NUMBER OF SHIPS OF THE LINE THUS: (12)

OS

while the French casualties were heavier (759 to 474 for the British).

De Guichen, who had 3,000 soldiers aboard for a descent on Barbados, returned to Guadeloupe, followed by Rodney. On the latter's sailing for St. Lucia to fill his water casks and to land his sick and wounded, the French admiral again put to sea. Rodney's patrolling frigates brought him the word, and the fleets were soon once more in contact (May 10). For the next several days there followed more maneuvering for position, with two brief engagements on the fifteenth and

nineteenth. On the twenty-second both fleets were back in port; the French at Fort Royal, the British at Barbados.

A large Spanish convoy carrying 10,000 troops, escorted by twelve ships of the line, had sailed from Cadiz on April 28 for the West Indies. Despite Rodney's efforts, the Spaniards eluded him and joined forces with de Guichen off Guadeloupe on June 9. The combined fleets and landing forces might have accomplished much, but the Spanish fleet carried with it the seeds of its own destruction. Spanish grandees in charge of His Most Catholic

Majesty's fleets could hardly be expected to concern themselves overmuch with such plebeian details as cleanliness or sanitation. The Spanish fleet was so ravaged with pestilence and scurvy that neither seamen nor soldiers were equal to any great undertaking, even if the admiral, Don José Solano, was of a mind to attempt one (which he was not). He flatly refused to engage in any combined operations with his ally, and, in fact, demanded to be accompanied to the Spanish possessions to leeward. De Guichen had orders to leave the Windwards before the hurricane season, so although it was only the beginning of July, he decided to kill two birds with one stone, and the combined fleets sailed for the eastern end of Cuba. Leaving the Spaniards there to find their way to Havana, de Guichen put into the French naval station at Cap François in Haiti.

Here were waiting appeals from Lafayette and the French Minister to the United States to sail for North America, where such a fleet as his might accomplish so much. But the French admiral declined, as being contrary to his instructions. Perhaps more important, at least to the French, was his task of escorting a fleet of 95 merchantmen, laden with coffee and sugar, back to France.

Rodney, having detailed several of his ships of the line to convoy the accumulated West Indian "trade" to England, set sail for North America, where he expected to find de Guichen. The British fleet arrived off Sandy Hook on September 14. Rodney might, had he been a younger and healthier man (he was sixty-two, and suffered greatly from gout), have destroyed a French squadron of seven ships of the line and three frigates under Commodore de Ternay which had arrived in Narragansett Bay with 6,000 troops under Rochambeau on July 12. No such attempt was made, and on November 16, Rodney sailed for the West Indies.

The arrival in July of the French at Rhode Island might have seriously threatened the British hold on New York. There Vice-Admiral Arbuthnot had only four of the line,

but the following day, July 13, a reinforcement of six ships of the line under Rear Admiral Thomas Graves arrived off Sandy Hook, thus swinging the balance of power once more in favor of the British. To the intense disappointment of the Americans, the French expeditionary force, from which so much had been hoped, was promptly blockaded in Newport.

In European waters there had been no noteworthy naval engagement since Rodney's relief of Gibraltar early in the year. However, the Allies delivered a powerful blow against British commerce on August 9, when the Franco-Spanish fleets from Cadiz captured a large British convoy some 250 miles west of Cape St. Vincent. Fifty-five merchantmen out of 63 were taken, sixteen of them carrying troops and supplies for the West Indies.

In the West Indies British power suffered severe losses in the violent hurricanes which swept the region in October. Two ships of the line, two frigates, of 44 and 42 guns, and nine smaller warships were lost, some with all hands. Surviving vessels were dismasted or otherwise damaged, while destruction to facilities on shore was widespread. These losses were partly offset by similar disasters to French vessels during the same storms.

In December the United Provinces, who had recently joined the protective association of neutrals called the League of Baltic Powers (better known as the Armed Neutrality), were added to the list of England's enemies.

As far as the European theater was concerned, the declaration of war on the Dutch had resulted only in an increased drain on British naval resources. But in the Caribbean the outbreak of hostilities opened up a (literally) golden prospect. On January 27, 1781, orders arrived directing the seizure of all Dutch possessions. Prime target was the little (eight square miles) island of St. Eustatius. Here the Dutch had built up a great center of trade, much of it of warlike supplies destined for the combatants in the West Indian islands and America. Hitherto protected by a neutral flag, the island had long been a source of

NAVAL CAMPAIGNS IN THE WEST INDIES
1780-1782

SCALE IN MILES
10 20 30 40 50   100

ANGUILLA (BRITISH)

ST.-MARTIN (DUTCH)

B
SABA (DUTCH)

9 BARBUDA (BRITISH)

ST. EUSTATIUS (DUTCH)

ST. CHRISTOPHER
(ST. KITTS) (BRITISH) A2
A1

NEVIS   F   K
(BRITISH)

ANTIGUA (BRITISH)

MONTSERRAT (BRITISH)

GUADELOUPE (FRENCH)

A7

MARIE-GALANTE
(FRENCH)

ILES DES
SAINTES

A6
A5

DOMINICA
(BRITISH)

3 A3
7 M J
C 2 D
MARTINIQUE (FRENCH)
MAJOR NAVAL BASE

FORT ROYAL

E   5

G
1
4 ST. LUCIA (BRITISH)
A
A4

11 ST. VINCENT (FRENCH)

BARBADOS
(BRITISH)
8
10
L MAJOR
NAVAL BASE

I

THE GRENADINES
(BRITISH)

GRENADA (BRITISH)

H
TOBAGO (BRITISH)

ABBREVIATIONS
R.—RODNEY
H.—HOOD
DE GU.—DE GUICHEN
DE GR.—DE GRASSE
MART.—MARTINIQUE
GUAD.—GUADELOUPE
SHIPS OF LINE THUS: (12)

1780
1—Rodney (4) arrives from Gibraltar, March 27.

2—De Guichen (22) sails, April 13.

3—Rodney (20) leaves St. Lucia. Encounters de Gu.
    Action inconclusive. De Gu. to Guadeloupe. R. Pursues.

4—R. returns to St. Lucia.

5—De Gu. sails from St. Lucia, passes east of Mart.
    Sights British putting to sea, May 9.

6—After days of maneuvering and two slight engagements,
    fleets part on May 20 some 120 miles east of Mart.
    R. to Barbados. De Gu. to Mart. May 22.

7—De Gu. joined by Spanish fleet. Both sail July 5. Part east of Cuba.
    Spanish to Havana. De Gu. to C. François, thence to Cadiz, Aug. 16.

8—Rodney to Barbuda, July 31.

9—R., Barbuda to N.Y., arriving Sept. 14.

10—R. arrives Barbados, Dec. 10.

11—R. attempts to capture St. Vincent, Dec. 15. Fails.

1781
A—R. joined by H. (8) at St. Lucia

B—R. and H. take Dutch islands, Feb. 3.

C—H. detached to blockade 4 of line in Fort Royal, Mart.

D—De Grasse (20) from Brest, sights Mart., Apr. 28.

E—H. (17) meets de Gr. (24), Apr. 29. De Gr. to Fort Royal to refit. H. north
    to join R.

F—H. joins R., both to Barbados. Arrive May 18.

G—French attack on St. Lucia beaten off.

H—De Gr. sails May 25 from Fort Royal for Tobago. Island capitulates, June 2.

I—R. reaches Tobago too late, follows de Gr. Encounters,
    fails to attack, returns to Barbados. De Gr. to Mart.

J—De Gr. leaves Fort Royal July 5 for C. François, thence to Yorktown.

K—H. (14) leaves Antigua Aug. 10. Joins Graves at N.Y., Aug. 30.
    R. sails for England.

L—H. arrives from N.Y. (after Battle of Capes), Dec. 5.

M—De Gr. (26) arrives from America. Dec.

1782
A1—De Gr. (24) attacks St. Kitts and Nevis, Jan. 11. Nevis taken Jan. 20.
Garrison of St. Kitts retires inland. H. (22) arrives St. Kitts, Jan. 24.
Minor engagements, Jan. 25-26. De Gr. reinforced, now (32). Garrison
surrenders, Feb. 13. H. escapes to sea, Feb. 14. Sails for Antigua.

A2—R. (12) arrives from England, takes command. R. and H. to St. Lucia.

A3—De Gr., reinforced to (35), leaves Fort Royal with large convoy for
C. François, Apr. 8.

A4—R. (36) leaves St. Lucia in pursuit, Apr. 8.

A5—De Gr. sends convoy with (2) to Guad. Indecisive attack on British van,
Apr. 9. One Fr. 64 damaged, sent Guad. (2) others damaged by collision.

A6—Battle of Saintes, Apr. 12. De Gr. taken. French lose (5). Action
generally indecisive. No pursuit. Vaudreuil, De Gr.'s successor, and
remaining (25) rendezvous at C. François, Apr. 25. There joined by (15) Spanish.
Allied fleet takes no action.

A7—H. detached, Apr. 17. R. sails for Jamaica, Apr. 19. Arrives, Apr. 28.
H. takes two 64's, one frigate, and one sloop in Mona Passage, west of Puerto Rico,
Apr. 19. R. relieved by Pigot, July 10. Sails for England, July 22. Naval
war in West Indies may be said to be over.

annoyance to Britain, and of the sinews of war to Washington's armies.

Rodney's fleet had been swelled by the arrival from England of eight ships of the line under Rear Admiral Sir Samuel Hood to a force of 21 of the line. Leaving half a dozen ships to watch the small French squadron in Fort Royal, Rodney set sail, and a week after receipt of his orders the British admiral was off St. Eustatius. There could be no resistance to such an overwhelming force, and the island's garrison of less than 60 men surrendered at once. The booty was tremendous. Merchandise, crammed in the long rows of storehouses, was valued at more than £3,000,000. Over 150 merchant ships were taken, and a convoy of 30 more which had left the island two days before was chased and captured also.

The island's fall was a blow to the Americans. It was also a blow to the British planters and traders of the West Indies. For the island, as well as being a major arsenal for the American revolutionaries, was a free port into which came American tobacco, destined ultimately for Europe (much of it in British ships), and American corn and bacon, which the plantation owners desperately needed to feed their slaves. So a percentage of the goods seized were British, and the arbitrary way in which Rodney and Vaughan (commanding the troops) disposed of the loot caused such a furor in England as to nearly wreck Rodney's professional career.

One reason for the storm of criticism which soon broke over Rodney's head was the fact that he allowed himself to become so involved in the financial dealings at St. Eustatius that he stayed there for the next six months. He dispatched Hood to deal with a new French threat—a squadron under Rear Admiral de Grasse which had been reported as steering for the West Indies. These reinforcements brought the total French strength up to 24. Hood had only 18, but he was an aggressive commander and could be relied on to deploy his inferior force to the best advantage.

A long-range action, in which the French had the weather gauge but failed to close with their adversaries, ended with Hood retiring to join Rodney at St. Eustatius. De Grasse had the advantage in this encounter, four of the British ships being damaged more or less severely. On the other hand, he had had a decidedly inferior British squadron to leeward and a battle at close range might have decided the mastery of the Caribbean in one afternoon. Eight of the vessels opposed to him on April 29 were to face him again a year later—with results disastrous to himself.

Hood's retirement laid all-important St. Lucia open to attack, and de Grasse at once attempted to take it, but the fortifications were too strong and the assault was given up. An attack was now mounted against Tobago. Six sail of the line under Rear Admiral Francis Samuel Drake were sent by Rodney from Barbados to bolster the defense, but meeting with de Grasse and his whole fleet, Drake very properly rejoined his admiral. Rodney at once sailed for Tobago. Arriving on June 4, he learned that the island had surrendered two days before.

On June 9 both fleets were in contact. Rodney, with 20 of the line, was to windward of de Grasse's 23 and might have forced a battle. Had he done so, American history might have been written differently, for this fleet of de Grasse's was to be instrumental in bringing about the surrender at Yorktown. But for reasons best known to himself Rodney did not attack. Instead he went off to Barbados, while de Grasse returned to Martinique. On July 5, the French admiral sailed from Fort Royal for Cap François, where he picked up four of the line left there by de Guichen. Here he also received dispatches from Washington and Rochambeau, requesting him to bring his fleet north, either to New York or the Chesapeake.

Obviously, if all had been going well with the British effort on land there would have been no crisis. But two commands—Clinton, nominally Commander in Chief for North America, at New York, and Cornwallis

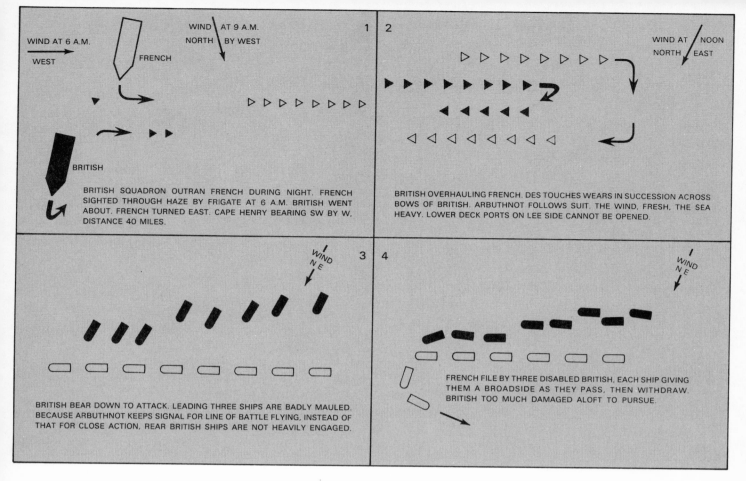

Diagrams showing approximate movements of Des Touches and Arbuthnot—March 16, 1781

In the diagrams:

1 — WIND AT 6 A.M. WEST. WIND AT 9 A.M. NORTH BY WEST. FRENCH. BRITISH.

BRITISH SQUADRON OUTRAN FRENCH DURING NIGHT. FRENCH SIGHTED THROUGH HAZE BY FRIGATE AT 6 A.M. BRITISH WENT ABOUT. FRENCH TURNED EAST. CAPE HENRY BEARING SW BY W. DISTANCE 40 MILES.

2 — WIND AT NOON NORTH EAST.

BRITISH OVERHAULING FRENCH. DES TOUCHES WEARS IN SUCCESSION ACROSS BOWS OF BRITISH. ARBUTHNOT FOLLOWS SUIT. THE WIND, FRESH, THE SEA HEAVY. LOWER DECK PORTS ON LEE SIDE CANNOT BE OPENED.

3 — WIND N E.

BRITISH BEAR DOWN TO ATTACK. LEADING THREE SHIPS ARE BADLY MAULED. BECAUSE ARBUTHNOT KEEPS SIGNAL FOR LINE OF BATTLE FLYING, INSTEAD OF THAT FOR CLOSE ACTION, REAR BRITISH SHIPS ARE NOT HEAVILY ENGAGED.

4 — WIND N E.

FRENCH FILE BY THREE DISABLED BRITISH, EACH SHIP GIVING THEM A BROADSIDE AS THEY PASS, THEN WITHDRAW. BRITISH TOO MUCH DAMAGED ALOFT TO PURSUE.

in the South—had divided the hard-pushed British forces at a time when only concentration might have staved off defeat. To make matters more difficult, Cornwallis was convinced that the main theater of operations lay in the Virginia and Chesapeake Bay region, while Clinton felt that firm control of New York and adjacent areas was the Crown's only hope. Now Cornwallis, after a campaign in the Carolinas, was withdrawing his war-weary regiments to the coast and preparing a fortified base at Yorktown and at Gloucester across the York River.

In March of 1781 the French squadron at Newport, with 1,000 soldiers aboard, put to sea bound for the Chesapeake. Arbuthnot, whose squadron had been badly battered in a gale at the end of January (one 74, *Culloden*, being wrecked on Long Island), followed immediately, his surmise as to their destination confirmed by a vessel which had sighted them and reported their course. Only three of the French ships were coppered and in consequence the British squadron passed their opponents, and when the French were sighted in the early morning of the sixteenth they were some distance astern. Des Touches, the French commander (de Ternay having died), handled his somewhat inferior squadron brilliantly. There was a big sea running, with frequent squalls, and the Frenchman, wearing his ships in succession, crossed the head of the pursuing British line. He thus deliberately sacrificed the windward position, at the same time enabling his ships to use their lower deck guns, always the heaviest aboard. The British, on the other hand, heeling over to the wind, were forced to keep their lower deck gun ports closed.

The British wore in succession, and the leading ships were badly cut up aloft as they came around. Arbuthnot made the mistake of keeping the signal for the line of battle flying, instead of hoisting that for close action. In consequence, some vessels were more closely engaged than others. Des Touches wore in succession once more, each ship firing her starboard battery into the crippled vessels at the head of the British line before she turned.

The French then hauled off and set a course for Newport. The British attempted to wear in pursuit but had suffered too much aloft, and the squadron made for the entrance to the Chesapeake, then almost due west and some miles distant. Strategically it was Arbuthnot's battle. His enemy's losses were almost twice those of his own and the French had been intercepted and forced to abandon their expedition. Tactically the honors went to des Touches, who successfully fought off a larger force while inflicting considerable damage on his opponent.

The commands of both French and British naval forces in the North American theater now changed hands, Commodore de Barras relieving des Touches while Arbuthnot sailed for England, leaving Rear Admiral Thomas Graves in charge at New York.

Intelligence had now reached Rodney that a French squadron was to leave the West Indies for North America. De Grasse, it was believed, would himself convoy the French trade from Cap François to France, but Hood was sent north with fourteen of the line to the Capes of the Chesapeake. Rodney himself sailed for England on leave of absence on August 1.

Ill health and financial troubles stemming from the taking of St. Eustatius took the senior British admiral across the Atlantic at a time when he could least be spared. For although Rodney might lack the fire of his earlier years, he was still vastly more skillful and aggressive than Graves. But even the most experienced commander can make mistakes. Rodney made one in sending only fourteen of the line north with Hood, underestimating the number that de Grasse would order to the Chesapeake. So three of the line went back to England with Rodney, and two were detached to Jamaica, leaving Hood with five less than

he might have had.

Of the twenty-one ships commanded by Rodney in the Leewards, seven were accounted for as follows:

Russel, 74	Badly damaged in the action of April 29. Sent to Antigua for repairs.
Sandwich, 90	Sent to Port Royal for repairs.
Torbay, 74 and *Prince William,* 64	Sent with convoy to Jamaica. Were then to be sent on to America.
Gibraltar, 80; Triumph, 74, and *Panther, 60*	Sailed with Rodney to England. All three in need of repair.

Of the fourteen which sailed north with Hood, several had sprung masts; *Montagu, 74,* and *Ajax, 74,* were leaky, while *Terrible, 74,* later destroyed after the battle of the Capes, made the long voyage with five pumps hard at work.

Dispatches were sent to Graves by two vessels, *Swallow* and *Active,* to inform him of Hood's imminent arrival. But dispatches had a way of going astray in those days. *Swallow* arrived safely in New York only to find Graves gone towards Boston, to intercept a convoy from France. She was sent on to find him but was forced ashore on Long Island by enemy vessels and wrecked. *Active* was taken before she reached her destination, and duplicate dispatches arrived for Graves only a matter of hours before Hood appeared with his squadron off Sandy Hook.

On the same evening, August 28, word came that de Barras had sailed with his whole squadron from Newport on the twenty-fifth. Graves had shortly before detached three ships for other duties, so it was with five of the line and a 50-gun ship that he joined Hood outside the bar on the thirty-first. Assuming command of the whole fleet, nineteen ships of the line, he set a course for the Chesapeake. Also converging on the Chesapeake were de Barras, the French squadron from the West Indies, Washington, and Rochambeau. No one

Entry Port of a Three-Decker

knew it, but the decisive moment of the American Revolution had come at last.

On August 30, one day before Graves left New York, de Grasse arrived in the Chesapeake and anchored in Lynnhaven Bay. He had with him twenty-eight ships of the line, all that he could scrape together at Cap François, even postponing the sailing of the all-important trade convoys to France by stripping them of their escorts. He also brought 3,300 good troops and, last but not least, a large sum of money. These reinforcements raised Lafayette's forces opposing Cornwallis to 8,000, while Washington, having given Clinton the slip, was on his way south with 2,000 of the Continental line and 4,000 French from Newport. Cornwallis's escape route into Carolina was closed by French ships cruising in the James River, while others blockaded the mouth of the York (thus reducing De Grasse's strength by several cruisers and four ships of the line).

It was the morning of September 5, 1781, when a string of bunting from the French frigate on watch off Cape Henry signaled the approach of a fleet. Hope rose among both

Americans and French that the newcomers might be de Barras' squadron from Newport. But as ship after ship lifted over the horizon it became plain that the British had arrived. Nineteen of the line the watchers counted— two 98's, twelve 74's, one 70, and four 64's, with attendant frigates. De Grasse ordered his ships to slip their cables immediately upon receiving the signal that the British were in the offing. Even so, it was some time before the French were outside, clear of Cape Henry and the shoal called the Middle Ground, and steering east, the wind being a little west of south.

The British had already formed line on the same (port) tack as the French, but some distance to windward, before the last of the Frenchmen were clear of the Cape. Graves now (2:30 P.M.) moved to close with the enemy, but instead of ordering his line to turn down to leeward together the signal was made for the van ship to incline to starboard and the rest of the fleet to follow in succession. Thus the British line moved toward the French on a long slant.

As the French formation was straggling—the center being to leeward of the van, and the rear well behind and to the leeward of the center—the van ships of both fleets were the first to make contact. The formation of the two fleets at this time (about 4 P.M.) was roughly in the shape of a "V," the leading ships making the point. The firing between the leading vessels now became very heavy and the action gradually spread to the centers of both fleets. Both flagships, the huge *Ville de Paris,* carrying 110 guns and the finest vessel afloat, and *London,* 98, were engaged; although Hood, in his criticism of Graves's conduct of the battle, states that the flagship and the center division opened fire at "a most improper distance."

Graves kept the signal for the line of battle flying almost continuously, and as this meant a continuation of a line from the van ship through the flagship, Hood's rear division did not get into action at all. It was not until

about 5:30 P.M., nearly sunset, that Hood noticed that the signal for the line of battle was no longer flying. Hood claimed afterwards that it was hauled down at that time. *London's* log records that the signal was hauled down at 4:11, rehoisted at 4:22 to bring the ships into formation, and hauled down again at 4:27. The signal for close action was also flying and, according to *London's* log, was repeated at 5:20, at which time Hood bore down with his ships. Signals were always hard to make out in the dense smoke which shrouded the battle lines, and exactly what happened will never be known. In any case, it is of little general interest today. What is important is

that, after the firing gradually died away at sunset, Graves decided not to renew the action.

While only the van squadrons of each fleet had been closely engaged, damage on both sides was severe. In fact, as the reports came in, Graves felt that things were so bad "we could only think of preserving the best appearance." *Terrible,* 74, was so badly shattered that she had to be burned, and several others were in bad shape. As de Grasse had had an original advantage of five ships, and might at any moment be reinforced by the Newport squadron, Graves's position was not a strong one. And when on the sixth the fleets lay in sight of each other making repairs, it

seemed to Graves that the enemy had not received nearly as much damage as had his own vessels.

The key to the Chesapeake was still in Graves's hands. Had he made such sail as he could for the entrance to the Bay he might well have taken up such a strong position that de Grasse would not have risked an attack. Though some ships were damaged in their hulls and badly cut up aloft, others had been but lightly engaged, while the rear ships had not fired a shot. British losses were only 336 (French, 230)—not enough to prevent them manning all their guns. As it was, the fleets kept in contact until the ninth, when the French disappeared. De Grasse had sighted the squadron of de Barras heading for the Chesapeake, and steered his own fleet for the same anchorage. On September 10, when the tardy and overcautious Graves finally came round to the same course it was too late. The French squadrons were united, and the British admiral was confronted with 36 of the line.

Graves returned to New York, reaching Sandy Hook on September 19, to repair damages and embark 6,000 troops for the relief of

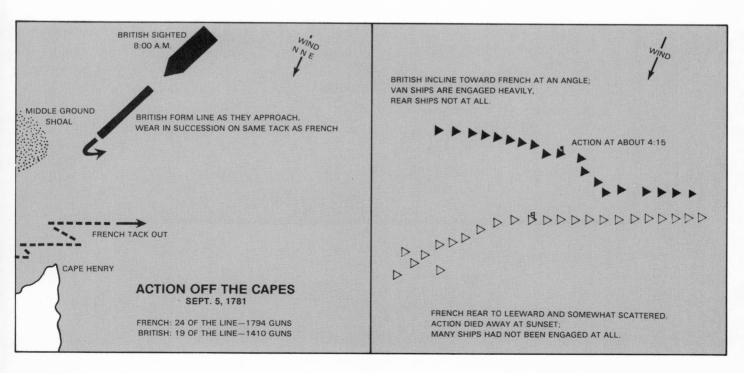

BRITISH SIGHTED 8:00 A.M.

WIND N N E

MIDDLE GROUND SHOAL

BRITISH FORM LINE AS THEY APPROACH, WEAR IN SUCCESSION ON SAME TACK AS FRENCH

FRENCH TACK OUT

CAPE HENRY

ACTION OFF THE CAPES
SEPT. 5, 1781

FRENCH: 24 OF THE LINE—1794 GUNS
BRITISH: 19 OF THE LINE—1410 GUNS

WIND

BRITISH INCLINE TOWARD FRENCH AT AN ANGLE; VAN SHIPS ARE ENGAGED HEAVILY, REAR SHIPS NOT AT ALL.

ACTION AT ABOUT 4:15

FRENCH REAR TO LEEWARD AND SOMEWHAT SCATTERED. ACTION DIED AWAY AT SUNSET; MANY SHIPS HAD NOT BEEN ENGAGED AT ALL.

Cornwallis. It was not until October 18 that his reinforced fleet was ready. On that date he set sail, with 23 ships of the line. Just what he hoped to accomplish with 23 ships against 36 when he had failed with 19 against 24 is a mystery. One plan was to attempt to slip by the French fleet and land the troops, despite land batteries, warships and the Allied armies. This was council of despair indeed, and it is doubtful if even the aggressive Hood really believed that this desperate venture could succeed. The question, as we know, was purely academic; Graves's ships had barely cleared Sandy Hook when Cornwallis's redcoats marched out in ordered ranks to lay down their arms.

This was the moment for which Washington and thousands of other Americans had fought, starved, shivered, and bled for six long and bitter years. That moment might, probably would, have come sooner or later. An independent America was by now a fact, not just an idea; a few thousand professional soldiers and disheartened Loyalists could not hold it for the Crown indefinitely. But the end at Yorktown came when it did because one admiral had had the foresight to concentrate every available ship, another had underestimated his enemy, while another had tried to fight what he should have sensed was a decisive battle, using the rigid methods of bygone years.

So far as the revolted Colonists were concerned, the naval war was over. That many of the ships which had confronted each other off the Capes of the Chesapeake met again north of Dominica in a battle which ended in a French defeat could not alter events in North America. Rodney's victory in the Passage of the Saints in April of the following year came too late for that. And whatever bitter thoughts de Grasse may have had as the British ensign went fluttering up over the battered *Ville de Paris,* he could at least remember that his brief command of the northern waters had cost England half a continent.

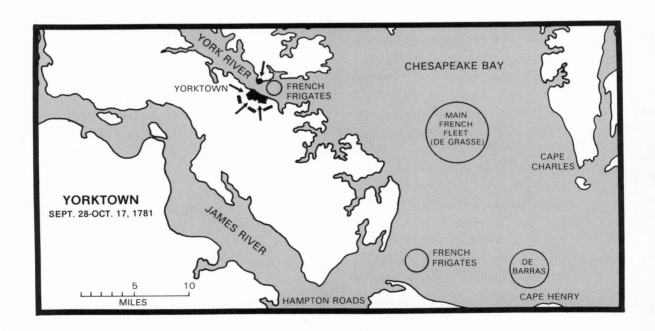

YORKTOWN
SEPT. 28-OCT. 17, 1781

Ships of the Continental Navy

Name	Type	Acquired	Fate
Alfred, 24	Ship	Purchased, 1775	Captured by *Ariadne*, 20, *Ceres*, 16, 1778.
Columbus, 20	Ship	Purchased, 1775	Driven ashore, burned at Point Judith, 1778.
Andrew Doria, 14	Brig	Purchased, 1775	Destroyed to avoid capture, Delaware River, 1777.
Cabot, 14	Brig	Purchased, 1775	Driven aground, captured. Taken in British service, 1777.
Providence, 12	Sloop	Purchased, 1775	Destroyed to avoid capture, Penobscot, 1779.
Hornet, 10	Sloop	Purchased, 1775	Destroyed to avoid capture, Delaware River, 1777.
Wasp, 8	Schooner	Purchased, 1775	Destroyed to avoid capture, Delaware River, 1777.
Fly, 8	Schooner	Purchased, 1775	Destroyed to avoid capture, Delaware River, 1777.
Lexington, 16	Brig	Purchased, 1776	Captured by *Alert*, 10, 1777.
Reprisal, 16	Brig	Purchased, 1775-76	Lost at sea, 1777.
Hampden, 14	Brig	Purchased, 1776	Sold at Providence, R.I., 1777.
Independence, 10	Sloop	Purchased, 1775-76	Wrecked Ocracoke Inlet, N.C., 1778.
Sachem, 10	Sloop	Purchased, 1775-76	Destroyed to avoid capture, Delaware River, 1777.
Mosquito, 4	Sloop	Purchased, 1775-76	Destroyed to avoid capture, Delaware River, 1777.
Raleigh, 32	Frigate	Launched, 1776	Captured by *Experiment*, 50, *Unicorn*, 28, 1778.
Hancock, 32	Frigate	Launched, 1776	Captured by *Rainbow*, 44, 1777.
Warren, 32	Frigate	Launched, 1776	Destroyed to avoid capture, Penobscot, 1779.
Washington, 32	Frigate	Launched, 1776	Destroyed to avoid capture, Delaware River, 1777.
Randolph, 32	Frigate	Launched, 1776	Blew up engaging *Yarmouth*, 64, 1778.
Providence, 28	Frigate	Launched, 1776	Captured at Charleston, S.C., 1780.
Trumbull, 28	Frigate	Launched, 177?	Captured by *Iris*, 32 (ex-*Hancock*) and *General Monk*, 18, 1781.
Congress, 28	Frigate	Launched, 1776	Destroyed to avoid capture, Hudson River, 1777.
Virginia, 28	Frigate	Launched, 1776-77	Run aground in Chesapeake. Captured, 1778.
Effingham, 28	Frigate	Launched, 1776-77	Destroyed (unfinished), Delaware River, 1777.

SHIPS OF THE CONTINENTAL NAVY (*continued*)

Boston, 24	Frigate	Launched, 1776-77	Captured at Charleston, S.C., 1780.
Montgomery, 24	Frigate	Launched, 1776-77	Destroyed to avoid capture, Hudson River, 1777.
Delaware, 24	Frigate	Launched, 1776	Captured in Delaware, 1777.
Ranger, 18	Ship	Launched, 1777	Captured at Charleston, S.C., 1780.
Resistance, 10	Brigantine	Launched, 1777	Captured by Howe's fleet, 1778.
Surprise	Sloop	Purchased, 1777	*
Racehorse, 12	Schooner	Captured from British, 1776	Destroyed, Delaware River, 1777.
Repulse, 8	Xebec	Pa. state gunboat lent to Continental Navy, 1777	Destroyed to avoid capture, Delaware River, 1777.
Champion, 8	Xebec	Pa. state gunboat lent to Continental Navy, 1777	Destroyed to avoid capture, Delaware River, 1777.
Indien, 40	Ship	Built in Holland	Purchased by French. Acquired by S. Carolina. As *South Carolina*, captured in 1782.
Deane (later *Hague*), 32	Frigate	Built at Nantes, 1777	Name changed to *Hague*, 1782. Decommissioned, 1783.
Queen of France, 28	Frigate	Purchased in France, 1777	Sunk as obstruction, Charleston, S.C., 1780.
Dolphin, 10	Cutter	Purchased in Dover, 1777	Cruiser, packet, then receiving ship, 1777.
Surprise, 10	Lugger	Purchased in Dunkirk, 1777	Seized by French, 1777.
Revenge, 14	Cutter	Purchased in Dunkirk, 1777	Sold at Philadelphia, 1779. Captured as privateer, 1779.
Alliance, 32	Frigate	Launched, 1778	Sold out of service, 1785.
General Gates, 18	Ship	Launched, 1777	Sold out of service, 1779.
Retaliation	Brigantine	Purchased, 1778	*
Pigot, 8	Schooner	Captured from British, 1778	*
Confederacy, 32	Frigate	Launched, 1778	Captured by *Roebuck*, 44, *Orpheus*, 32, 1781.
Argo, 12	Sloop	Purchased, 1779	Sold out of service, 1779.
Diligent, 12	Brig	Captured from British, 1779	Destroyed to avoid capture, Penobscot, 1779.
Bonhomme Richard, 42	Ship	Purchased in France, 1779	Sank after action with *Serapis*, 1779.
Pallas, 32	Frigate	Lent by France, 1779	French in Continental Service. Returned after war.
Cerf, 18	Cutter	Lent by France, 1779	French in Continental Service. Returned after war.
Vengeance, 12	Brig	Lent by France, 1779	French in Continental Service. Returned after war.
Serapis, 44	Ship	Captured by John Paul Jones	Sold in France, 1780.
Ariel, 20	Ship	Lent by France, 1779	French in Continental Service. Returned, 1781.

Saratoga, 18	Ship	Launched, 1780	Lost at sea, 1781.
America, 74	Ship of the line	Launched, 1782	Given to France. Broken up, 1786.
General Washington, 20 (ex-*General Monk*)	Ship	Captured, 1782	Sold 1784.
Duc de Lauzun, 20	Ship	Purchased Havana, 1782	Sold in France, 1783.
Bourbon, 36	Frigate	Launched, 1783	Sold, no service, 1783.

*Disposition unknown.

Arnold's Fleet on Lake Champlain*

Enterprise, 12	Sloop	12 4-pdrs, 10 swivels
Royal Savage, 12	Schooner	4 6-pdrs, 8 4-pdrs, 10 swivels
Revenge, 8	Schooner	4 4-pdrs, 4 2-pdrs
Liberty, 8	Schooner	4 4-pdrs, 4 2-pdrs
Lee, 6	Cutter	1 12-pdr, 1 9-pdr, 4 4-pdrs, 2 swivels
Washington, 11	Galley	2 18-pdrs, 2 12-pdrs, 2 9-pdrs, 4 4-pdrs, 1 2-pdr, 8 swivels
Trumbull, 10	Galley	1 18-pdr, 1 12-pdr, 2 9-pdrs, 6 6-pdrs, 6-8 swivels
Congress, 10	Galley	(Same as *Trumbull*)
Philadelphia, 3	Gondola	1 12-pdr, 2 9-pdrs
New York, 3	Gondola	(Same as *Philadelphia*)
Connecticut, 3	Gondola	(Same as *Philadelphia*)
Providence, 3	Gondola	(Same as *Philadelphia*)
Jersey, 3	Gondola	(Same as *Philadelphia*)
New Haven, 3	Gondola	(Same as *Philadelphia*)
Spitfire, 3	Gondola	(Same as *Philadelphia*)
Boston, 3	Gondola	(Same as *Philadelphia*)

*With the exception of *Enterprise, Royal Savage,* and *Liberty*—all captured from the British in 1775—the vessels of Arnold's squadron were built in 1776. *Liberty* was not present at the action of October 11. *Gates,* another galley, was still under construction.

The Mississippi River Squadron*

Morris, 24	Ship	Purchased 1778	Lost in hurricane, 1779
West Florida	Sloop	Captured by schooner *Morris* on Lake Pontchartrain, 1779	Sold 1780
Morris	Schooner		Disposed of in 1779

*The Mississippi Squadron was organized by Oliver Pollock, commercial agent of the Continental Congress at New Orleans. His efforts were encouraged by the Spanish governor, Bernado de Galvez. Several prizes were taken.

George Washington's Naval Squadron*

Name and Class	Tons	Armament	Crew	Captains	Took or Helped Take	First Cruise	Disposition
Hannah, schooner	78	4 4-pdrs, swivels	—	Nicholas Broughton	1	Sept. 5, 1775	Returned to owner, Oct. 1775.
Hancock (ex-*Speedwell*), schooner	72	6 4-pdrs, 10 swivels	70	Nicholas Broughton John Manley Samuel Tucker	19	Oct. 22, 1775	Returned to owners, Jan. 1777.
Franklin (ex-*Elizabeth*), schooner	60	2 4-pdrs, 4 2-pdrs, 10 swivels	70	John Selman Samuel Tucker James Mugford John Skimmer	17	Oct. 22, 1775	Returned to owners, Jan. 1777.
Lee (ex-*Two Brothers*), schooner	74	4 4-pdrs, 2 2-pdrs, 10 swivels	50	John Manley Daniel Waters John Skimmer	26	Oct. 28, 1775	Returned to owners, Dec. 1777.
Warren (ex-*Hawk*), schooner	64	4 4-pdrs, 10 swivels	50	Winborn Adams William Burke	5	Oct. 31, 1775	Captured by frigate *Liverpool*, 28, Aug. 26, 1776.
Harrison (ex-*Triton*), schooner	64	4 4-pdrs, 6 swivels	50	William Coit	4	Nov. 4, 1775	Badly in need of repair. Decommissioned in spring of '76.
Washington (ex-*Endeavor*), brigantine	160	6 6-pdrs, 4 4-pdrs, 10 swivels	74	Sion Martindale	1	Nov. 23, 1775	Captured, Dec. 5, 1775 by frigate *Fowey*, 20.
Lynch, schooner	—	4 4-pdrs, 2 2-pdrs, 4 swivels	—	John Ayres John Adams	4	Mar. 1, 1776	Captured, May 19, 1777 by *Foudroyant*, 80.

*The strength of the crews varied from time to time, as did the armament (*Warren* had eight guns when she was taken). The schooners were typical New England design of the period. Plans show them to have been rather bluff in the bows, with square transoms and a half deck ending just forward of the mainmast. Under this deck was the captain's cabin and minuscule quarters for the officers. The small (half a dozen or so) peacetime crews normally existed in the forecastle. The comparatively large complements carried (mostly for prize crews, as well as to work the guns) were crowded in the erstwhile cargo holds. The usual sail plan called only for mainsail, foresail, and jib. To give the vessels a better turn of speed for war work square topsails, sometimes a crossjack, and a flying jib were usually added. The flag was white, with a green pine tree on one side and the words "Appeal to Heaven" on the other.

All told, the vessels of the squadron took 55 sail, of which 11 were released and 6 retaken. As well as seamen, they captured 354 officers and men of the Seventy-first Highlanders, bound for Boston.

Rules for the Regulation of the Navy of the United Colonies

The Commanders of all ships and vessels belonging to the thirteen United Colonies are strictly required to show in themselves a good example of honor and virtue to their officers and men, and to be very vigilant in inspecting the behaviour of all such as are under them, and to discountnance and suppress all dissolute, immoral, and disorderly practices, and also such as are contrary to the rules of discipline and obedience, and to correct those who are guilty of the same, according to the usage of the sea.

The Commanders of the ships of the thirteen United Colonies are to take care that divine service be performed twice a day on board, and a sermon preached on Sundays, unless bad weather or other extraordinary accidents prevent it.

If any shall be heard to swear, curse, or blaspheme the name of God, the Commander is strictly enjoined to punish them for every offense by causing them to wear a wooden collar, or some other shameful badge of distinction, for so long time as he shall judge proper. If he be a commissioned officer, he shall forfeit one shilling for each offense, and a warrant or inferior officer six pence. He who is guilty of drunkenness, if a seaman, shall be put in irons until he is sober, but if an officer, he shall forfeit two days' pay.

No Commander shall inflict any punishment upon a seaman beyond twelve lashes upon his bare back with a cat of nine tails; if the fault shall deserve a greater punishment, he is to apply to the Commander in chief of

Rules for the Regulation of the Navy of the United Colonies were drawn up by the Naval Committee on November 28, 1775. They shed enough light on the management of the warships of the period to be worth quoting in full.

the Navy, in order to the trying of him by a court-martial, and in the mean time he may put him under confinement.

The Commander is never by his own authority to discharge a commission or warrant officer, nor to punish or strike him, but he may suspend or confine them, and when he comes in the way of a Commander in chief, apply to him for holding a court-martial.

The Officer who commands by accident of the Captain's or commander's absence (unless he be absent for a time by leave) shall not order any correction by confinement, and upon the captain's return on board he shall then give an account of his reasons for so doing.

The Captain is to cause the articles of war to be hung up in some public places of the ship, and read to the ship's company once a month.

Whenever a Captain shall inlist a seaman, he shall take care to enter on his books the time and terms of his entering, in order to his being justly paid.

The Captain shall, before he sails, make return to, and leave with the Congress, or such person or persons as the Congress shall appoint for that purpose, a compleat list of all his officers and men, with the time and terms of their entering; and during his cruize shall keep a true account of the desertion or death of any of them, and of the entering of others, and after his cruize and before any of them are paid off, he shall make return of a compleat list of the same, including those who shall remain on board his ship.

The men, shall, at their request, be furnished with slops that are necessary by the Captain or purser, who shall keep an account of the same, and the Captain, in his return in the last mentioned article directed to be made, shall mention the amount delivered to each man, in order to its being stopped out of his pay.

As to the term "inferior Officer," the Captain is to take notice that the same does not include any commission or any warrant officer, except the second master, surgeon's mate, cook, armourer, gun-smith, master at arms and sail maker.

The Captain is to take care when any inferior officers or volunteer seamen are turned over into the ship under his command from any other ship, not to rate them on the ship's books in a worse quality, or lower degree or station, than they served in the ship they were removed from; and for his guidance he is to demand from the commander of the ship from which they are turned over, a list, under his hand, of their names and qualities.

Any officer, seaman, or others, intitled to wages or prize money, may have the same paid to his assignee, provided the assignment be attested by the Captain or Commander, the master or purser of the ship, or a chief magistrate of some county or corporation.

The Captain is to discourage the seamen of his ship from selling any part of their wages or shares, and never to attest the letter of attorney of any seaman, until he is fully satisfied that the same is not granted in consideration of money given for the purchase of his wages or shares.

When an inferior officer or seaman dies, the Captain is forthwith to make out a ticket for the time of his service, and to send the same by the first safe conveyance to the Congress, or agents by them for that purpose appointed, in order to the wages being forthwith paid to the executors or administrators of the deceased.

A convenient place shall be set apart for sick or hurt men, to which they are to be removed, with their hammocks and bedding, when the surgeon shall advise the same to be necessary, and some of the crew shall be appointed to attend and serve them, and to keep the place clean.

The cooper shall make buckets with covers and cradles if necessary, for their use.

All ships furnished with fishing tackle, being in such places where fish is to be had, the captain is to employ some of the company in fishing; the fish to be distributed daily to such persons as are sick or upon recovery, provided the surgeon recommend it, and the surplus by turns amongst the messes of the officers and seamen without favour or partiality and gratis, without any deduction of their allowance of provisions on that account.

It is left to the discretion of Commanders of squadrons to shorten the allowance of provisions according to the exigencies of the service, taking care that the men be punctually paid for the same.

The like power is given to Captains of single ships in cases of absolute necessity.

If there should be a want of pork, the Captain is to order three pounds of beef to be issued to the men, in lieu of two pounds of pork.

One day in every week shall be issued out of proportion of flour and suet, in lieu of beef, for the seamen, but this is not to extend beyond four months' victualling at one time, nor shall the purser receive any allowance for flour or suet kept longer on board than that time, and there shall be supplied, once a year, a proportion of canvas for pudding-bags, after the rate of one ell for every sixteen men.

If any ship of the thirteen United Colonies shall happen to come into port in want of provisions, the warrant of a Commander in chief shall be sufficient to the Agent or other instrument of the victualling, to supply the quantity wanted, and in urgent cases, where delay may be hurtful, the warrant of the Captain of the ship shall be of equal effect.

The Captain is frequently to order the proper officers to inspect into the condition of the provisions, and if the bread proves damp, to have it aired upon the quarter deck or poop, and also examine the flesh casks, and if any of the pickle be leaked out, to have new made and put in, and the casks made tight and secure.

The Captain or purser shall secure the cloaths, bedding, and other things of such persons as shall die or be killed, to be delivered to their executors or administrators.

All papers, charter parties, bills of lading, passports and other writings whatsoever, found on board any ship or ships, which shall be taken, shall be carefully preserved, and the originals sent to the court of Justice for maritime affairs, appointed or to be appointed by the legislatures in the respective colonies, for judging concerning such prize or prizes; and if any person or persons shall wilfully or negligently destroy or suffer to be destroyed, any such paper or papers, he or they so offending shall forfeit their share of such prize or prizes, and suffer such other punishment as they shall be judged by a court-martial to deserve.

If any person or persons shall embezzele, steal or take away any cables, anchors, sails, or any of the ship's furniture or any of the powder, arms, ammunition, or provisions of any ship belonging to the thirteen United Colonies, he or they shall suffer such punishment as a court-martial shall order.

When in sight of a ship or ships of the enemy, and at such other times as may appear to make it necessary to prepare for an engagement, the Captain shall order all things in his ship in a proper posture for fight, and shall, in his own person and according to his duty, hearten and encourage the inferior officers and men to fight courageously, and not to behave themselves faintly or cry for quarters, on pain of such punishment as the offence shall appear to deserve for his neglect.

Any Captain or other officer, mariner, or others, who shall basely desert thier duty or station in the ship and run away while the enemy is in sight, or in time of action, or shall entice others to do so, shall suffer death, or such other punishment as a court-martial shall inflict.

Any officer, seaman, or marine, who shall begin, excite, cause or join in any mutiny or sedition in the ship to which he belongs, on any pretence whatsoever, shall suffer death, or such other punishment as a court-martial shall direct. Any person in or belonging to the ship, who shall utter any words of sedition and mutiny, or endeavour to make any mutinous assemblies on any pretence whatsoever, shall suffer such punishment as a court-martial shall inflict.

None shall presume to quarrel with or strike his superior officer on pain of such punishment as a court-martial shall order to be inflicted.

If any person shall apprehend he has just cause of complaint, he shall quietly and decently make the same known to his superior officer, or to the captain, as the case may require, who shall take care that justice be done him.

There shall be no quarreling or fighting between shipmates on board any ship belonging to the thirteen United Colonies, nor shall there be used any reproachful or provoking speeches, tending to make quarrels and disturbance, on pain of imprisonment and such other punishment as a court-martial shall think proper to inflict.

If any person shall sleep upon his watch, or negligently perform the duty which shall be enjoined him to do, or forsake his station, he shall suffer such punishment as a court-martial shall judge proper to inflict, according to the nature of his offence.

All murder shall be punished with death.

All robbery and theft shall be punished at the discretion of a court-martial.

Any master at arms who shall refuse to receive such prisoner or prisoners as shall be committed to his charge, or having received them, shall suffer him or them to escape, or dismiss them without orders for so doing, shall suffer in his or their stead, as a court-martial shall order and direct.

The Captain, officers, and others shall use their utmost endeavours to detect, apprehend, and bring to punishment, all offenders, and shall at all times readily assist the officers appointed for that purpose in the discharge of their duty, on pain of being pro-

ceeded against and punished by a court-martial at discretion.

All other faults, disorders, and misdemeanours, which shall be committed on board any ship belonging to the thirteen United Colonies, and which are not herein mentioned, shall be punished according to the laws and customs in such cases at sea.

A court-martial shall consist of at least three Captains and three first lieutenants, with three Captains and three first lieutenants of Marines, if there shall be so many of the Marines then present, and the eldest Captain shall preside.

All sea officers of the same denomination shall take rank of the officers of the Marines.

The sentence of a court-martial for any capital offence, shall not be put in execution, until it be confirmed by the Commander in chief of the fleet; and it shall be the duty of the president of every court-martial to transmit to the Commander in chief of the fleet every sentence which shall be given, with a summary of the evidence and proceedings thereon, by the first opportunity.

The Commander in chief of the fleet for the time being, shall have power to pardon and remit any sentence of death, that shall be given in consequence of any of the aforementioned Articles.

There shall be allowed to each man serving on board the ships in the service of the thirteen United Colonies, a daily proportion of provisions, according as is expressed in the following table, viz.

Sunday, 1 lb. bread, 1 lb. beef, 1 lb. potatoes or turnips.

Monday, 1 lb. bread, 1 lb. beef, 1 lb. potatoes or turnips, and pudding.

Tuesday, 1 lb. bread, 1 lb. beef, 1 lb. potatoes or turnips, and pudding.

Wednesday, 1 lb. bread, two oz. butter, four oz. cheese, and 1/2 pint of rice.

Thursday, 1 lb. bread, 1 lb. pork, and 1/2 pint of peas.

Friday, 1 lb. bread, 1 lb. beef, 1 lb. potatoes or turnips, and pudding.

Saturday, 1 lb. bread, 1 lb. pork, 1/2 pint peas and four oz. cheese.

Half a pint of rum per man per day, and discretionary allowance on extra duty and in time of engagement.

A pint and a half of vinegar for six men per week.

The pay of the officers and men (per calendar month) shall be as follows:

Captain or commander,	32 dollars	Cooper,	15 dollars
Lieutenants,	20 dollars	Captain's or Commander's	
Masters,	20 dollars	clerk	15 dollars
Mates,	15 dollars	Steward,	12 1/3 dollars
Boatswain,	15 dollars	Chaplain,	20 dollars
Boatswain's first mate,	9 1/2 dollars	Able Seamen,	6 2/3 dollars
Boatswain's second mate,	8 dollars	Captain of marines,	26 2/3 dollars
Gunner,	15 dollars	Lieutenants,	18 dollars
Gunner's Mate,	10 2/3 dollars	Serjeants,	8 dollars
Surgeon,	21 1/3 dollars	Corporals,	8 dollars
Surgeon's mate,	13 1/3 dollars	Fifer,	7 1/3 dollars
Carpenter,	15 dollars	Drummer,	7 1/3 dollars
Carpenter's mate,	10 2/3 dollars	Privates (of) marines,	6 2/3 dollars

Glossary

ABAFT: In the direction of the stern.

ABEAM: At right angles to the keel.

ADZ: A cutting tool with a curved blade at right angles to the handle. Used for shaping timber.

AFTERGUARD: Men stationed on the quarterdeck and poop to work the aftersails.

AMIDSHIPS: The middle of a ship.

ANCHOR-MEN: Men stationed on the forecastle to work about the anchors, foreyards, and bowsprit. Usually the oldest and most experienced on board.

APRON: A thin, flat piece of lead about a foot square, used to cover the vent of a cannon. So called because it was held in place by two white cords.

ARMS CHEST: A wooden chest holding small arms and ammunition, brought up from below and lashed on deck when preparing for action.

ATHWART: At right angles to. From side to side (of a ship).

AUGER: A boring tool.

BACKSTAFF: Navigating instrument, an improvement on the earlier cross-staff. Invented by Elizabethan navigator John Davis.

BACKSTAYS: Stays leading aft (port and starboard) from the top of an upper mast to the ship's sides. The lee backstays on a fore-and-after were slacked off.

BAR SHOT: A projectile consisting of two hemispheres separated by a short bar, used against spars and rigging.

BARGE: A ship's boat used for flag officers.

BARK: In the eighteenth century, a two-masted vessel, square-rigged on the fore and fore-and-aft rigged on the main.

BARKENTINE: In the eighteenth century, a three-masted vessel, square-rigged on the fore and main, and fore-and-aft rigged on the mizzen.

BATTEN: A thin strip of wood. Sometimes set into a pocket in a sail to make the sail set better.

BEAM: The width of a ship.

BEATING TO WINDWARD: Making progress against the direction of the wind when sailing on the wind or close-hauled.

BILGES: The curved part of the ship's hull where the sides and the flat bottom meet.

BLOCK: A pulley, or system of pulleys, in a frame, with a hook or ring for attaching to a line or other objects.

BLOCK SHIP: A ship deliberately sunk to form an obstruction.

BOARD: The distance sailed on one tack before coming about.

BOARDING: Entering a vessel with intent to capture it.

BOARDING NETTINGS: Nets rigged up and outward from the bulwarks to prevent an enemy from boarding.

BOARDING PARTY: A group, usually armed with cutlasses and pistols, detailed to board a vessel.

BOATSWAIN: Warrant officer in charge of everything pertaining to the working of the ship.

BOMB VESSEL: A vessel, often ketch-rigged, specially designed to carry one or more large mortars.

BOMBARD: An early cannon, often throwing a stone ball.

BOOM: Spar used for extending the foot of a fore-and-aft sail.

BOW CHASERS: Guns mounted in the bows and able to fire directly, or almost directly, ahead.

BOW GUNS: Guns in the forward part of a vessel.

BOWSPRIT: A spar extending forward from the stem of a vessel.

BRACES: Ropes leading from the yardarms to the deck or an adjacent mast, by means of which the yards are hauled into any required position.

BREECHING: Heavy rope attached to ship's sides and passing through ring on breech of cannon. To prevent gun recoiling beyond a certain distance.

BRIG: A two-masted vessel, square-rigged on both masts.

BRIGANTINE: A two-masted vessel, square-rigged on the fore and fore-and-aft rigged on the main. In the eighteenth century it often carried a square main topsail.

BROADSIDE: The number of cannon mounted on a vessel's side. Also a discharge of such guns, simultaneously, in groups, or in succession.

BULKHEADS: Transverse or longitudinal partitions separating portions of the ship.

BULWARKS: The upper section of the frames and side planking which extends above and around the upper deck.

CABLE: (1) Rope. (2) A chain secured to an anchor. (3) In the eighteenth century, a distance of 120 fathoms or 720 feet.

CABLE SPRINGS: Ropes leading from the stern outboard to the anchor cable. By hauling on one or the other, an anchored ship could be turned and her broadsides brought to bear over a wide arc.

CALIBER: The diameter of the bore of a gun or the diameter of a projectile.

CANNON: Ships' guns, cast of bronze or iron. Designated by the weight of the shot they threw, i.e., 6-pounder, 32-pounder, etc.

CAPITAL SHIP: A ship considered heavily armed enough to lie in the line of battle.

CAPSTAN: A vertical winch, drum, or barrel, used for handling heavy hawsers, chains, etc.

CAPSTAN BARS: Wooden bars, shipped in the capstan head for heaving the capstan around.

CARCASS: A hollow projectile filled with incendiary material.

CAREEN: To heave a vessel over on her side by means of cables ashore, in order to clean or repair her bottom.

CARRONADE: A short, light cannon throwing a heavy ball a short distance. Developed by the Carron Iron Works, in Scotland.

CARTRIDGE: A measured charge of powder, enclosed in a case or bag of some combustible material.

CASCABEL: The round knob on the breech of a cannon.

CASE SHOT: The general term used to describe loads of balls of iron or lead, of various numbers and sizes, cased in bags or in tins (canister), or lashed to a frame (grapeshot).

CAT: A form of hull, rather than a specific rig. Usually a bluff-bowed vessel without the typical beakhead.

CATHEAD: Heavy timbers, projecting from either side of the bow, used as support for the tackle which raised (catted) an anchor out of the water prior to its being secured.

CAT-O'-NINE-TAILS: A whip with nine thongs, each knotted at the end.

CAULK: To make watertight a seam in planking, by forcing in strips of tarred rope fibers. Seams in deck planking were then "payed" by the application of hot pitch.

CHAIN PLATES: Iron straps bolted to a ship's side to which the tackle setting up the shrouds and backstays was attached.

CHAIN SHOT: Shot connected by a short chain, for cutting sails and rigging.

CHARGE: The powder used to propel the projectile—in olden days shoveled in loose, but by the eighteenth century enclosed in a serge or flannel cartridge.

CHRONOMETER: An accurate timepiece designed specifically for use at sea.

CLOSE-HAULED: Sailing close to the wind.

COASTERS: Small vessels suitable for carrying cargoes from one port of a country to another, but not designed for ocean voyages.

COCKPIT: The space on the lowest, or orlop deck, where the midshipmen had their berths, and which was used by the surgeon as an operating room in action.

COEHORN: A small mortar.

COLLIER: A vessel, in Britain often a brig, employed in hauling cargoes of coal.

COLUMN: A division of ships in line ahead.

COME ABOUT: To bring a ship into the wind and onto another tack.

COME UP INTO THE WIND: To turn a ship so that the wind is right ahead, either to lose way preparatory to stopping or anchoring, or to go about on another tack.

COMMODORE: The title of an officer, below the rank of admiral, in command of a squadron of warships.

COMPASS: Navigational device using a magnetized needle and card divided into 32 or more points, suspended in a bowl, which in turn is suspended on a free-moving frame, or "gimbal."

COMPASS TIMBERS: Naturally curved timbers.

CONVOY: A collection of merchant vessels escorted for protection by one or more warships.

COUNTER: The part of a ship's stern overhanging the sternpost.

COURSE: (1) The lower square sail on fore, main, and mizzen. (2) The direction in which a vessel is steering.

COURT-MARTIAL: Naval or military court convened to try naval or military cases, or to administer martial law.

CRUISER: In the eighteenth century, any ship, from the size of frigate on down, engaged in patroling, scouting, or blockade duty.

CUTTER: (1) A small, single-masted vessel, having usually two headsails, a square topsail and lower course, and a large gaff mainsail. (2) A ship's boat next in size to the launch.

CUTTING A CABLE: Cutting through the anchor cable, rather than take the time to raise it in the normal manner.

CUTTING AWAY BOATS: On small vessels the larger ships' boats were at times towed to save deck space. A little extra speed could be obtained by cutting these loose.

DAVITS: In the eighteenth century, wooden members, often curved, either fixed or which could be lowered over sides or stern and from which were suspended one or more ship's boats.

DEADEYES: Circular wooden blocks with three holes through which the lanyards, used to set up taut the shrouds and backstays, are rove.

DECK BEAM: An athwartship beam supporting a deck.

DOCKYARDS: An area equipped to service and/or build warships, furnish masts, sails, supplies, etc.

DOUBLE-BANKED BOAT: A boat rowed with two oarsmen to each oar.

DOUBLE-HEADED SHOT: For extra smashing effect at close range, cannon were often loaded with two (double-headed) and sometimes three (triple-headed) shot.

DRAFT: The depth of a vessel below the waterline.

DRIVER: The gaff-headed sail on the aftermast of a ship, bark,

brig, snow, or brigantine (in the last it may also be called a mainsail).

DRY DOCK: An excavated area, or basin, with solid masonry sides and end, adjacent to navigable water and separated from it by a system of watertight gates. When a new hull was completed, or repairs finished, water was admitted, the gates were opened, and the hull was towed out.

FIGHTING SAILS: For ease of handling, with a minimum of men aloft, a ship going into action often reduced her canvas to topsails, spanker, and jib.

FIGHTING TOPS: The platforms built across the trestletrees at the top of the lower masts. In action these were usually manned by sharpshooters, sometimes armed with swivels, coehorns, and grenades.

FIRE SHIP: A vessel crammed with combustibles, sailed as close aboard an enemy vessel as possible, and then set on fire, the crew taking to their boats at the last moment.

FLAGSHIP: A vessel bearing an admiral's flag, hence one carrying an officer of flag rank and his staff.

FLOATING BATTERY: A heavily timbered raft or barge with thick sides and sometimes partially decked capable of mounting heavy cannon.

FLUSH DECK: A continuous upper deck.

FOOT ROPE: Rope secured under a yard, bowsprit, or boom for a foot support when working.

FORE-AND-AFT RIGGED: A term applied to any vessel rigged with fore-and-aft sails.

FORE-AND-AFT SAILS: All staysails, gaffsails, etc. which are set in a fore-and-aft direction, i.e., along the line of the keel.

FORECASTLE: The upper deck forward of the foremast.

FOREMAST: The mast nearest the bow in all vessels with two or more masts where there is a larger mast abaft it.

FOTHERING: The positioning of a spare sail or canvas over a leak in a ship's hull.

FRAMES: The ribs of a ship.

FREEBOARD: The distance from the waterline to the upper deck.

FRIGATE: A three-masted, ship-rigged vessel, carrying its armament on the main deck, and on quarterdeck and forecastle.

FURL (canvas): To gather up and secure a sail.

GAFF: The spar to which the head of a fore-and-aft sail is secured.

GALLERIES: The sternwalks, sometimes ornately carved, which ran below the stern windows on some of the larger war vessels.

GIG: A ship's boat usually designated for the use of a commanding officer.

GLASS: Usually refers to the nautical half-hour glass; a glass, therefore, equals 30 minutes.

GONDOLA (also Gundalow): A flat-bottomed open boat, with sail and oars, mounting two or three guns.

GRAPESHOT: A cluster of iron shot, usually nine, fastened together in tiers of three by rope and/or canvas. Used against light hulls and personnel.

GROG: A mixture of rum and water.

GUN CAPTAIN: Seaman in charge of a gun crew. Directed the laying of the gun, primed it, and fired it.

GUN CREW: Men detailed to work a gun in action. Number varied with size of cannon.

GUNBOAT: A small boat, usually undecked, propelled by oars and/or sails and usually carrying but one cannon.

GUNPORT: The opening in the ship's side through which a gun was aimed and fired.

GUNWALE: The uppermost member of a boat's side.

HALF MODEL: A model of one side of a vessel, sometimes solid but in early days often ribbed and planked. Often used in conjunction with plans as an aid to the shipbuilder.

HALYARD, OR HALLIARD: Rope used for hoisting a sail, gaff, yard, flag, etc.

HAMMOCK NETTINGS: Stretched along the top of the ship's rail on iron uprights, these nettings formed a trough in which the crew's hammocks, tightly rolled, were stowed. In some cases, wooden sides were used instead of netting.

HAND GRENADES: Hollow iron spheres, filled with powder. A length of fuze, lit just before throwing, provided ignition.

HANDSPIKE: A wooden bar, something like a crowbar, often strengthened with iron at the tip, used to heave up the breech of a gun, and to lever the carriage into position.

HATCHWAY: Large square opening in a deck.

HAWSE HOLE: A hole in the bow through which the anchor cable passes.

HEADSAILS: Jibs and staysails set between the bowsprit and the foremost mast.

HELM: The tiller.

HOLD: The space below decks utilized for the stowing of ballast, cargo, and stores.

HOLYSTONE: A large, flat stone used to clean and whiten a vessel's decks.

HOWITZER: A short-barreled cannon, often used to fire shell instead of shot.

HULK: A vessel, often condemned as unseaworthy, and stripped of masts, spars, and cannon.

IDLERS: Crewmen whose duties kept them busy during the day—sailmakers, clerks, cooks, carpenters, etc. They stood no regular watches; hence the term.

INDIAMEN: Large, stoutly built merchantmen, usually well armed, used in the long and dangerous voyages to the Indies.

"IN IRONS": The situation of a vessel having missed stays and which refuses to fall off from the wind.

"IN ORDINARY": A term applied to war vessels laid up in peacetime. In "moth balls."

JIB: A headsail set on a stay forward of the foremast.

JOLLY BOAT: A small ship's boat comparable to a dinghy.

JURY-RIGGED SHIP: A ship temporarily rigged and repaired after damage at sea.

KEEL: The longitudinal beam forming the backbone of a vessel from which the ribs start.

KEELSON: Longitudinal timber laid inside a vessel on the floor timbers, parallel to the keel, to which it is bolted.

KEEPING STATION: Maintaining proper distance from other ships in a formation.

KNEE: A piece of timber having a natural or artificial crook. Among other things, used as a support for deck beams.

KNOT: A nautical mile (about 6,080 feet).

LATEEN SAIL: A triangular sail having a yard along the luff. Common in the Mediterranean and the East.

LATEEN YARD: Spar on which a lateen sail is set.

LAUNCH: The largest of a ship's boats.

LAYING DOWN: The drawing out full size on the mold loft floor of the structural members of a ship's frame.

LEE: The side opposite that from which the wind is blowing.

LEEWARD: (1) The direction away from the wind. (2) Downwind.

LETTER OF MARQUE: (1) A commission authorizing a private vessel to operate against the vessels of an enemy. (2) A vessel commissioned to operate against the enemy but still carrying cargo.

LIGHT-WEATHER SAILS: Sails made of lighter canvas, as opposed to heavy-duty or storm canvas.

LINE ABREAST: A formation in which ships are in line, said line being at right angles to their course.

LINE AHEAD: A formation in which ships are in column.

LINE OF BEARING: A line of ships, said line being at other than a 90-degree angle to their course.

LINSTOCK: A forked staff about three feet long used to hold the end of the match to the touchhole of a cannon.

LOG LINE: A line, knotted at intervals to represent a mile, used for measuring a ship's speed through the water.

LOGBOOK: The official operating records of a ship, written up daily by one of the ship's officers.

LOOSE (canvas): To unfurl a sail.

LUFF: (1) The leading edge of a fore-and-aft sail. (2) To bring a vessel up into or toward the wind.

LUG SAIL: A form of fore-and-aft sail, bent to a yard, which is slung one-third or less forward of the mast. Often used in small boats. There are at least four varieties.

MAGAZINE: Space or compartment devoted to the stowing of ammunition.

MAINMAST: In a three-masted vessel the middle mast. The aftermast in a two-master.

MAINSAIL: On a square-rigger, the lower sail on the mainmast. On a fore-and-after, the sail spread by the main gaff and boom.

MAN-OF-WAR: An armed vessel belonging to the recognized navy of a country.

MARINES: Soldiers serving aboard ship. Specifically, members of corps with military training and discipline, raised especially for sea duty.

MAST HOUSE: Sheds where masts were finally cut and worked into shape.

MAST POND: Ponds or pools where mast timbers were kept submerged, and thus free from decay, until needed.

MASTER: Sailing master. Warrant officer who was responsible, under the captain, for conducting a vessel safely from port to port. Also conducted survey work and instructed midshipmen in navigation.

MASTER-AT-ARMS: Warrant officer charged with duty of maintaining discipline aboard ship.

MATES: Petty officers, assistants to the various warrant officers—surgeon, boatswain, gunner, etc.

MESSENGER: A light line used for hauling over a heavier rope or cable. In old sailing ships, a line which led to the capstan to assist in heaving in the anchor cable.

MIDSHIPMAN: A cadet officer.

MISS STAYS: For a vessel to fail to come about.

MIZZEN: The third mast from forward of a vessel with more than two masts.

MOLD LOFTS: Large lofts where the timbers of a ship's frame were laid out in exact size and shape from the plans.

NETTING: A rope network.

NIPPERS: Short ropes used to clamp the cable to the messenger. Also the ship's boys assigned to holding them.

ORLOP DECK: The lowest deck, or partial deck. Below it was the hold.

OUTRIGGER: A strong beam passed through the portholes of a ship, used to secure the masts and take part of the strain when careening.

PENDANT (also pennant): A triangular flag.

PETTY OFFICER: A naval officer corresponding in rank to a noncommissioned officer in the army.

PINK: A form of hull, in which the upper part of the stern narrows and projects beyond the hull, curving sharply underneath to the sternpost.

POINT BLANK: Usually considered to be the range at which a shot fired from a gun laid with zero elevation strikes the water.

POOP DECK: Short deck over the quarterdeck. The aftermost deck and the highest.

PORT: (1) An opening in a ship's side. (2) The left side of a vessel, looking toward the bow (in the eighteenth century, called the larboard side).

PORT LID: A shutter, hinged at the top, for closing a port.

PORT TACK: The tack on which the wind comes over the vessel's port side.

POWDER MONKEY: Name given to those, usually boys, who carried cartridges from the magazine to the guns.

PRESS: The system for compulsory manning of vessels in the Royal Navy.

PRESS GANG: Parties of seamen, usually under an officer, who enforced—often brutally—the press laws.

PREVENTER TACKLE: Tackle used temporarily for additional support or securing.

PRIMING IRON: Iron pick used to clear the touchhole of a cannon, and to pierce the cartridge before priming the vent.

PRIVATEER: A privately owned armed vessel, sailing against the enemy under government commission.

PRIZE: A captured ship.

PRIZE CREW: Crew put aboard a captured ship, to guard the imprisoned crew and to bring the vessel to a friendly port.

PRIZE MONEY: Money from the sale of a prize and distributed among the captors.

PROVING OF CANNON: Test-firing with extra charges and double- and sometimes triple-headed shot.

PURSER: Warrant officer in charge of ship's provisions.

PUT DOWN HELM: To put the tiller to leeward (to bring the vessel to the wind).

PUT UP HELM: To put the tiller to windward.

QUARTER: That portion of a vessel's side near the stern.

QUARTER BOAT: Boat hung on davits on a vessel's quarter, or quarters.

QUARTERDECK: A name applied to the afterpart of the upper deck. In many ships the quarterdecks were raised above the upper decks.

QUARTERMASTER: A petty officer, assistant to the master and master's mates.

QUOIN: A wedge-shaped piece of wood used to elevate the breech of a cannon.

RADEAU: A bargelike gunboat.

RAKE: (1) To position one's vessel across another vessel's bow or stern so that its fire can sweep the enemy's decks. (2) The angle of a vessel's mast from the vertical.

RAMMERS: Staffs of wood, or heavy rope, with reinforced ends, used to push the shot down on top of the charge.

RATE: Old-fashioned method of denoting a vessel's class and gunpower. Superseded by the addition of the number of the vessel's guns after her name, i.e., *Warren*, 32.

RED-HOT SHOT: Round shot heated in a furnace and carried to the guns on special cradles. Used as incendiary projectiles.

REEF (canvas): To reduce the area of a sail by tying part of it up to its mast, yard, or boom.

REPEATING FRIGATES: Frigates stationed to repeat the flagship's signals to vessels not in sight of the flagship.

RIGGING: The ropes, chains, etc. that hold and move masts, sails, and spars of a ship.

ROPE WALK: A long covered way used in the preparation of rope.

ROUND SHOT: Solid iron shot (until the advent of armor in the nineteenth century always of cast iron).

ROW GALLEY: Shallow-draft gunboat for harbor defense. Sometimes furnished with a sail or sails.

RUDDER: A flat wooden shape hung on the sternpost by pins (pintles) swiveling on metal eyes (gudgeons) for steering the boat.

RUNNING FREE: Sailing with the wind astern or on the quarter.

RUNNING RIGGING: That part of a ship's rigging which is movable and rove through blocks, such as halyards, sheets, etc.

SAIL LOFT: Area where sails are laid out, cut, and sewn.

SAILING MASTER: *See* Master.

SALUTE: The measured firing of a certain number of guns (the exact number required by protocol) to honor a personage, a flag (national or naval), or an occasion.

SCARFING: A method of cutting two pieces of wood so that they form a strong overlapping joint.

SCHOONER: In the eighteenth century, a two-masted vessel fore-and-aft rigged, but often with the addition of a square fore-topsail.

SCUTTLE: A small opening in a ship's deck or side.

SEXTANT: An instrument for measuring angular distances. Used at sea to ascertain latitude and longitude.

SHEATHING: Covering, usually of wood or metal, applied over a vessel's planking.

SHEER HULK: Hulk equipped with an arrangement of stout poles (sheers) and tackle for stepping or unstepping ships' masts.

SHEET: Rope or tackle from lower corner or clew of a square sail, clew of a staysail or jib, or the boom of a gaffsail, by which direction of the sail is controlled.

SHELL: A hollow iron projectile, filled with powder and ignited by a fuze.

SHIP: Specifically, a three-masted vessel square-rigged on all three masts.

SHIP OF THE LINE: See Capital ship.

SHIP-RIGGED: See Ship.

SHIP'S BOATS: Small open boats either towed, stowed on deck, or carried on davits.

SHROUDS: Stays running from the masthead to the ship's side and set up by deadeyes.

SIDE TACKLES: Tackles hooked to either side of a truck carriage to assist in running a gun out after loading.

SIGNAL REPEATERS: See Repeating frigates.

SINGLE-BANKED BOAT: A boat in which each oar is pulled by one man.

SLING: A chain supporting the center of a lower yard.

SLOOP: In the eighteenth century, a craft with single mast, a gaff mainsail, headsails, and usually a square topsail and course.

SLOOP OF WAR: A relatively small warship, usually armed on a single deck and sometimes on the quarterdeck. Usually of less than 24 guns (U.S.) or 18 guns (R.N.). Could be rigged as a ship, brig, brigantine, etc.

SLOW MATCH: Made of cotton wick soaked in lye or some other substance. Applied to the touchhole to fire a gun.

SNOW: Similar to a brig, but the gaff driver or spanker was set on a separate mast a foot or two abaft the mainmast. This mast was stepped on deck and was secured to the main trestletrees.

SPANKER: See Driver.

SPARS: General term for masts, yards, gaffs, booms, etc.

SPIKING A GUN: Disabling a gun by driving a long spike into the vent or touchhole.

SPONGE: Usually of sheepskin, fastened to a wooden staff or stiff rope. For swabbing the bore of a gun before reloading.

SQUARE-RIGGED: A vessel having one or more masts with a complete set of square sails.

STANDING RIGGING: That part of a ship's rigging which is permanently secured and not movable, i.e., stays, shrouds, etc.

STARBOARD: The right side of a vessel, looking forward.

STARBOARD TACK: The tack on which the wind comes over the vessel's starboard side.

STAY: A stout rope used for supporting a mast.

STAYSAIL: A sail set upon a stay.

STEM: The foremost vertical timber, fitting into the forward end of the keel.

STEPPING: Fitting a mast into place usually with the lower end (butt or heel) resting into a frame (step) on the keelson.

STERN: The afterpart of the vessel.

STERNPOST: The aftermost vertical timber, fitting into the after end of the keel.

STOCK: The crosspiece of an old-fashioned anchor, at right angles to the arms.

STRAKE: A continuous line of planking fitted end to end from stem to stern of a vessel's side.

STRIKE: (1) To stow below. (2) To strike one's flag; to surrender.

STUDDING SAILS: Light sails used to increase a vessel's speed when running free. A studding sail was set outside a square sail, its head attached to a small spar which in turn was carried by the studding sail boom extended from the yardarm.

SUPERCARGO: A merchant vessel's officer charged with managing the ship's business.

SWIVEL: A light cannon on a nonrecoiling swivel mount.

TACK (noun): (1) A vessel's course when obliquely opposed to the direction of the wind. (2) The lower forward corner of a fore-and-aft sail.

TACK (verb): To change from one tack to another by putting down the helm.

TACKLE: An arrangement of ropes and pulleys for hoisting or

pulling heavy objects.

TAMPION: Wooden plug used to stop up the muzzle of a cannon.

THOLEPIN: A pin fitting into a socket on a small boat's rail and over which a rope grommet (loop or ring) is placed to serve as a rowlock.

THREE-DECKER: A vessel with her main armament on three decks.

TILLER: A lever used for turning a vessel's rudder from side to side.

TOPGALLANT MAST: The mast above the topmast.

TOPMAST: The mast above the lower mast.

TOPMEN: Active men stationed in the tops to attend to the sails on the three masts above the lower yards.

TOPS: See Fighting tops.

TOPSAILS: Sails set on the yards slung on the topmasts.

TORY: (1) A person who, during the American Revolution, favored the British. (2) A member of the conservative or King's party in Parliament, as opposed to a Whig.

TRAIN: (1) To aim a cannon. (2) A line or trail of powder or combustibles to a mine or charge.

TRAIN TACKLE: Tackle used to aid in aiming a cannon by moving the carriage from side to side.

TRANSPORT: A vessel used for carrying troops.

TREENAILS: Wooden pegs often used in place of metal spikes or bolts.

TRESTLETREES: Wooden timbers fitted fore-and-aft at the upper part of the lower masts to support the crosstrees and tops.

TRIM: The most advantageous set of a vessel in the water on her fore-and-aft line.

TRUCK CARRIAGE: Wooden gun carriage with wheels, used almost without variation for over 300 years.

TRUCKS: (1) Wooden wheels used on a naval gun carriage. (2) Circular pieces of wood atop the highest masts, usually with sheaves for signal halyards.

TRUNNIONS: Heavy pins or gudgeons, at right angles to the bore, cast as part of a cannon, and on which the tube rested on the carriage.

TUMBLE HOME: The inclination inboard of a vessel's sides.

TURNING TOGETHER: Each ship turning at the same time as the signal to execute the turn is made.

TWO-DECKER: A warship having her main armament on two decks.

UPPER WORKS: The parts of a vessel proper above the main deck.

VAN: The foremost division of a force when advancing.

VENT: The touchhole of a cannon.

WAD: Usually made of rope yarn, rammed on top of shot to keep it in place.

WAIST: The portion of the deck between the forecastle and quarterdeck.

WAISTERS: Crewmen stationed in the waist of the ship.

WALES: Strong planks running fore-and-aft on a vessel's sides.

WALL PIECE: A light gun, often mounted in a swivel-type mount, used on the tops of walls and fortifications.

WARRANT OFFICER: An officer holding his rank by warrant rather than a commission.

WATCH: A period, usually four hours, during which each division of the ship's company alternately remains on deck.

WEAR: To change from one tack to another by putting the helm up and turning away from the wind.

WEARING IN SUCCESSION: A maneuver in which ships wear (or turn) when each ship reaches the point at which the lead ship wore or turned. As opposed to wearing (or turning) together.

WEATHER GAUGE: The position to windward of the enemy's battle fleet.

WEIGHING ANCHOR: Heaving in the anchor cable and bringing the anchor up off the bottom.

WHEEL: A circular frame with handles for controlling the rudder.

WHEEL BLOCK AND ROPES: The tackle which communicated the movements of the wheel to the tiller or quadrant at the head of the rudder.

WHIG: A member of a political party which started in the seventeenth century, defending especially the rights of Parliament in the struggle with the sovereign.

WINDAGE: The difference between the diameter of a cannon ball and the actual bore of a gun.

WINDWARD: The side toward the wind. The point or side from which the wind blows.

YARDS: Spars on which square sails are set.

Bibliography

Abbot, William J. *Naval History of the United States.* New York: P. F. Collier, 1886.

Adams, James Truslow, ed. *Album of American History.* Vol. 1. New York: Charles Scribner's Sons, 1944.

Albion, Robert Greenhalgh. *Forests and Sea Power.* Hamden, Conn.: Archon Books, 1965.

Alderman, Clifford Lindsey. *The Privateersmen.* Philadelphia: Chilton Books, 1965.

Allen, Gardner W. *A Naval History of the American Revolution.* Cleveland: Houghton Mifflin Co., 1913.

Bloomster, Edgar L. *Sailing and Small Craft.* Annapolis, Md.: U.S. Naval Institute, 1940.

Brady, William. *The Kedge-Anchor; or, Young Sailors' Assistant.* 3d ed. New York: William Brady, 1848.

Chapelle, Howard I. *History of the American Sailing Navy.* New York: W. W. Norton Co., 1949.

———. *History of American Sailing Ships.* New York: W. W. Norton Co., 1935.

Chatterton, E. Keble. *Fore and Aft Rig.* London: Seeley Service & Co., 1912.

———. *Sailing Ships and Their Story.* Philadelphia: J. B. Lippincott Co., 1909.

Clark, William Bell. *George Washington's Navy.* Baton Rouge: Louisiana State University Press, 1960.

Clark, George Ramsey; Stevens, William Oliver; Alden, Carroll Storrs; and Krafft, Herman Frederick. *The Navy, 1775 to 1909.* 2 vols. Annapolis, Md.: U.S. Naval Academy, 1910.

Clowes, William Laird. *The Royal Navy.* London: Sampson Low, Marston, and Co., 1897.

Davis, Charles G. *The Built-up Ship Model.* Salem, Mass.: Marine Research Society, 1933.

———. *The Ways of the Sea.* New York: The Rudder Publishing Co., 1930.

Department of the Navy, Naval History Division. *Dictionary of American Naval Fighting Ships.* Washington, D.C.: Government Printing Office, 1959—. Vol. 1, 1959; Vol. 2, 1963; Vol. 3, 1968.

————. *Naval Documents of the American Revolution*. Washington, D.C.: Government Printing Office, 1964—. Vol. 1, 1964; Vol. 2, 1966; Vol. 3, 1968.

Ferrere, Claude. *Histoire de la Marine Francaise*. Paris: E. Flammarion, 1934.

Frost, Holloway H. *We Build a Navy*. Annapolis, Md.: U.S. Naval Institute, 1940.

Grey, Charles. Artillery (original manuscript). 1839.

Landström, Björn. *The Ship*. New York: Doubleday & Co., 1961.

Lewis, Michael. *The Navy of Britain*. London: George Allen & Unwin, 1948.

Lorenz, Lincoln. *John Paul Jones, Fighter for Freedom and Glory*. Annapolis, Md.: U.S. Naval Institute, 1943.

Lovette, Leland P. *Naval Customs, Traditions and Usage*. Annapolis, Md.: U.S. Naval Institute, 1939.

Maclay, Edgar Stanton. *A History of American Privateers*. New York: D. Appleton & Co., 1894.

————. *A History of the United States Navy, 1775-1902*. New York: D. Appleton & Co., 1902.

Mahan, A. T. *The Influence of Sea Power Upon History*. Boston: Little, Brown & Co., 1941.

Masefield, John. *Sea Life in Nelson's Time*. New York: Macmillan Co., 1925.

May, W. E. *Dress of Naval Officers*. London: H.M. Stationery Office, 1966.

Paullin, Charles. *The Navy of the American Revolution*. Cleveland: Burrows Brothers Co., 1906.

Pennsylvania Records. Philadelphia: Pennsylvania Historical Society.

Perrin, W. G. *British Flags*. Cambridge: The University Press, 1922.

Peterson, Harold L. *Arms and Armor in Colonial America, 1526-1783*. Harrisburg, Pa.: The Stackpole Co., 1956.

————. *The Book of the Continental Soldier*. Harrisburg, Pa.: The Stackpole Co., 1968.

————. *Round Shot and Rammers: An Introduction to Muzzle-loading Land Artillery in the United States*. Harrisburg, Pa.: The Stackpole Co., 1969.

Pratt, Fletcher. *The Compact History of the United States Navy*. Rev. ed. New York: Hawthorn Books, 1967.

Rankin, R. H. *Uniforms of the Sea Service*. Annapolis, Md.: U.S. Naval Institute, 1962.

Robinson, C. N. *The British Fleet*. London: George Bell & Sons, 1894.

Robison, S. S. *History of Naval Tactics*. Annapolis, Md.: U.S. Naval Institute, 1942.

Roscoe, Theodore, and Freeman, Fred. *Picture History of the United States Navy, from Old Navy to New, 1776-1897.* New York: Charles Scribner's Sons, 1956.

Society for Nautical Research. *The Mariner's Mirror.* Cambridge: The University Press.

Soule, C. C. *Naval Terms and Definitions.* New York: D. Van Nostrand Co., 1922.

Spears, John R. *History of Our Navy.* New York: Charles Scribner's Sons, 1899.

Stevens, William Oliver, and Westcott, Allan Ferguson. *A History of Sea Power.* New York: G. H. Doran Co., 1920.

Swinburne, H. L. *The Royal Navy.* London: Adam and Charles Black, 1907.

Underhill, H. A. *Sailing Ship Rigs and Rigging.* Glasgow: Brown, Son, and Ferguson Ltd., 1938.

U.S. Naval Institute. *H. H. Rogers Collection of Ship Models.* Annapolis, Md.: U.S. Naval Institute, 1954.

————. *U.S. Naval Institute Proceedings, 1935-1969.* Annapolis, Md.: U.S. Naval Institute.

Ward, Christopher. *The War of the Revolution.* New York: Macmillan Co., 1952.

Wood, William, and Gabriel, R. H. *The Winning of Freedom.* Pageant of America, edited by Ralph Henry Gabriel, vol. 6. New Haven: Yale University Press, 1927.

Index (Entries in capitals are ship names. Italicized entries are pictures.)